A BOOK OF FAITH

Books by Elizabeth Goudge

Novels

ISLAND MAGIC
A CITY OF BELLS
TOWERS IN THE MIST
THE MIDDLE WINDOW
THE BIRD IN THE TREE
THE CASTLE ON THE HILL
GREEN DOLPHIN COUNTRY
THE HERB OF GRACE
THE HEART OF THE FAMILY
GENTIAN HILL
THE ROSEMARY TREE
THE WHITE WITCH
THE DEAN'S WATCH
THE SCENT OF WATER
THE CHILD FROM THE SEA

Short Stories

WHITE WINGS
THE REWARD OF FAITH
THE WELL OF THE STAR
THE PEDLAR'S PACK
THE GOLDEN SKYLARK
THE IKON ON THE WALL
THE LOST ANGEL

Novelette

THE SISTER OF THE ANGELS

Juveniles

SMOKY HOUSE
HENRIETTA'S HOUSE
THE LITTLE WHITE HORSE
MAKE-BELIEVE
THE VALLEY OF SONG

Non-Fiction

GOD SO LOVED THE WORLD
ST. FRANCIS OF ASSISI
A DAY OF PRAYER

Anthology

AT THE SIGN OF THE DOLPHIN
A BOOK OF COMFORT
A CHRISTMAS BOOK
THE TEN GIFTS

Omnibus

THE ELIOTS OF DAMEROSEHAY
THREE CITIES OF BELLS

Elizabeth Goudge

A Book of Faith

HODDER AND STOUGHTON

LONDON SYDNEY AUCKLAND TORONTO

242

2001494S

For

KENNETH PRESTON

Who, throughout the forty years
that I have known him, has
had faith as a grain of
mustard seed.

With my love

Foreword

FAITH

This book brings together some of the things that poets and writers have said about faith—not only faith itself, but about the people and things and experiences that can kindle faith. It is a very mixed collection for simple as well as profound things arouse faith in us, and power to express the emotions that we all feel varies as much as the emotions themselves. I have found this preface difficult to write (like most writers, I am, after several hopeless starts, writing the beginning at the end) because once I started to think about faith, the fact that my ability to think at all is not great got me at once into a state of confusion. Faith, I found, is a confusing virtue.

Of the three cardinal virtues faith comes first, as though it were the most important, and yet they are so intertwined that one can hardly put one before the other. What priest at his ordination, or bride and bridegroom at their wedding, would dare to stand before God and make their promises of faithfulness if they did not have a firm hope that their love was strong enough to keep them? And once the love of God has been revealed to us in his son, and we set out on the prodigal's journey back to the Father, we could never keep going if we did not believe that Christ walks with us all the way, and hope for the heaven of union with him at the end of it all.

And so it is hard to separate faith from hope and love and try to look at it by itself. Doubt, too, would seem to be a part of faith. Loving the light so much, could we face night without our confident hope that the sun will rise in the morning? But what guarantee have we got that it will? None, really. And on some nights that we can all of us remember, nights of the soul that can last for months or years as well as winter nights of grief or illness, we doubt if it will. But time does drag by and the dawn comes, and we find that faith given back to us after a night of doubt is a stronger thing, and far more valuable to us than faith that has never been tested. The loss, grief, and pain we experienced now

9

seem a part of faith because they taught us to trust God, and we now have a deeper joy and peace in believing. Yet all that is truly good, all that comes from God, has its own simplicity that belongs to itself alone. What is the essence of faith, the thing breathed out from the heart of the simplicity?

When I was a child, I read a story about the making of the first opal. There was once a fairy person who possessed three treasures, three diamonds as clear and sparkling as stars on a frosty night. These symbolised for him the beauty of the world that he adored. But being a careless creature, he was always losing one or the other. He wished he could make them one, a larger jewel that would not be so easily mislaid, and also he wished he could give them the beauty of colour as well as of light. He thought about it and he had a bright idea. One diamond he hid deep in the green moss of the forest, another in a blue rock pool beside the sea that reflected the blue of the sky, and the third he placed in the heart of a glowing fire. He left them there for a while and then he took them out again, and the three diamonds had turned into an emerald, a sapphire and a ruby. These three jewels he melted together in the heat of the sun, and then at last he had what he had wanted; all the things he loved made one thing in the moony beauty of the opal. And the one large simple jewel was shaped like the orb of the world. I never forgot the story, and I think one could take the opal as representing faith as well as all the things that the fairy loved; the warmth of fire, the light of moon, stars and sun, the woods and sky and sea, and all the living creatures who dwell in them; all the beauty that, second only to the Word through whom we believe they were created, gives us our faith in God. So beauty also is a part of faith, yet another colour in the opal that is one simple jewel. . . . Yet still I do not know what is the essence that breathes from the simplicity.

Since sinful human beings are far too complicated to understand simplicity, of course, we cannot know, but could it perhaps be likened to a scent? The scent of the white hart who leaps away into the forest with a speed that makes the hunter's pursuit hopeless? Or of a flower, an elusive scent that comes on the wind and is gone again before the child in the garden can tell from which direction it drifted. Or we could say it is like music heard by a man who has lost his way in the dark; the echo of a bell or of a voice singing. He does not know where it comes from, but it speaks to him of life and companionship.

Saint Paul says, "Faith is the substance of things hoped for, the evidence of things not seen." The faith he speaks of came to him after he had himself been hunted down and captured on the Damascus road. For this hunt, it would seem, is a two-way thing. There is no knowing when the white hart will change direction, as terrifying in his backward leap as an arc of white lightning; or as gentle as the unicorn in Rilke's poem. "Whitely it stole up to a maid—to *be* within the silver mirror and in her." But in spite of his gentleness, she was not able to see the creature. All she knew of him was the fleeting reflection in the mirror and the sense of inward possession, and all Saint Paul had of the lightning was physical blindness and the pulsing warmth invading the pit of his empty heart. But when his sight came back, the sky and the trees, and the white roads winding over the hills, must have smiled at him with a beauty as strange and new as the knowledge that his heart seemed now to be beating for the first time. He was reborn into a new life for he had received the gift of faith, and it was for him so tremendous a gift that he could use the words "substance" and "evidence" when speaking of something both untouchable and invisible.

We live in a maze of symbols, all of them from the sun to a bird's feather, from the Bach B minor Mass down to the echo of a bell, uniting to give us this multi-coloured treasure that starts us off on the journey that has been described down the centuries in so many myths and stories, but is always the same journey. The prodigal son and the Magi were journeying to the same place and Person; they were hunters on the same trail. The prodigal son caught the scent of some remembered goodness, the fragrance of some garden at life's beginning and of Someone who had walked with him there. Or so, on his good days, the song of the birds and the colours of the wayside flowers seemed to tell him. . . . On his bad days he could not smell a thing; except the stink of his own dirt. . . . But he went on, sometimes with the faint sound of water in his ears from far-off streams. How could he know that at the other end of the trail another hunter was running out to meet him? And how could the Magi know either in those times of darkness and confusion that when their star blinked and went out, and they floundered off the road, they would ever get on it again? It was only when the stable door opened and the light came down the path to meet them that they knew their journey had not been hopeless.

The author of the Epiphany collect must have been much like Saint Paul, for he speaks with the same shattering confidence. "Mercifully grant that we, which know thee now by faith, may after this life have the fruition of thy glorious Godhead." The fruition, the completeness of the Godhead. What a thing to dare to hope for! It sounds ridiculous, yet both men, and an amazing number of saints and mystics both before and after them, have said the same thing. . . . We exhausted, futile travellers, losing the way, falling in the dark, struggling on again, will ultimately get there. . . . It is an immense hope and is the gift of faith; and faith, it seems, is in part a readiness to receive the symbols not only as gifts of immeasurable value in themselves but as far more;

echoes, gleams, reflections, intimations of what George Macdonald calls "the secret too great to be told." The symbols cannot tell us what it is, but if we are ready and willing to watch and listen and receive, they breathe out to us the knowledge that it is *there*. To breathe in this breath, to catch its perfume or the echo of its music, is to experience the faith that Christ likened to a grain of mustard seed, a simple thing, yet hiding within itself the possibility of miraculous transformation. What the essence of our faith can be, I still do not really know, but I do know the words that come to me when I hear great music or see the sun lighting up the spiders' webs on a morning when the garden is spangled with dew. "I bring you good tidings of great joy."

Compiler's Note

Every poem and piece of prose in an anthology is there because the person who compiled the anthology likes it. It is a collector's piece. But behind this obvious fact is another. The compiling of an anthology can be an act of thanksgiving. What would any of us do without the books and poems that help us along our way?—the books we return to again and again, the poems we learn by heart and repeat for comfort in sleepless nights? We long to say thank-you. In the case of writers who have been dead for several centuries, this can be difficult, but to those who are happily still with us an anthology says—Thank you.

Contents

Part 10
Faith Maintained as Old Age Carries Us Forward Through Death to Resurrection and to Hope of Heaven

Part 1

Faith in God the Creator

"My Lord, my Master," I said, "was it not you, and you alone, who in the beginning spoke the Word that formed the world? . . . O Lord, at the beginning of creation you spoke the Word."

The Book of Esdras
The Apocrypha

1.

The Wisdom and Majesty of God

THE TRUMPET OF GOD

For the TRUMPET of God is a blessed intelligence & so are all the instruments in HEAVEN.

For GOD the father Almighty plays upon the HARP of stupendous magnitude and melody.

For innumerable Angels fly out at every touch and his tune is a work of creation.

For at that time malignity ceases and the devils themselves are at peace.

For this time is perceptible to man by a remarkable stillness and serenity of soul.

Christopher Smart

Inquire of the LORD while he is present,
Call upon him when he is close at hand.
Let the wicked abandon their ways
    and evil men their thoughts:
let them return to the LORD, who will have pity on them,
    return to our God, for he will freely forgive.
For my thoughts are not your thoughts,
    and your ways are not my ways.
    This is the very word of the LORD.
For as the heavens are higher than the earth,
so are my ways higher than your ways
    and my thoughts than your thoughts;
and as the rain and the snow come down from heaven

and do not return until they have watered the earth,
    making it blossom and bear fruit,
and give seed for sowing and bread to eat,
so shall the word which comes from my mouth prevail;
   it shall not return to me fruitless
without accomplishing my purpose
      or succeeding in the task I gave it.
      You shall indeed go out with joy
      and be led forth in peace.
Before you mountains and hills shall break into cries of joy,
and all the trees of the wild shall clap their hands,
   pine-trees shall shoot up in place of camel-thorn,
      myrtles instead of briars;
   all this shall win the LORD a great name,
      imperishable, a sign for all time.

The Book of Isaiah
The New English Bible

WHAT HAVE I BUT WORDS?

What have I but words
sounds, open and closed
lengths shapes
vibrations with meanings?
You
use colours, life, suns
for expression
hardness and softness
just
     draw back a few clouds to expose
a firmament of eyes
just
     roll aside a few mountain ranges
to make room for another ocean,
will you?

And those sighs
those shadows
which wander through trees in evening skies
cast green ghosts on the wall, eyes,

22

flaming saturns ringed with fires
what voices you command.
Guide my mind and hand
after drawing me into the heart-
heat stir of your molten foundry.
I am spun round and round.

Too obviously
ʾ you can claim every advantage over me.

Sister Mary Agnes, Order of Poor Clares

There are mines for silver
and places where men refine gold;
where iron is won from the earth
and copper smelted from the ore;
the end of the seam lies in darkness,
and it is followed to its farthest limit.
Strangers cut the galleries;
they are forgotten as they drive forward far from men.
While corn is springing from the earth above,
what lies beneath is raked over like a fire,
and out of its rocks comes lapis lazuli,
dusted with flecks of gold.
No bird of prey knows the way there,
and the falcon's keen eye cannot descry it;
proud beasts do not set foot on it,
and no serpent comes that way.
Man sets his hand to the granite rock
and lays bare the roots of the mountains;
he cuts galleries in the rocks,
and gems of every kind meet his eye;
he dams up the sources of the streams
and brings the hidden riches of the earth to light.
But where can wisdom be found?
And where is the source of understanding?
No man knows the way to it;
it is not found in the land of living men.
The depths of ocean say, 'It is not in us,'
and the sea says, 'It is not with me.'
Red gold cannot buy it,
nor can its price be weighed out in silver;
it cannot be set in the scales against gold of Ophir,

against precious cornelian or lapis lazuli;
gold and crystal are not to be matched with it,
no work in fine gold can be bartered for it;
black coral and alabaster are not worth mention,
and a parcel of wisdom fetches more than red coral;
topaz from Ethiopia is not to be matched with it,
it cannot be set in the scales against pure gold.
Where then does wisdom come from,
and where is the source of understanding?
No creature on earth can see it,
and it is hidden from the birds of the air.
Destruction and death say,
'We know of it only by report.'
But God understands the way to it,
he alone knows its source;
for he can see to the ends of the earth
and he surveys everything under heaven.
When he made a counterpoise for the wind
and measured out the waters in proportion,
when he laid down a limit for the rain
and a path for the thunderstorm,
even then he saw wisdom and took stock of it,
he considered it and fathomed its very depths.
And he said to man:
　　The fear of the Lord is wisdom.
　　and to turn from evil is understanding.

The Book of Job
The New English Bible

I sought Thee round About, O Thou my God,
　　　　To find Thy abode:
I said unto the Earth, 'Speak, art thou He?'
　　　　She answered me,
'I am not.' I enquired of creatures all,
　　　　In general,
Contained therein: they with one voice proclaim
That none amongst them challenged such a name.

I asked the seas, and all the deeps below,
　　　　My God to know:

24

I asked the reptiles, and whatever is
                    In the abyss:
Even from the shrimp to the leviathan
                    My enquiry ran:
But in those deserts, which no line can sound,
The God I sought for was not to be found.

I asked the Air, if that were He, but know
                    It told me, 'No';
I from the towering eagle to the wren
                    Demanded then,
If any feathered fowl 'mong them were such
                    But they, all much
Offended at my question, in full quire
Answered, to find my God I must look higher.

And now, my God, by Thy illumining grace,
                    Thy Glorious face
(So far forth as Thou wilt discovered be)
                    Methinks I see:
And though invisible and infinite,
                    To human sight
Thou in Thy Mercy, Justice, Truth, appearest,
In which to our frail senses Thou com'st nearest.
                  *   *   *   *
O, make us apt to seek and quick to find,
                    Thou God most kind:
Give us Love, Hope, and Faith in Thee to trust,
                    Thou God most just:
Remit all our offences, we entreat,
                    Most Good, most Great:
Grant that our willing though unworthy quest
May, through Thy grace, admit us 'mongst the blest.

                                        Thomas Heywood

Do you not know, have you not heard,
were you not told long ago,
 have you not perceived ever since the world began,
that God sits throned on the vaulted roof of earth,
        whose inhabitants are like grasshoppers?

25

He stretches out the skies like a curtain,
he spreads them out like a tent to live in;
he reduces the great to nothing
and makes all earth's princes less than nothing.
Scarcely are they planted, scarcely sown,
scarcely have they taken root in the earth,
before he blows upon them and they wither away,
and a whirlwind carries them off like chaff.
To whom then will you liken me,
whom set up as my equal?
asks the Holy One.
Lift up your eyes to the heavens;
consider who created it all,
led out their host one by one
and called them all by their names;
through his great might, his might and power,
not one is missing.
Why do you complain, O Jacob,
and you, Israel, why do you say,
'My plight is hidden from the LORD
and my cause has passed out of God's notice?'
Do you not know, have you not heard?
The LORD, the everlasting God, creator of the wide world,
grows neither weary nor faint;
no man can fathom his understanding.
He gives vigour to the weary,
new strength to the exhausted.
Young men may grow weary and faint,
even in their prime they may stumble and fall;
but those who look to the LORD will win new strength,
they will grow wings like eagles;
they will run and not be weary,
they will march and never grow faint.

The Book of Isaiah
The New English Bible

2.
Longing for God

There is one thing I ask of the Lord,
for this I long,
to live in the house of the Lord,
all the days of my life,
to savour the sweetness of the Lord,
to behold his temple.

For there he keeps me safe in his tent
in the days of evil.
He hides me in the shelter of his tent,
on a rock he sets me safe.

O Lord, hear my voice when I call;
have mercy and answer.
Of you my heart has spoken:
'Seek his face.'
It is your face, O Lord, that I seek;
hide not your face.
Dismiss not your servant in anger;
you have been my help.

Do not abandon or forsake me,
O God my help!
Though father and mother forsake me,
The Lord will receive me.

I am sure I shall see the Lord's goodness
in the land of the living.

Hope in him, hold firm and take heart.
Hope in the Lord!

Part of Psalm 26

O God, you are my God, for you I long;
for you my soul is thirsting.
My body pines for you
like a dry, weary land without water.
So I gaze on you in the sanctuary
to see your strength and your glory.

For your love is better than life,
my lips will speak your praise.
So I will bless you all my life,
in your name I will lift up my hands.
My soul shall be filled as with a banquet,
my mouth shall praise you with joy.

On my bed I remember you.
On you I muse through the night
for you have been my help;
in the shadow of your wings I rejoice.
My soul clings to you;
your right hand holds me fast.

Part of Psalm 62

How lovely is your dwelling place,
Lord, God of hosts.

My soul is longing and yearning,
is yearning for the courts of the Lord.
My heart and my soul ring out their joy
to God, the living God.

The sparrow herself finds a home
and the swallow a nest for her brood;

she lays her young by your altars,
Lord of hosts, my king and my God.

They are happy, who dwell in your house,
for ever singing your praise.
They are happy, whose strength is in you,
in whose hearts are the roads to Sion.

As they go through the Bitter Valley
they make it a place of springs,
the autumn rain covers it with blessings.
They walk with ever growing strength,
they will see the God of gods in Sion.

One day within your courts
is better than a thousand elsewhere.
The threshold of the house of God
I prefer to the dwellings of the wicked.

For the Lord God is a rampart, a shield;
he will give us his favour and glory,
The Lord will not refuse any good
to those who walk without blame.

Lord, God of hosts,
happy the man who trusts in you!

Part of Psalm 83

Lord, teach me to seek Thee and reveal Thyself to me when I seek Thee. For I cannot seek Thee except Thou teach me, nor find Thee except Thou reveal Thyself. Let me seek Thee in longing, let me long for Thee in seeking: let me find Thee in love and love Thee in finding. Lord, I acknowledge and I thank Thee that Thou hast created me in this Thine image, in order that I may be mindful of Thee, may conceive of Thee and love Thee: but that image has been so consumed and wasted away by vices and obscured by the smoke of wrongdoing that it cannot achieve that for which it was made, except Thou renew it and create it anew. Is the eye of the soul darkened by its infirmity, or dazzled by Thy glory? Surely, it is both darkened in itself and dazzled by Thee.

Lord, this is the unapproachable light in which Thou dwellest. Truly I see it not, because it is too bright for me; and yet whatever I see, I see through it, as the weak eye sees what it sees through the light of the sun, which in the sun itself it cannot look upon. Oh supreme and unapproachable light, oh holy and blessed truth, how far art thou from me who am so near to Thee, how far art Thou removed from my vision, though I am so near to Thine! Everywhere Thou art wholly present, and I see Thee not. In Thee I move and in Thee I have my being, and cannot come to Thee. Thou art within me and about me, and I feel Thee not.

St. Anselm

I turned to speak to God
About the world's despair;
But to make bad matters worse
I found God wasn't there.

God turned to speak to me
(Don't anybody laugh)
God found I wasn't there
At least not over half.

Robert Frost

Batter my heart, three-person'd God; for, you
As yet but knock, breathe, shine, and seek to mend;
That I may rise, and stand, o'erthrow me, and bend
Your force, to break, blow, burn and make me new.
I, like an usurped town, to another due,
Labour to admit you, but O, to no end.
Reason, your viceroy in me, me should defend,
But is captiv'd, and proves weak or untrue.
Yet dearly I love you, and would be loved fain,
But am betroth'd unto your enemy:
Divorce me, untie, or break that knot again,
Take me to you, imprison me, for I
Except you enthrall me, never shall be free,
Nor ever chaste, except you ravish me.

John Donne

INSATIABLENESS

I

No walls confine! Can nothing hold my mind?
Can I no rest nor satisfaction find?
  Must I behold eternity
          And see
  What things above the Heav'ns be?
         Will nothing serve the turn?
         Nor earth, nor seas, nor skies?
         Till I what lies
     In time's beginning find;
  Must I till then forever burn?

Not all the crowns; not all the heaps of gold
On earth; not all the tales that can be told,
  Will satisfaction yield to me:
          Nor tree,
  Nor shade, nor sun, nor Eden, be
         A joy: nor gems in gold,
         (Be't pearl or precious stone,)
         Nor spring, nor flowers,
        Answer my craving powers,
  Nor anything that eyes behold.

Till I what was before all time descry,
The world's beginning seems but vanity.
  My soul doth there long thoughts extend;
         No end
  Doth find, or being comprehend:
         Yet somewhat sees that is
         The obscure shady face
         Of endless space,
        All room within; where I
  Expect to meet eternal bliss.

II

  This busy, vast, inquiring soul
         Brooks no control,
        No limits will endure,
  Nor any rest: it will all see,

Not time alone, but ev'n eternity.
  What is it? Endless sure.

  'Tis mean ambition to desire
                A single world:
            To many I aspire,
      Though one upon another hurl'd:
    Nor will they all, if they be all confin'd,
                Delight my mind.

    This busy, vast, inquiring soul
                Brooks no control:
            'Tis very curious too.
      Each one of all those worlds must be
      Enriched with infinite variety
                And worth; or 'twill not do.

    'Tis nor delight nor perfect pleasure
                To have a purse
      That hath a bottom in its treasure,
    Since I must thence endless expense disburse.
    Sure there's a God (for else there's no delight)
                One infinite.

                                    Thomas Traherne

How should I praise thee, Lord! How should my rhymes
    Gladly engrave thy love in steel,
    If what my soul doth feel sometimes,
      My soul might ever feel!

Although there were some fourtie heav'ns, or more,
    Sometimes I peere above them all;
    Sometimes I hardly reach a score,
      Sometimes to hell I fall.

O rack me not to such a vast extent;
    Those distances belong to thee:
    The world's too little for thy tent.
      A grave too big for me.

Wilt thou meet arms with man, that thou dost stretch
    A crumme of dust from heav'n to hell?
    Will great God measure with a wretch?
      Shall he thy stature spell?

O let me, when thy roof my soul hath hid,
    O let me roost and nestle there:
    Then of a sinner thou art rid,
      And I of hope and fear.

Yet take thy way; for sure thy way is best:
    Stretch or contract me thy poore debtor;
    This is but tuning of my breast,
      To make the musick better.

Whether I flie with angels, fall with dust,
    Thy hands made both, and I am there:
    Thy power and love, my love and trust
    Make one place ev'rywhere.

George Herbert

3.
Faith That We Shall Find Him Within Us

To go to Rome
Is great trouble, small profit.
The King you have in mind
(Unless you bring Him in your heart)
You'll never find.

Brendan Kennelly

I laugh when I hear that the fish
   in the water is thirsty.
You wander restlessly from forest
   to forest while the Reality
   is within your own dwelling.
The truth is here! Go where you will—
   to Benares or to Mathura;
   until you have found God
   in your own soul, the whole world
   will seem meaningless to you.

Rabindranath Tagore

Within this earthen vessel are bowers
   and groves, and within it is the
   Creator:

Within this vessel are the seven oceans
   and the unnumbered stars.
The touchstone and the jewel-appraiser are within;
And within this vessel the Eternal
   soundeth, and the spring wells
   up.
Kabir says: 'Listen to me, my friend!
   My beloved Lord is within.'
'He shall sit as a refiner and purifier
   of silver.'

Rabindranath Tagore

   How could the love between Thee and
     me sever?
   As the leaf of the lotus abides on the
     water: so thou art my Lord, and I
     am Thy servant.
   As the night-bird Chakor gazes all
     night at the moon: so Thou art
     my Lord and I am Thy servant.
   From the beginning until the ending
     of time, there is love between
     Thee and me; and how shall such
     love be extinguished?
   Kabir says: 'As the river enters
     into the ocean, so my heart
     touches Thee.'

Rabindranath Tagore

THE COMPANION

It has been one of those quiet, hidden days,
Like the wind brushing past dark cypresses as they sway;
Or the murmur of a shell, pressed close to the ear,
Which only the keenest perception can hear.
("It is I, do not fear.")
I have flitted through this dusk of a day,
A moth in dim air,
Or as shadows of leaves tapping at my windowpane.

35

Known only to him who has passed it with me.
Traversing the cloisters alone,
"It is Myself, how can you be afraid?"

Sister Mary Agnes, Order of Poor Clares

It is rumoured of God Almighty that He has made us
'In His own image.'
Pessimists complain, 'Our Creator has betrayed us.'
'And Life,' they say, 'is a self-defensive scrimmage.'
I prefer to think that each potential corpse
From its own life must fashion
God, an encompassing dream. With crowns and harps
Men fill their future unperturbed by passion.
Such Heaven is but a gilded make-believe
Where God's imperial palace is 'To Let.'
God! Everyman has got Him up his sleeve.
He haunts them like a tradesman's unpaid debt.

God is spontaneous. Springs from God knows where.
And when I meet Him he resembles—what?
Nothing on earth except myself. I stare
at Him, and say, 'O God, I've such a lot
To tell you.' And He replies,
'I know your thoughts. I know your heart's whole story.'
And I am lifted up into His glory.

Siegfried Sassoon

To love someone, even in the usual human manner, is to get a brief
dim glimpse of something within that person which is tremendous
awe-inspiring and eternal. In our ignorance, we think that this 'some
thing' is unique. He or she, we say, is like nobody else. That is because
our perception of the Reality is clouded and obscured by the externa
manifestations—the character and individual qualities of the person
we love—and by the way in which our own ego-sense reacts to them
Nevertheless, this weak flash of perception is a valid spiritual experi
ence and it should encourage us to purify our minds and make them fi
for that infinitely greater kind of love which always awaits us. Thi

36

love is not restless or transient, like our human love. It is secure and eternal and calm. It is absolutely free from desire, because lover and be-loved have become one.

Swami Prabharananda and Christopher Isherwood

FOR LOTTE BIELITZ

(Written at her request)

It *is* hard, the descent to God. But see:
you're plying your empty vessels in distraction,
when to be child, girl, woman's suddenly
enough to give him endless satisfaction.

He is the water: you need only mould
the cup out of two hands extended yonder:
and if you kneel as well—why, then he'll squander,
and pass all your capacity to hold.

Rainer Maria Rilke

Expecting Him, my door was open wide:
Then I looked round
If any lack of service might be found,
And saw Him at my side:
How entered, by what secret stair,
I know not, knowing only He was there.

Thomas Edward Brown

4.
In Praise of God, King of the World

The Lord is king, with majesty enrobed;
the Lord has robed himself with might,
he has girded himself with power.

The world you made firm, not to be moved;
your throne has stood firm from of old.
From all eternity, O Lord, you are.

The waters have lifted up, O Lord,
the waters have lifted up their voice,
the waters have lifted up their thunder.

Greater than the roar of mighty waters,
more glorious than the surgings of the sea,
the Lord is glorious on high.

Truly your decrees are to be trusted.
Holiness is fitting to your house,
O Lord, until the end of time.

Psalm 92

SONG OF SPRINGTIME: A PSALM OF WORSHIP

To you our praise is due
in Sion, O God.

To you we pay our vows,
you who hear our prayer.

To you all flesh will come
with its burden of sin.
Too heavy for us, our offences,
but you wipe them away.

Blessed he whom you choose and call
to dwell in your courts.
We are filled with the blessings of your house,
of your holy temple.

You keep your pledge with wonders,
O God our saviour,
the hope of all the earth
and of far distant isles.

You uphold the mountains with your strength,
you are girded with power.
You still the roaring of the seas,
(the roaring of their waves)
and the tumult of the peoples.

The ends of the earth stand in awe
at the sight of your wonders.
The lands of sunrise and sunset
you fill with your joy.

You care for the earth, give it water,
you fill it with riches.
Your river in heaven brims over
to provide its grain.

And thus you provide for the earth;
You drench its furrows,
you level it, soften it with showers,
you bless its growth.

You crown the year with your goodness.
Abundance flows in your steps,
in the pastures of the wilderness it flows.

The hills are girded with joy,
the meadows covered with flocks,
the valleys are decked with wheat.
They shout for joy, yes, they sing.

Psalm 64

EVERYONE SANG

Everyone suddenly burst out singing;
And I was filled with such delight
As prisoned birds must find in freedom,
Winging wildly across the white
Orchards and dark green fields; on—on—and out of sight.
Everyone's voice was suddenly lifted;
And beauty came like the setting sun:
My heart was shaken with tears; and horror
Drifted away . . . O, but Everyone
Was a bird; and the song was wordless; the singing will
    never be done.

Siegfried Sassoon

THE LAST LEAF

I saw how rows of white raindrops
    From bare boughs shone,
And how the storm had stript the leaves
    Forgetting none
Save one left high on a top twig
    Swinging alone;
Then that too bursting into song
    Fled and was gone.

Andrew Young

SPRING SONG IN WINTER

Too long, too long
I gathered icicles in spring
To thread them for a melting song;
And in midsummer saw the foliage fall,
Too foolish then to sing
How leaf and petal cling
Though wind would bear them to the root of all.

Now winter's come, and winter proves me wrong:
Dark in my garden the dead,
Great naked briars, have spread,
So vastly multiplied
They almost hide
The single shrub to share whose blossoming
Blood on cold thorns my fingers shed.

Michael Hamburger

CHANTICLEER

All this night shrill chanticleer,
Day's proclaiming trumpeter,
    Claps his wings and loudly cries,
    Mortals, mortals, wake and rise!
        See a wonder
        Heaven is under;
    From the earth is risen a Sun
    Shines all night, though day be done.

Wake, O earth, wake everything!
Wake and hear the joy I bring;
    Wake and joy; for all this night
    Heaven and every twinkling light,
        All amazing,
        Still stand gazing.
    Angels, Powers, and all that be,
    Wake, and joy this Sun to see.

Hail, O Sun, O blessed Light,
Sent into the world by night!
   Let thy rays and heavenly powers
   Shine in these dark souls of ours;
      For most duly
      Thou art truly
   God and man, we do confess:
   Hail, O Sun of Righteousness!

William Austin

Your love, Lord, reaches to heaven;
your truth to the skies.
Your justice is like God's mountain,
your judgments like the deep.

To both man and beast you give protection.
O Lord, how precious is your love.
My God, the sons of men
find refuge in the shelter of your wings.

They feast on the riches of your house;
they drink from the stream of your delight.
In you is the source of life
and in your light we see light.

Keep on loving those who know you,
doing justice for upright hearts.

Part of Psalm 35

Fountain of Sweets! Eternal Dove!
Which leav'st Thy glorious perch above,
And hovering down, vouchsafest thus
To make Thy nest below with us.

Soft as Thy softest feathers, may
We find Thy love to us today;
And in the shelter of Thy wing
Obtain Thy leave and grace to sing.

Joseph Beaumont

Part 2

All Created Things Speak to Us, With Their Many Voices, of the Word of God Who Created Them

1. The Word
2. The Seasons
3. "Be Still, and Know that I am God"

When all things began, the Word already was. The Word dwelt with God, and what God was, the Word was. The word, then, was with God at the beginning, and through him all things came to be; no single thing was created without him. All that came to be was alive with his life, and that life was the light of men. The light shines on in the dark, and the darkness has never quenched it.

St. John's Gospel
The New English Bible

1.
The Word

It is a summer day in Burgundy, where the light has a vibrant clarity quite unlike that of English summers. Sitting at the long white table in the shaded room with its slatted shutters, we seem to be enclosed within that mysterious and complicated world in which, by eating and talk, man transforms what comes to him by way of his senses into his own distinctive life. But, as those who are waiting at table come and go with the dishes, there is revealed through the long doors, in bursts of limpid sunshine, another world of *things,* clear and triumphant in their independent existence, stones and plants and trees, insistent upon being seen in the exactness of their contours, defining themselves in colour and form and movement, simply, gloriously and beyond all argument *being.* In such a setting only the most insensitive eye could fail to note the challenge of all in the world that *is,* that carries in it a truth and rightness that determines it to be just this and not that. Men of scientific training, whose business it is to work with this world of things, normally acquire that instinctive respect for and appreciation of creation which is also the mark of gifted gardeners, cooks, artists, and poets. Often it is only people who imagine themselves to be religious who treat this whole vista with the profoundest contempt. Yet these have so frequently upon their lips the, for them, evidently meaningless words 'consubstantial with the Father, by whom all things were made'. Their own tradition shames them. One would rightly expect to be able to gather examples of every kind of strained and unusual austerity from the desert sources. How gratifying it is, then, to hear a scholar, with a trained and experienced eye in this field, remarking when he comes to Anthony the Great's reaction to his first sight of the Interior Mountain, where he was for so long to live: 'Note this love for the place,' and going on to cite Anthony saying: 'My book, O philoso-

47

pher, is the nature of created things, and it is present when I will, for me to read the words of God.' . . . .

There will be something very wrong both with the theology and the theologian that does not approach the mystery of God through a deep reverence for the mystery of what he has made. It can never be too often said that one of the first traps set before the man who desires to pray or to study the theology of prayer is to set it in a world apart. The man of prayer cannot be a man of two minds. If our attitude towards the least of the creatures is wrong, so will our attitude to God be wrong. We might remember that, in the right hands, a little of the common earth, upon which men walk without reflection, can open the eyes of the blind.

Aelred Squire

THE DAYS

Issuing from the Word
The seven days came,
Each in its own place,
Its own name.
And the first long days
A hard and rocky spring,
Inhuman burgeoning,
And nothing there for claw or hand,
Vast loneliness ere loneliness began,
Where the blank seasons in their journeying
Saw water at play with water and sand with sand.
The waters stirred
And from the doors were cast
Wild lights and shadows on the formless face
Of the flood of chaos, vast
Lengthening and dwindling image of earth and heaven.
The forest's green shadow
Softly over the waters driven,
As if the earth's green wonder, endless meadow
Floated and sank within its own green light.
In water and night
Sudden appeared the lion's violent head,
Raging and burning in its watery cave.
The stallion's tread
Soundlessly fell on the flood, and the animals poured

Onward, flowing across the flowing wave.
Then on the waters fell
The shadow of man, and earth and the heavens scrawled
With names, as if each pebble and leaf would tell
The tale untellable. And the Lord called
The seventh day forth and the glory of the Lord.
And now we see in the sun
The mountains standing clear in the third day
(Where they shall always stay)
And thence a river run,
Threading, clear cord of water, all to all:
The wooded hill and the cattle in the meadow,
The tall wave breaking on the high sea-wall,
The people at evening walking,
The crescent shadow
Of the light-built bridge, the hunter stalking
The flying quarry, each in a different morning,
The fish in the billow's heart, the man with the net,
The hungry swords crossed in the cross of warning,
The lion set
High on the banner, leaping into the sky,
The seasons playing
Their game of sun and moon and east and west,
The animal watching man and bird go by,
The women praying
For the passing of this fragmentary day
Into the day where all are gathered together,
Things and their names, in the storm's and lightning's nest,
The seventh great day and the clear eternal weather.

Edwin Muir

From A SONG TO DAVID

*Eighteen verses have been chosen from an eighteenth-century poem
that is as long as it is beautiful*

GOD'S CREATION

He sung of God—the mighty source
Of all things—the stupendous force
On which all strength depends;

49

From whose right arm, beneath whose eyes,
All period, pow'r, and enterprise
   Commences, reigns, and ends.

The world—the clust'ring spheres he made,
The glorious light, the soothing shade,
   Dale, champaign, grove, and hill;
The multitudinous abyss,
Where secrecy remains in bliss
   And wisdom hides her skill.

Trees, plants, and flow'rs—of virtuous root:
Gem yielding blossom, yielding fruit,
   Choice gums and precious balm;
Bless ye the nosegay in the vale,
And with the sweetness of the gale
   Enrich the thankful psalm.

Of fowl—e'en ev'ry beak and wing
Which chear the winter, hail the spring,
   That live in peace or prey;
They that make music, or that mock,
The quail, the brave domestic cock
   The raven, swan, and jay.

Of fishes—ev'ry size and shape,
Which nature frames of light escape,
   Devouring man to shun:
The shells are in the wealthy deep,
And shoals upon the surface leap
   And love the glancing sun.

Of beasts—the beaver plods his task;
While the sleek tigers roll and bask,
   Nor yet the shades arouse;
Her cave the mining coney scoops;
Where o'er the mead the mountain stoops
   The kids exult and brouse.

Of gems—their virtue and their price,
Which hid in earth from man's device,
   Their darts of lustre sheathe:
The jasper of the master's stamp,

The topaz blazing like a lamp
Among the mines beneath.

PRAISE AND ADORATION

PRAISE above all—for praise prevails:
Heap up the measure, load the scales,
   And good to goodness add;
The generous soul her saviour aids,
But peevish obloquy degrades;
   The Lord is great and glad.

Now labour his reward receives,
For ADORATION counts his sheaves
   To PEACE, her bounteous prince;
The nectarine his strong tint imbibes,
And apples of ten thousand tribes,
   And quick peculiar quince.

The wealthy crops of whit'ning rice,
'Mongst thyine woods and groves of spice,
   For ADORATION grow;
And, marshall'd in the fenced land,
The peaches and pomegranates stand,
   Where wild carnations blow.

The laurels with the winter strive;
The crocus burnishes alive
   Upon the snow-clad earth;
For ADORATION myrtles stay
To keep the garden from dismay,
   And bless the sight from dearth.

For ADORATION, DAVID's psalms
Lift up the heart to deeds of alms;
   And he, who kneels and chants,
Prevails his passions to controul,
Finds meat and med'cine to the soul,
   Which for translation pants.

For ADORATION, in the dome
of CHRIST, the sparrows find an home,

51

And on his olives perch;
The swallow also dwells with thee,
O man of God's humility,
    Within his Saviour's CHURCH.

STRENGTH AND GLORY

Strong is the lion—like a coal
His eyeball, like a bastion's mole
    His chest against the foes;
Strong, the gier-eagle on his sail,
Strong against tide, th'enormous whale
    Emerges, as he goes.

But stronger still, in earth and air
And in the sea, the man of pray'r,
    And far beneath the tide;
And in the seat to faith assign'd,
Where ask is have, where seek is find,
    Where knock is open wide.

Glorious the sun in mid career;
Glorious th'assembled fires appear;
    Glorious the comet's train;
Glorious the trumpet and alarm;
Glorious th'almighty stretched-out arm;
    Glorious th'enraptur'd main;

Glorious the northern lights a-stream;
Glorious the song, when God's the theme;
    Glorious the thunder's roar;
Glorious hosanna from the den,
Glorious the catholic amen;
    Glorious the martyr's gore.

Glorious—more glorious, is the crown
Of Him that brought salvation down,
    By meekness, called thy Son:
Thou at stupendous truth believ'd;
And now the matchless deed's atchiev'd,
    DETERMINED, DARED, and DONE.

Christopher Smart

A PASTORAL HYMNE

Happy Choristers of Aire,
Who by your nimble flight draw neare
    His throne, whose wondrous story
    And unconfined glory
Your notes still Caroll, whom your sound
And whom your plumy pipes rebound.

Yet do the lazy Snailes no lesse
The greatness of our Lorde confesse,
    And those whom weight hath chain'd
    And to the Earth restrain'd,
Their ruder voices do as well,
Yea and the speechless Fishes tell.

Great Lord, from whom each Tree receaves
Then pays againe as rent, his leaves;
    Thou dost in purple set
    The Rose and Violet,
And giv'st the sickly Lilly white,
Yet in them all, the name doth write.

John Hall

PLOUGHING IN MIST

Pulling the shoulder-sack
Closer about his neck and back,
He called out to his team
That stamped off dragging the weigh-beam;
And as he gripped the stilts and steered
They plunged in mist and disappeared,
Fading so fast away
They seemed on a long journey gone,
Not to return that day;
But while I waited on
The jingle of loose links I caught,
And suddenly on the hill-rise

Pale phantoms of the mist at first,
Man and his horses burst
As though before my eyes
Creation had been wrought.

Andrew Young

2.

The Seasons

Very early in the morning sunlight runs
    Plucking at the grassblades with the spheres' music,
    And the silver-candled moon in the dawn
    Kindles in each dewdrop a reflected song.
    The trees catch the young light playing,
    Flinging this shower of green laburnum gold,
    A seamless robe.

The noiselessness which lives in the summer air
    Is borne from interstellar spaces
    Free as the winged seed on the wind,
    Implanted as a gift in quiet hearts.

And when in the maturing year in autumn mists
    The elms loom a golden shadow in the mind
    (Forgetting fine detail of loved leaf and bark)
    We know they are foreshadowings of our own dissolving
    (O burnished cloud)—
    Both an indwelling and a dispossessing.

For when night falls with the stars unsphered
    (Crystal frosts burning the windowpane)
    And lips are dumb and our house derelict,
    From the interlunar caverns the Word will run
    Swift as light and speak for us from the thick cloud.
    Then we will hope for the silver nails
    To splinter the dark for us again—
    See them turning in the vast door of heaven—
And open wide new worlds.

M.L., A nun of Burnham Abbey

Unfold, unfold! take in his light,
Who makes thy Cares more short than night.
The Joys, with which his *Day-star* rise,
He deals to all, but Drowsy Eyes:
And what the men of this world miss,
Some *drops* and *dews* of future bliss.
    Hark! How his *winds* have chang'd their *note,*
And with warm *whispers* call thee out.
The *frosts* are past, the *storms* are gone:
And backward *life* at last comes on.
The lofty *groves* in express Joyes
Reply unto the *Turtle's* voice,
And here in *dust* and *dirt,* O here
The *Lilies* of his love appear!

Henry Vaughan

Nothing is so beautiful as spring—
    When weeds, in wheels, shoot long and lovely and lush;
    Thrush's eggs look little low heavens, and thrush
Through the echoing timber does so rinse and wring
The ear, it strikes like lightnings to hear him sing;
    The glassy pear tree leaves and blooms, they brush
    The descending blue; that blue is all in a rush
With richness; the racing lambs too have fair their fling.
What is all this juice and all this joy?
    A strain of the earth's sweet being in the beginning
In Eden garden. —Have, get, before it cloy,
    Before it cloud, Christ, lord, and sour with sinning,
Innocent mind and Mayday in girl and boy,
    Most, O maid's child, thy choice and worthy the winning.

Gerard Manley Hopkins

NORTHUMBRIAN MAY

The cold Northumbrian day,
Grey with white spume along the island sea,
Presents its own uncompromising May,
Harsh hardiness whose possibility
Inhibits what the southern month would be.

It is such days as this,
Of disappointment shrugged away behind,
That mould its race of men. They do not miss
The ease which lesser mortals hope to find,
Saved by a dogged steadiness of mind.

But when their good hours come
And bluebell breath drifts beneath bluebell sky
The faculty of rapture is not dumb
But only wordless, shaping the same high
Delight the land's saints knew as ecstasy.

J. Phoenice

BIRDS and FLOWERS COME BACK
to WAR-SCARRED LONDON

Twelve houses fell, twelve gardens broke their bounds
Before the lovers, tempted by these fronds,
Brushed by these rambling branches, could transgress
The traffic's laws and stumbled into peace;
Bedded on grass, felt the green light grow dimmer,
The yellow light grow brighter, but recede. . . .
Or walking here a clerk surprised the summer
Fierce in its narrow cage and, half afraid,
Dreamed his way back to boyhood beasts and flowers.
Translated into dreams the screech of cars.

Here whitethroats build their nests, a nightingale
Often at early dawn strikes dumb the owl.
And here—a dole of colour to the needy—
Are poppies, buttercups for all to pick;
Or dandelion leaves: a muttering lady
Braves bricks and brambles daily for their sake.
On Sundays round a parliament of mothers
Small girls make daisy-chains or look for feathers,
Snail-shells, dead butterflies and beetles' shards. . . .

Because twelve houses fell, now timid birds
Return to London and the lovers lie
Among tall ferns in deep tranquillity,

57

Hidden at nightfall in those bushes where
Four hours on end the schoolboys play at war.

Michael Hamburger

From JUBILATE AGNO

THE FLOWERS

For the doubling of flowers is the improvement of the
gardners talent.
For the flowers are great blessings.
For the Lord made a Nosegay in the meadow with his
disciples & preached upon the lily.

For the angels of God took it out of his hand and
carried it to the Height.
For a man cannot have publick spirit, who is void of
private benevolence.
For there is no Height in which there are not flowers.
For flowers have great virtues for all the senses.
For the flower glorifies God and the root parries the adversary.

For the flowers have their angels even the words of God's
Creation.
For the warp & woof of flowers are worked by perpetual
moving spirits.
For flowers are good both for the living and the dead.
For there is a language of flowers.
For there is a sound reasoning upon all flowers.

For elegant phrases are nothing but flowers.
For flowers are peculiarly the poetry of Christ.
For flowers are medicinal.
For flowers are musical in ocular harmony.
For the right names of flowers are yet in heaven. God
make gardners better nomenclators. . . .

Christopher Smart

THE RARE MOMENT

Now I have no fear, —my mind is peace.
See the rain that falls straight and gentle on flowers,
On golding oaks, on greying willows, on wet leaves,
Flamy azaleas, washed ore of brooms, fresh lilacs,
And on a hundred others such, as blue Plutonian cups
Of gentian; shy butterfly cyclamen;
Frilled parrot tulips, cool as girls' curved arms;
Globed, smouldering dark red lanterns of my peonies.

If I could give you riches it were these,—
With camellia and clematis, lovely and perfect too.
Oh! now the garden is all music under rain,
Waiting a shout, a live fanfare when the sun comes out.
My peace combines with joy, and this is bliss.
Today how bright earth shines in the garment of God.
White dove, my Joy, fly—hasten to welcome it.

Joseph Braddock

THESE IMAGES

These images were mortal without love,
Pithless, unfocused; would lie down to die:
The bracing rain which drives towards the shore,
The shags' sea-race: then on the yellow cliff
Campion, montbretia, ragwort; tufted crests
Of knapweed, and the corraline
Delicate tamarisk; pagoda-bells,
Warm fuchsia sways for colour, all the pomp,
Purple and gold, of August's panoply.
These images were empty less your love.
Love is a lamp within the alabaster,
Irradiation in the bowl of sky
That stirs my life to wonder, blazons earth.
Love is the soundless flight of a white bird
Which else were flesh and feathers and no more.

Joseph Braddock

ROSE POGONIAS

A saturated meadow,
  Sun-shaped and jewel-small,
A circle scarcely wider
  Than the trees around were tall;
Where winds were quite excluded,
  And the air was stifling sweet
With the breath of many flowers—
  A temple of the heat.

There we bowed us in the burning,
  As the sun's right worship is,
To pick where none could miss them
  A thousand orchises.
For though the grass was scattered,
  Yet every second spear
Seemed tipped with wings of color
  That tinged the atmosphere.

We raised a simple prayer
  Before we left the spot,
That in the general mowing
  That place might be forgot;
Or if not all so favored,
  Obtain such grace of hours
That none should mow the grass there
  While so confused with flowers.

Robert Frost

THE BEE–ORCHIS

I saw a bee, I saw a flower;
I looked again and said, For sure
Never was flower, never was a bee
Locked in such immobility.

The loud bees lurched about the hill,
But this flower-buried bee was still;

I said, O Love, has love the power
To change a bee into a flower.

Andrew Young

THE BUTTERFLY

To Julia

I caught a Swallow-tail inside my hat
To send you in a letter, redolent
Of sun and savage mountains, blossom too,
Lush grass and teeming flowers, bringing you
The Alpine breath:—
           But when I picked him out
He glowed so fiercely, not a feather dimmed,
His six legs waving protest, could I kill him?
Brilliant his blue eye-spots; his wings were saffron:
It would have been a blasphemy against Day.
He was Life-holy. So I let him soar
Up, if he wished, to meet the glinting glacier.
He must shine, if he will, upon my page.

Joseph Braddock

MORNING GLORY

With a pure colour there is little one can do:
Of a pure thing there is little one can say.
We are dumb in the face of that cold blush of blue,
Called glory, and enigmatic as the face of day.

A couple of optical tricks are there for the mind;
See how the azure darkens as we recede:
Like the delectable mountains left behind,
Region and colour too absolute for our mind.

61

Or putting an eye too close, until it blurs,
You see a firmament, a ring of sky,
With a white radiance in it, a universe,
And something there that might seem to sing and fly.

Only the double sex, the usual thing;
But it calls to mind spirit, it seems like one
Who hovers in brightness suspended and shimmering,
Crying Holy and hanging in the eye of the sun.

And there is one thing more; as in despair
The eye dwells on that ribbed pentagonal round,
A cold sidereal whisper brushes the ear,
A prescient tingling, a prophecy of sound.

Ruth Pitter

And now the trembling light
Glimmers behind the little hills, and corn,
Ling'ring as loth to part: yet part thou must
And though than open day far pleasing more
(Ere yet the fields and pearled cups of flowers
    Twinkle in the parting light;)
Thee night shall hide, sweet visionary gleam
That softly lookest through the rising dew:
    Till all like silver bright
    The faithful Witness, pure, and white,
Shall look o'er yonder grassy hill,
At this village, safe, and still.

All is safe, and all is still,
Save what noise the watch-dog makes
Or the shrill cock the silence breaks
    Now and then.
    And now and then
    Hark!—once again
    The wether's bell
    To us doth tell
Some little stirring in the fold.

    Methinks the ling'ring, dying ray
    Of twilight time doth seem more fair,

And lights the soul up more than day,
When widespread, sultry sunshines are.
Yet all is right, and all most fair;
For Thou, dear God, hast formed all;
Thou deckest ev'ry little flower,
Thou girdest ev'ry planet ball
And mark'st when sparrows fall.
Thou pourest out the golden day
On corn-fields rip'ning in the sun
Up the side of some great hill
Ere the sickle has begun. . . .

Samuel Palmer

Look how my autumn leaves from green to gold
Burn in the frosty fire. Tissue and vein
Shiver and curl to ash; no flowers remain
On withered stem, or from the patient mould
Draw breath and on life's tree their fans unfold.
Twice has my summer pride waxed high; now wane
The gentle influences of the rain.
The sun, the earth: and death comes, dank and cold.
But fast inscalloped in the undying root,
Constant beyond all change of sky or soil,
Lies fenced the mystery of the living shoot—
Green involutions of the mind. No toil
Attends their weaving. Ah, would they uncoil
Again from that inmost core, leaf, stem, flower, fruit.

Robert Rendall

BRAMBLES

Let us go to the fields, let us kneel there,
Clinging as bees do where the wan sun flares
Dead stone walls to life,
And find dear Autumn's ebon-tinted crowns
Sown by her random hand along the vines.

Sharp are the thorns to tear the flesh,
So blood and fruit shall mingle as the mesh
Of days we mourn the dead, but know
No death, no life is nature's law;
I eat this fruit and taste the freshness
She bestows.

Come, love, this wall is quiet;
Here let us be affianced with the diet
Of gipsy folk; here we shall beg the sun
A little nourishment.
So winter's lodging rent
Shall have been won.

S. L. Henderson Smith

WINTER COMPANY

Blackbird silent in the snow;
Motionless crocus in the mould;
Naked tree; and, cold and low.
        Sun's wintry gold . . .
Lost for the while in their strange beauty—self how far!—
Lulled were my senses into a timeless dream;
As if the inmost secret of what they are
        Lay open in what they seem.

Walter de la Mare

This morning the first snow of winter fell
Upon the virgin willow, where she wept
Beside the pond. I turned about, to tell
My beloved the news, and suddenly there leapt
A cold suspicion in my mind. I heard
Accusing conscience say, 'I am become
A monster unto many!' The unspoken word
Died on my lips, and I was stricken dumb.

In poverty of spirit watching the snow
I saw the chasm of self we may not span,

The friend we think we know yet never know,
The fantasy dividing man from man.
But then the willow slipped her icy glove,
And touched the pond with fingertips of love.

Richard Church

A HILLSIDE THAW

To think to know the country and not know
The hillside on the day the sun lets go
Ten million silver lizards out of snow!
As often as I've seen it done before
I can't pretend to tell the way it's done.
It looks as if some magic of the sun
Lifted the rug that bred them on the floor
And the light breaking on them made them run.
But if I thought to stop the wet stampede,
And caught one silver lizard by the tail,
And put my foot on one without avail,
And threw myself wet-elbowed and wet-kneed
In front of twenty others' wriggling speed—
In the confusion of them all aglitter,
And birds that joined in the excited fun
By doubling and redoubling song and twitter—
I have no doubt I'd end by holding none.

It takes the moon for this. The sun's a wizard
By all I tell; but so's the moon a witch.
From the high west she makes a gentle cast
And suddenly, without a jerk or twitch,
She has her spell on every single lizard.
I fancied when I looked at six o'clock
The swarm still ran and scuttled just as fast.
The moon was waiting for her chill effect.
I looked at nine: the swarm was turned to rock
In every lifelike posture of the swarm,
Transfixed on mountain slopes almost erect.
Across each other and side by side they lay.

The spell that so could hold as they were
Was wrought through trees without a breath of storm
To make a leaf, if there had been one, stir.
It was the moon's: she held them until day,
One lizard at the end of every ray.
The thought of my attempting such a stay!

Robert Fro

3.

"Be Still, and Know that I am God"

RAINBOW IN EXETER

ke all tourists we had to find the cathedral.
ke all tourists we failed.
n the bridge we asked a fine stout open-faced Devonshire bobby the
way
d stopping the traffic no doubt impressed with your candidly lost
American accent
gave us directions which we of course blissfully failed to carry out
d ended up once more at yet another petrol station asking directions.

und and round we went as in a squirrel cage
eking God knows what road
ehydrated as ever coveting all the gorgeous pub signs
t stopping again and again to pore over the Esso map
d seek to trace with finely pointed fingernail our ultimate
destination
that sad penultimate day.

ith absurd yet amused irritation I watched your face
nt studiously over the map spread upon your knees
d I reminding you that the lights had turned green.
e English sky was smiling most blandly overhead.
t fair, I thought, set fair.

nd then a distant voice in the sky
listant gentle awakening behind the sudden clouds
ine graffiti of raindrops on the windscreen

and we both of us looked up a bit startled
at the phenomenon above us.

A gateway! A glorious gateway
opening there above us beyond this traffic-loud moment
a triple-barred rainbow to another land
spreading over acres of sky
welcoming us through
and for us then it was the only true thing in the world.

Laughing, half crying, we passed through that gate in the sky
glorious in the knowledge of ourselves
not having any directions
but sure of our way.

Christy Brow

BETTER THAN LOVE

Are you there? Can you hear?
Listen, try to understand,
O be still, become an ear,
For there is darkness on this land.
Stand and hearken, still as stone,
For I call to you alone.

Who can be what the weed was
In the empty afternoon?
Who can match me the wild grass,
Sighing its forgotten tune:
Who is equal to that shell,
Whose spiral is my parable?

No human eye reflects the weed
Burning beneath the lonely sun:
The wild hard grass spangled with seed
Is still unmatched by anyone;
The justice of the shell is still
Above the mind, above the will.

Since love and beauty, blown upon,
Are not desired, not spoken of,
Hear me, you solitary one,
Better than beauty or than love,
Seen in the weed, the shell, the grass,
But never in my kind, alas!

The ragged weed is truth to me,
The poor grass honour, and the shell
Eternal justice, till I see
The spirit rive the roof of hell
With light enough to let me read
More than the grass, the shell, the weed.

Ruth Pitter

A RING OF WILLOWS

To Jean Kellogg

This shallow pool holds such a depth of sky
That all our sorrows are taken pity upon
Where any angel, weeping his steep bright tears,
Compels a look for heavenly compassion
Down from an upward searching of the clouds
To where the sky is doubled, and the trees,
In perfect likeness of their looking down,
Look up from heaven that the pool conceives.

They are all willows, flowing in a ring
Deep dark and down, a green and thickset fall
Toward heaven nearer than the birds ascend.
Framed in that water-wish, their mood is all
One downward concentration like a crane.
He stands on one slim stilt, himself absorbed
In proving stillness by his still intent,
Balanced upon a white and windless cloud.

Eric Barker

A POOL FOR UNICORNS

Now all voices
lie quiet as stones
that speak not at all.
Between two jay calls silence fell.
Blue shrieking bolts
they struck the woods.
And pause like that which thunder gives
is coloured like their wings.
Before they scream again
(small peacocks spiteful
of the dove's soft mood)
let the illusion deepen into dusk
and make a pool for unicorns to break.
Let those unheard hooves
and owl wings
and the trees
and stones
forgive a poem its long and
tide-like sound, the measured wave
its curved and pebbled voice,
in breaking words.

Eric Bark

IDLENESS

God, you've so much to do,
To think of, watch and listen to,
That I will let all else go by
And lending ear and eye
Help you to watch how in the combe
Winds sweep dead leaves without a broom;
And rooks in the spring-reddened trees
Restore their villages,
Nest by dark nest
Swaying at rest on the trees' frail unrest;
Or on this limestone wall,
Leaning at ease, with you recall
How once these heavy stones

Swam in the sea as shells and bones;
And hear that owl snore in a tree
Till it grows dark enough for him to see;
In fact, will learn to shirk
No idleness that I may share your work.

Andrew Young

TEESDALE

Walked up to the scar.
Walked down to the beck.
Walked on wet hay, on heather,
On limestone, on spongy grass,
Learning the shapes of tiniest lichen and rock plant,
Marsh crowfoot and meadow campanula,
The various yellow and reds of the monkey flower,
Habitat of juniper, of mountain ash,
Haunts of curlew and grouse,
The wide distribution of starlings.

Bathed in clear shallows, in pools,
In deeper, peat-coloured water.
Saw dawn and dusk, noonlight, moonlight, starlight—
Caught a snatch or two of the small-talk of place.

When the wind began to sing,
Articulate, with human voices from nowhere,
There was an end to small-talk,
Not one peewit to be heard.

When the mist came down
There was no pasture, no copse,
Only the smell of hay getting lost in moorland,
The green and the crimson moss drowning.

Wind and mist—
They took all the rest away.

Michael Hamburger

THE MOOR

It was like a church to me,
I entered it on soft foot,
Breath held like a cap in hand,
It was quiet.
What God was there made himself felt,
Not listened to, in clean colours
That brought a moistening of the eye,
In movement of the wind over grass.

There were no prayers said. But stillness
Of the heart's passions—that was praise
Enough; and the mind's cession
Of its kingdom. I walked on,
Simple and poor, while the air crumbled
And broke on me generously as bread.

R. S. Thomas

DARTMOOR

I shall not return again the way I came,
Back to the quiet country where the hills
Are purple in the evenings, and the tors
Are grey and quiet, and the tall standing stones
Lead out across the moorland till they end
At water's edge.
It is too gentle, all that land,
It will bring back
Such quiet dear remembered things,
There, where the longstone lifts its lonely head,
Gaunt, grey, forbidding,
Ageless, however worn away;
There, even, grows the heather . . .
Tender, kind,
The little streams are busy in the valleys,
The rivers meet by the grey Druid bridge,
So quiet,
So quiet,

Not as death is quiet, but as life can be quiet
When it is sweet.

Agatha Christie

If there were dreams to sell,
    What would you buy?
Some cost a passing bell;
    Some a light sigh,
That shakes from Life's fresh crown
Only a rose-leaf down.
If there were dreams to sell,
Merry and sad to tell,
And the crier rang the bell,
    What would you buy?

A cottage lone and still,
    With bowers nigh,
Shadowy, my woes to still,
    Until I die.
Such pearl from Life's fresh crown
Fain would I shake me down.
Were dreams to have at will,
This would best heal my ill,
    This would I buy.

Thomas Lovell Beddoes

From THE DUINO ELEGIES

Part of the Ninth Elegy

Here is the time for the Tellable, *here* is its home.
Speak and proclaim. More than ever
the things we can live with are falling away, and their place
being oustingly taken up by an imageless act.
Act under crusts, that will readily split as soon
as the doing within outgrows them and takes a new outline.

73

Between the hammers lives on
our heart, as between the teeth
the tongue, which, nevertheless,
remains the bestower of praise.

Praise the world to the Angel, not the untellable: you
can't impress him with the splendour you've felt; in the cosmos
where he more feelingly feels you're only a tyro. So show him
some simple thing, remoulded by age after age,
till it lives in our hands and eyes as a part of ourselves.
Tell him *things*. He'll stand more astonished; as you did
beside the roper in Rome or the potter in Egypt.
Show him how happy a thing can be, how guileless and ours;
how even the moaning of grief purely determines on form,
serves as a thing, or dies into a thing,—to escape
to a bliss beyond the fiddle. These things that live on departure
understand when you praise them: fleeting, they look for
rescue through something in us, the most fleeting of all.
Want us to change them entirely, within our invisible hearts,
into—oh, endlessly—into ourselves! Whosoever we are.

Earth, isn't this what you want: an invisible
re-arising in us? Is it not your dream
to be one day invisible? Earth! invisible!
What is your urgent command, if not transformation?
Earth, you darling, I will! Oh, believe me, you need
your Springs no longer to win me: a single one,
just one, is already more than my blood can endure.
I've now been unspeakably yours for ages and ages.
You were always right, and your holiest inspiration's
Death, that friendly Death.
Look, I am living. On what? Neither childhood nor future
are growing less. . . . . Supernumerous existence
wells up in my heart.

Rainer Maria Rilke

74

Part 3

The Loving and Beloved Creatures Who Share Our Hope

1. The Animals (and Some Other Creatures)
2. The Birds

"Let Man and Beast appear before him,
and magnify his name together."

Christopher Smart

1.
The Animals (and Some Other Creatures)

For I reckon that the sufferings we now endure bear no comparison with the splendour, as yet unrevealed, which is in store for us. For the created universe waits with eager expectation for God's sons to be revealed. It was made the victim of frustration, not by its own choice, but because of him who made it so, yet always there was hope, because the universe itself is to be freed from the shackles of mortality and enter upon the liberty and splendour of the children of God. Up to the present, we know, the whole created universe groans in all its parts as if in the pangs of childbirth. Not only so, but even we, to whom the Spirit is given as firstfruits of the harvest to come, are groaning inwardly while we wait for God to make us his sons and set our whole body free. For we have been saved, though only in hope. Now to see is no longer to hope: why should a man endure and wait for what he already sees? But if we hope for something we do not yet see, then, in waiting for it, we show our endurance.

The Letter of Paul to the Romans

THE COVENANT

The covenant of God and animal,
The frieze of fabulous creatures winged and crowned,
And in the midst the woman and the man—

Lost long ago in fields beyond the Fall—

For is this done by wreathing his body seven times round with elegant
quickness. . . .

> Keep faith in sleep-walled night and there are found
> On our long journey back where we began.
>
> Then the heraldic crest of nature lost
> Shines out again until the weariless wave
> Roofs with its sliding horror all that realm.
>
> What jealousy, what rage could overwhelm
> The golden lion and lamb and vault a grave
> For innocence, innocence past defence or cost?

Edwin Muir

THE LORD OF LIFE

The ways of God go down into microscopic depths as well as up into
telescopic heights. . . . So with mind; the ways of God go into the
depths yet unrevealed to us: He knows His horses and dogs as we cannot know them, because we are not yet pure sons of God. When
through our sonship, as Paul teaches, the redemption of these lower
brothers and sisters shall have come, then we shall understand each
other better. But now the Lord of Life has to look on at the wilful tor-
ture of multitudes of His creatures. It must be that offences come, but
woe unto that man by whom they come! The Lord may seem not to
heed, but He sees and knows. . . .

George Macdonald

I have had many dreams about animals, domestic, wild, and legend-
ary, but I shall describe only one at this point, as it seems to me to
throw into an imaginative shape two of the things I have been writing
about: our relation to the animal world, a relation involving a predes-
tined guilt, and our immortality. All guilt seeks expiation and the end
of guilt, and our blood-guiltiness towards the animals tries to find release in visions of a day when man and the beasts will live in friendship
and the lion will lie down with the lamb. My dream was connected
with this vision. I dreamed that I was lying asleep,. when a light in my

room wakened me. A man was standing by my bedside. He was wearing a long robe, which fell about him in motionless folds, while he stood like a column. The light that filled the room came from his hair, which rose straight up from his head, burning, like a motionless brazier. He raised his hand, and without touching me, merely by making that sign, lifted me to my feet in one movement, so that I stood before him. He turned and went out through the door, and I followed him. We were in the gallery of a cloister; the moon was shining, and the shadows of arches made black ribs on the flagstones. We went through a street, at the end of which there was a field, and while we walked on the moonlight changed to the white light of early morning. As we passed the last houses I saw a dark, shabby man with a dagger in his hand; he was wearing rags bound round his feet, so that he walked quite soundlessly; there was a stain as of blood on one of his sleeves; I took him to be a robber or a murderer and was afraid. But as he came nearer I saw that his eyes, which were fixed immovably on the figure beside me, were filled with a profound, violent adoration such as I had never seen in human eyes before. Then, behind him, I caught sight of a confused crowd of other men and women in curious or ragged clothes, and all had their eyes fixed with the same look on the man walking beside me. I saw their faces only for a moment. Presently we came to the field, which as we drew near changed into a great plain dotted with little conical hills a little higher than a man's head. All over the plain animals were standing or sitting on their haunches on these little hills; lions, tigers, bulls, deer, elephants, were there; serpents too wreathed their lengths on the knolls; and each was separate and alone, and each slowly lifted its head upward as if in prayer. This upward-lifting motion had a strange solemnity and deliberation; I watched head after head upraised as if proclaiming some truth just realized, and yet as if moved by an irresistible power beyond them. The elephant wreathed its trunk upward, and there was something pathetic and absurd in that indirect act of adoration. But the other animals raised their heads with the inevitability of the sun's rising, as if they knew, like the sun, that a new day was about to begin, and were giving the signal for its coming. Then I saw a little dog busily running about with his nose tied to the ground, as if he did not know that the animals had been redeemed. He was a friendly little dog, officiously going about his business, and it seemed to me that he too had a place in this day, and that his oblivious concern with the earth was also a sort of worship. How the dream ended I do not remember: I have now only a memory of the great animals with all their heads raised to heaven.

Edwin Muir

From JUBILATE AGNO

THE CREATURES

Rejoice in God, O ye Tongues; give the glory to the Lord, and the Lamb.

Nations, and languages, and every Creature, in which is the breath of Life.

Let man and beast appear before him, and magnify his name together.

Let Noah and his company approach the throne of Grace, and do homage to the Ark of their Salvation.

Let Abraham present a Ram, and worship the God of his Redemption.

Let Isaac, the Bridegroom, kneel with his Camels, and bless the hope of his pilgrimage.

Let Jacob, and his speckled Drove adore the good Shepherd of Israel.

Let Esau offer a scape Goat for his seed, and rejoice in the blessing of God his father.

Let Nimrod, the mighty hunter, bind a Leopard to the altar, and consecrate his spear to the Lord. . . .

Let Moses, the Man of God, bless with a Lizard, in the sweet majesty of good-nature, and the magnanimity of meekness.

Let Joshua praise God with an Unicorn—the swiftness of the Lord, and the strength of the Lord, and the spear of the Lord mighty in battle. . . .

Let Ethan praise with the Flea, his coat of mail, his piercer, and his vigour, which wisdom and providence, have contrived to attract observation and to escape it.

Let Heman bless with the Spider, his warp and his woof, his subtlety and industry, which are good.

Let Chalcol praise with the Beetle, whose life is precious in the sight of God, tho' his appearance is against him. . . .

Let Solomon praise with the Ant, and give the glory to the Fountain of all Wisdom. . . .

Let Mephibosheth with the Cricket praise the God of chearfulness, hospitality, and gratitude. . . .

Let Job bless with the Worm—the life of the Lord is in Humiliation, the Spirit also and the truth. . . .

Let Zadoc worship with the Mole—before honour is humility, and he that looketh low shall learn. . . .

Let Tobias bless Charity with his Dog, who is faithful, vigilant, and a friend in poverty.
Let Anna bless God with the Cat, who is worthy to be presented before the throne of grace, when he has trampled upon the idol in his prank. . . .

Let Peter rejoice with the Moon Fish who keeps up the life in the waters by night. . . .

Let John rejoice with Nautilus who spreads his sail & plies his oar, and the Lord is his pilot. . . .

Let Thomas rejoice with the Sword-Fish, whose aim is perpetual & strength insuperable. . . .

Let James the less, rejoice with the Haddock, who brought the piece of money for the Lord and Peter. . . .

For the nets come down from the eyes of the Lord to fish up men to their salvation.
For I have a greater compass both of mirth and melancholy than another. . . .

For in my nature I quested for beauty, but God, God hath sent me to sea for pearls. . . .

THE CAT JEOFFRY

For I will consider my Cat Jeoffry.
For he is the servant of the Living God duly and daily serving him.
For at the first glance of the glory of God in the East he worships in his way.

81

For in his morning orisons he loves the sun and the sun loves him. . . .

For he purs in thankfulness, when God tells him he's a good Cat. . . .

For he knows that God is his saviour.
For there is nothing sweeter than his peace when at rest.
For there is nothing brisker than his life when in motion. . . .

For the divine spirit comes about his body to sustain it in compleat
    Cat. . . .

Christopher Smart

OLD WOMAN TO CAT

Cat, smoother soother than a velvet glove,
How can you thus reply to my caress?
In giving, I receive the touch of love
Yet the gnarled knuckle and the brown age-blotch
Are there for those mysterious eyes to watch
And I thought beauty shrank from ugliness.

Queen Cat, to whom I kneel with joints that creak,
There is no grace in my antiquity
But only movements difficult and weak,
Whereas you move with pure fluidity.
Bear with me, lovely one, and though I grow
Unlovelier still, pretend you do not know.

M. Bon

CAT

Unfussy lodger, she knows what she wants and gets it:
Food, cushions, fires, the run of the garden.
I, her night porter in the small hours
Don't bother to grumble, grimly let her in.
To that coldness she purrs assent,

Eats her fill and outwits me,
Plays hide and seek in the dark house.

Only at times, by chance meeting the gaze
Of her amber eyes that can rest on me
As on a beech-bole, on bracken or meadow grass
I'm moved to celebrate the years between us,
The farness and the nearness:
My fingers graze her head.
To that fondness she purrs assent.

Michael Hamburger

THE PLAIN FACTS

By a PLAIN but AMIABLE Cat

See what a charming smile I bring,
Which no one can resist;
For I have found a wondrous thing—
The Fact that I exist.

And I have found another, which
I now proceed to tell.
The world is so sublimely rich
That you exist as well.

Fact One is lovely, so is Two,
But O the best is Three:
The fact that I can smile at you,
And you can smile at me.

Ruth Pitter

Cats move like water,
Dogs like wind . . .
Only when bodies
Have shut out mind

Can they learn the calm
Motion of dream.

Would we could know
The way men moved
When thought was only
A great dark love

And blood lay calm
In a depthless dream.

Stanley Burnshaw

From MODES OF FEELING

Last Verses

Look in the snug of an inn, under that dark table
A poodle's head, a black dahlia, glistening eyes—
Any dog grasping a bone, why he's been there
Since Chaucer took the road to Canterbury,
Or Odysseus went home to Ithaca.
That sleek cat, see, sharpening sadist claws
For the voracious shrew's
Protracted terror, is as durable
As glazed Egyptian porcelain from tombs.

Manifold incarnations, inbeings
In an ascending cycle
Point to the warm touch of a human hand.
That bird you hear whistling his heart out
Forlornly went unheeded;
While scythe-winged swifts tore shrieking through the sky,
Swift dropped on swift, in high pure heaven to mate,
Unmarked of man. Flowers breathed their fragrances
Aeons before brutes lurked, to smell them . . .

All forms of life, each separate quiddity,
Shadow the divine perfect,
Stirring the conscious soul

Bound to race memories,
Speak equally through a cell or Saturn's rings.

Ahead peaks gleam, waves glow,—
Salt odour of the glowing wave to those long parched by land
Presage a Sea no mortal mind may sail.

Joseph Braddock

BYRON'S DOG

 This monument is still a conspicuous ornament in the garden of
Newstead. The following is the inscription by which the verses are
preceded.

"Near this spot
Are deposited the Remains
of one
Who possessed Beauty
Without Vanity,
Strength without Ferocity,
And all the Virtues of Man
Without his Vices.

This Praise which would be unmeaning flattery
If inscribed over Human Ashes,
Is but a just tribute to the Memory of
'Boatswain,' a Dog
Who was born at Newfoundland,
May, 1803,
And died at Newstead Abbey,
Nov. 18, 1808."

When some proud son of man returns to earth,
Unknown to glory, but upheld by birth,
The sculptor's art exhausts the pomp of woe,
And storied urns record who rests below;
When all is done, upon the tomb is seen,
Not what he was, but what he should have been;
But the poor dog, in life the firmest friend,

The first to welcome, foremost to defend,
Whose honest heart is still his master's own,
Who labours, fights, lives, breathes for him alone,
Unhonoured falls, unnoticed all his worth,
Denied in heaven the soul he held on earth;
While man, vain insect! hopes to be forgiven,
And claims himself a sole exclusive heaven.
Oh man! thou feeble tenant of an hour,
Debased by slavery, or corrupt by power,
Who knows thee well must quit thee with disgust,
Degraded mass of animated dust!
Thy love is lust, they friendship all a cheat,
Thy smiles hypocrisy, thy words deceit!
By nature vile, ennobled but by name,
Each kindred brute might bid thee blush for shame.
Ye! who perchance behold this simple urn,
Pass on—it honours none you wish to mourn.
To mark a friend's remains these stones arise;
I never knew but one—and here he lies.

George Byron

WORDSWORTH'S DOG

Lie here, without a record of thy worth,
Beneath a covering of the common earth!
It is not from unwillingness to praise,
Or want of love, that here no Stone we raise;
More thou deserv'st; but *this* Man gives to Man,
Brother to brother, *this* is all we can.
Yet they to whom thy virtues made thee dear
Shall find thee through all the changes of the year:
This Oak points out thy grave; the silent tree
Will gladly stand a monument of thee.
I grieved for thee, and wished thy end were passed;
And willingly have laid thee here at last:
For thou hadst lived till everything that cheers
In thee had yielded to the weight of years;
Extreme old age had wasted thee away,
And left thee but a glimmering of the day;
Thy ears were deaf, and feeble were thy knees,—

86

I saw thee stagger in the summer breeze,
Too weak to stand against its sportive breath,
And ready for the gentlest stroke of death.
It came, and we were glad; yet tears were shed;
Both Man and Woman wept when Thou wert dead;
Not only for a thousand thoughts, that were,
Old household thoughts, in which thou hadst thy share;
But for some precious boons vouchsafed to thee,
Found scarcely anywhere in like degree!
For love, that comes to all—the holy sense,
Best gift of God—in thee was most intense;
A chain of heart, a feeling of the mind,
A tender sympathy, which did thee bind
Not only to us Men, but to thy Kind;
Yea, for thy Fellow-brutes in thee we saw
The soul of Love. Love's intellectual law;—
Hence, if we wept, it was not done in shame;
Our tears from passion and from reason came,
And, therefore, shalt thou be an honoured name.

William Wordsworth

MATTHEW ARNOLD'S DOG

Four years!—and didst thou stay above
   The ground which hides thee now, but four?
And all that life, and all that love,
   Were crowded, Geist! into no more?
            *   *   *   *

That liquid, melancholy eye,
   From whose pathetic, soul-fed springs
Seem'd surging the Virgilian cry,
   The sense of tears in mortal things.—

That steadfast, mournful strain, consoled
   By spirits gloriously gay,
And temper of heroic mould—
   What, was four years their whole short day?

Yes, only four!—and not the course
   Of all the centuries yet to come,

And not the infinite resource
    Of Nature, with her countless sum.

Of figures, with her fulness vast
    Of new creation evermore,
Can ever quite repeat the past,
    Or just thy little self restore.

*   *   *   *

And so there rise these lines of verse
    On lips that rarely form them now;
While to each other we rehearse;
    Such ways, such arts, such looks hadst thou!

We stroke thy broad brown paws again,
    We bid thee to thy vacant chair,
We greet thee by the windowpane,
    We hear thy scuffle on the stair.

We see the flaps of thy large ears
    Quick raised to ask which way we go;
Crossing the frozen lake, appears
    Thy small black figure on the snow!

Nor to us only art thou dear,
    Who mourn thee in thine English home;
Thou hadst thine absent master's tear,
    Dropt by the far Australian foam.

The memory lasts both here and there,
    And thou shalt live as long as we,
And after that—thou dost not care!
    In us was all the world to thee.

Yet fondly zealous for thy fame,
    E'en to a date beyond our own,
We strive to carry down that name,
    By moulded turf and graven stone.

We lay thee, close within our reach,
    Here, where the grass is smooth and warm,
Between the holly and the beech,
    Where oft we watched thy couchant form.

Asleep, yet lending half an ear

To travellers on the Portsmouth road:—
There build we thee, O guardian dear,
  Mark'd with a stone, thy last abode!

Then some, who through this garden pass,
  When we too, like thyself, are clay,
Shall see thy grave upon the grass,
  And stop before the stone, and say:

People who lived here long ago
  Did by this stone, it seems, intend
To name for future times to know
  The dachshund, Geist, their little friend.

Matthew Arnold

THE RUNAWAY

Once when the snow of the year was beginning to fall,
We stopped by a mountain pasture to say, "Whose colt?"
A little Morgan had one forefoot on the wall,
The other curled at his breast. He dipped his head
And snorted at us. And then he had to bolt.
We heard the miniature thunder where he fled,
And we saw him, or thought we saw him, dim and gray,
Like a shadow against the curtain of falling flakes.
"I think the little fellow's afraid of the snow.
He isn't winter-broken. It isn't play
With the little fellow at all. He's running away.
I doubt if even his mother could tell him, 'Sakes,
It's only weather.' He'd think she didn't know!
Where is his mother? He can't be out alone."
And now he comes again with clatter of stone,
And mounts the wall again with whited eyes
And all his tail that isn't hair up straight.
He shudders his coat as if to throw off flies.
"Whoever it is that leaves him out so late,
When other creatures have gone to stall and bin,
Ought to be told to come and take him in."

Robert Frost

COWPER

He walked among the alders. Birds flew down,
And water voles watched by the river shore.
A mist hummed on his eyelids, blurred and brown—
The self-sequestered with himself at war.

The bright psalms were his banners: Sion, Ind,
Siloam, rang like horns down Joshua's plain.
At noon the thunder rambled from his mind—
He felt the sun beneath the Olney rain.

Norman Nicholson

THE TAME HARE

She came to him in dreams—her ears
Diddering like antennae, and her eyes
Wide as dark flowers where the dew
Holds and dissolves a purple hoard of shadow.
The thunder clouds crouched back, and the world opened
Tiny and bright as a celandine after rain.
A gentle light was on her, so that he
Who saw the talons in the vetch
Remembered now how buttercup and daisy
Would bounce like springs when a child's foot stepped off them.
Oh, but never dared he touch—
Her fur was still electric to the fingers.

Yet of all the beasts blazoned in gilt and blood
In the black-bound missal of his mind,
Pentecostal dove and paschal lamb,
Eagle, lion, serpent, she alone
Lived also in the noon of ducks and sparrows;
And the cleft-mouthed kiss which plugged the night with fever
Was sweetened by a lunch of docks and lettuce.

Norman Nicholson

THE BADGER

White is my neck, head yellow, sides
The same. Weapons I wear, am hurried, and along
My back as on my cheek stands hair. Two ears
Above my eyes, through greenest grass
On claws I go. If in my house sharp
Fighter finds me where my children
Live, my part is grief, this stranger bringing
Doom of dying to my door.
I must be cool then, and
Take off my dear ones: To wait for
His fierceness (on ribs crawling
Closer) would be most witless, I
Would not chance it. But working with forefeet
A way through the steep hill, with ease I shall
Lead out my dears through the down
By a tunnel in secret. I shall not fear then
To fight with the death dog. And if close behind me
He follows a pathway up on the hilltop
I shall turn, and go for him,
And viciously spear this creature I hate
      Who has followed me there.

Geoffrey Grigson

HEDGEHOGS AND GEESE

Hedgehogs undermine the winter.
Shrouded in old leaves
they let the edges of their bodies die.
They retreat into their own hearts.
Geese, too, retreat before the ice
but south instead of under.
They burrow with their wings.
Down the long tunnels of the skies
they hurtle, talking to themselves,
a conversation encoded by the wind
and by their unimaginable history.
At zero latitude they nod.

91

They pull the equator over their heads
and go to sleep.

Each year I study these alternatives,
pursuing kinship in a hardening world.
My eyes lift to the geese at first,
a moment lured by height
and uncorrupted space
—one's fill of distances!
But that's the vision unbraced by the will
or the spirit premature as usual.
At heart no flyer
I bristle timidly when touched.
When the ice comes I retreat beneath it.
I choose at last hedgehogs.

Alasdair MacLean

LIZARD

O lizard,
chinking up the new made wall
come down: the moderns do not make you inns.
Come down to me,
green lightning of the day,
and lie upon the frond-dress of the ground
like such a pin as white necked Deirdre wore.
Ah! You are down.
Where will you go now?
Not up the palm,
for there the urchin sun
lies spikey white in his great lair of sky,
and I am here between you and your cave
where you skid round boy-glad on roller skates.
No, lagartijo, I take that image back.
Not skates.
For you have claws like fairy forks
that feed in autumn on the red and berried ground.
Oh, calm your pulsing neck.
That's right. Lie still,
so I can marvel at your mosaiced back

your carpet-threaded tail
your head of fish
your mould of yacht hull curves,
water in sand
your miming wisdom's torch
your anchored grace.
You raise yourself upon a twig to preach;
I read the message in your watching eye
that I am some dead thing lit by the sun
mere moon of your amaze.
And moving ants
are all the passion of your livelier eye.
If I be naught to you, yet you are now
the biggest of God's fingers in my world,
my friend,
my image-maker,
poet-wife.
O little dragon, where is the scoundrel knight
would tilt at you?
Tell me, and I will kill him in my verse.

Jerome Kiely

SO GOOD OF THEIR KIND

"Snakes hanging from a tree!
Snakes hanging from the rough crack-willow bark!
Snakes hanging—come and see—
It almost frightened me—
I passed, and saw them shining in the dark."

Not snakes, huge slugs. They hung
Twined in sevenfold embrace, by a tough slime;
Strong slime that held them wrung
Together, swinging and strung
In the great double helix of our time.

And there suspended, till
They had accomplished what they had to do.
And though they seemed so still

It was dynamic will
That held them, and their world about them too.

Fissured and frowning rock
Behind and overhanging, the bole seemed;
But strong desire had struck
That too; each ridge and nook
With something glittering and precious gleamed.

There must have been some dance,
Some festal wooing; for the rugged face
With nacreous phosphor glanced,
Festooned with radiance:
So they had dignified their nuptial place.

A strong electric tide
Flowed through my flesh, so honoured to have seen them:

All life was on their side,
Death was so well defied—
And then I saw a wonder grow between them.

Something—a great round gem—
Seemed from the two twined bodies to be growing;
Flower on a double stem
The soul of both of them,
Each lost, both consummated in one knowing.

It flowered and faded: rest
Took them a moment, as they hung entwined
And vulnerable: at best
Their strength was of the least;
They had attained their height: their star declined.

One wreathed himself away,
Climbing the wonderful rope. The other soon
Devouring the strong grey
Bond of their nuptial day,
Followed, and with strange swiftness both were gone.

But one on the rough rind
Turning towards his fellow as he moved,
Eager to seek his blind

Safe crevice, yet could find
A moment for the mate whom he had loved:

With almost courtly pause,
Turning the head with almost conscious grace,
Seeming to know the laws
By which life pleads love's cause,
With the soft mouthparts touched the other's face.

Ruth Pitter

THE PRAYER OF THE ANT

Lord,
I am always made out to be wrong;
a fable to the whole world.
Certainly I hoard
and make provision!
I have my rights!
And surely I can take a little joy
in the fruits of all my work
without some sob singer
Coming to rob my store?
There is something in Your justice
that I scarcely understand,
and, if You would allow me to advise,
it might be thought over again.
I have never been a burden to anybody,
and, if I may say so,
I manage my own business very well.
Then,
to the incorrigible improvidence
of some people,
must I, for all eternity, say
Amen.

Carmen de Gasztold

2.
The Birds

THE PRAYER OF THE COCK

Do not forget, Lord,
it is I who make the sun rise.
I am Your servant
but, with the dignity of my calling,
I need some glitter and ostentation.
Noblesse oblige. . . .
All the same,
I am Your servant,
only. . . . do not forget, Lord,
I make the sun rise.

Carmen de Gasztol

HEN UNDER BAY-TREE

A squalid, empty-headed Hen,
Resolved to rear a private brood,
Has stolen from the social pen
To this, the noblest solitude.

She feels this tree is magical.
She knows that spice, beneath her breast
That sweet dry death; for after all
Her cradle was the holy East.

Alert she sits, and all alone;
She breathes a time-defying air:
Above her, songbirds many a one
Shake the dark spire, and carol there.

Unworthy and unwitting, yet
She keeps love's vigil glorious;
Immovably her faith is set,
The plant of honour is her house.

Ruth Pitter

THE MISSEL-THRUSH

That missel-thrush
Scorns to alight on a low bush,
And as he flies
And tree-top after tree-top tries,
His shadow flits
And harmlessly on tree-trunk hits.

Shutting his wings
He sways and sings and sways and sings,
And from his bough
As in deep water he looks through
He sees me there
Crawl at the bottom of the air.

Andrew Young

THE OLD SWEET DOVE OF WIVETON

'Twas the voice of the sweet dove
I heard him move
I heard him cry
Love, love.

High in the chestnut tree
Is the nest of the old dove

And there he sits solitary
Crying, Love, love.

The gray of this heavy day
Makes the green of the trees' leaves and the grass brighter
And the flowers of the chestnut tree whiter
And whiter the flowers of the high cow-parsley.

So still is the air
So heavy the sky
You can hear the splash
Of the water falling from the green grass
As Red and Honey push by,
The old dogs,
Gone away, gone hunting by the marsh bogs.

Happy the retriever dogs in their pursuit
Happy in bog-mud the busy foot.

Now all is silent, it is silent again
In the sombre day and the beginning soft rain
It is a silence made more actual
By the moan from the high tree that is occasional,
Where in his nest above
Still sits the old dove,
Murmuring solitary
Crying for pain,
Crying most melancholy
Again and again.

Stevie Smith

WILD DOVES ARRIVING,
AND ABSORBED IN HEDGES

There is a contrast between the high flight of doves
And their douce behaviour two by two in hedges.
They fly in parties. Their wings are sharp and quick and nervy.
They have purpose. Their quick flight pauses, doves drop away
In ones for now new green of hedges, where flight from branch
To branch inside is nothing wild. Mated, their ringed
Eyes, their melody, are mild. "Dove-grey", we say, "dove-grey."

At times they walk for smoothness on quiet roads.
A car approaches. Spreading white tails they rise
And are once more invisibly absorbed in hedges.

Geoffrey Grigson

THE BIRD

Adventurous bird walking upon the air,
Like a schoolboy running and loitering, leaping and springing,
Pensively pausing, suddenly changing your mind
To turn at ease on the heel of a wing-tip. Where
In all the crystalline world was there to find
For your so delicate walking and airy winging
A floor so perfect, so firm and fair,
And where a ceiling and walls so sweetly ringing,
Whenever you sing, to your clear singing?

The wide-winged soul itself can ask no more
Than such a pure, resilient and endless floor
For its strong-pinioned plunging and soaring and upward and
    upward springing.

Edwin Muir

THE TOMTIT

Twilight had fallen, austere and grey,
The ashes of a wasted day,
When, tapping at the window-pane,
My visitor had come again,
To peck late supper at his ease—
A morsel of suspended cheese.

What ancient code, what Morse knew he—
This eager little mystery—
That, as I watched, from lamp-lit room,
Called on some inmate of my heart to come
Out of its shadows—filled me then
With love, delight, grief, pining, pain,
Scarce less than had he angel been?

Suppose, such countenance as that,
Inhuman, deathless, delicate,
Had gazed this winter moment in—
Eyes of an ardour and beauty no
Star, no Sirius could show!

Well, it were best for such as I
To shun direct divinity;
Yet not stay heedless when I heard
The tip-tap nothings of a tiny bird.

Walter de la Ma

LARK'S NEST

To find a lark's nest in the tufted grass
Had long been my ambition, and I went
Over the meadow criss-cross, lest I pass
That carefully concealed establishment
Where leaves and wheat and stubble were entwined,
Perfectly camouflaged, and safe from all
Who walked that way: a tiny flickering shrine
Where love alone kept the shy bird in thrall.

Yet I could not discover where she stayed
Quiescent and obedient, for the fine
Pasture contained her, as a diamond
Hides in the rugged splendour of the mine.
Only her mate's high pleasure told me how
Time would distil new joy: but could not, now.

Jean Kenwa

MIRACLES

Beauty is the medicine of God,
the oil He pours upon our wounded minds
and sudden beauty is His miracle
of healing. I have been cured a thousand times
and thrice by miracle. In the springtime once

100

walking an arid path I saw asleep
on an apple tree a choir of angel folk
swandowned, swanquiet, or the souls of swans;
and in the month of June beyond Cloghroe
a boy by a river like a pipe of grace
wistfully fingered by the playing sun;
but, best of all, the Barrow evening when I saw
red chestnuts that sprouted plumes and legs
upon a stalk quite suddenly—two birds!—
two kingfishers who snatched my thoughts away
out of brown waters on their joyous beaks,
for a blackbird panicked in a berrybush
and the kingfishers brandished their jewelled swords,
and cut across the river with a thrust of light
bluegreen and blue and red and beetle bright.
O kingfishers, right royally ye caught
my heart and played it to the bank of awe!

Jerome Kiely

TOKI

"The Bird of Time has but a little way
To fly—and Lo! The Bird is on the Wing. . . . "

Rubaiyat of Omar Khayyam, Fitzgerald translation

O rare bird, red heron,
scarlet crested ibis, you
native of Eastern Asia,
once the subject of poems,
paintings, fans and screens
in China, Japan, Korea—
but now a dying breed.

In China and Korea
your heron's crested head, tinged
on the cheeks and bill with red and orange,
no longer graces rice fields.
Your white, slender body like a vase
no longer stands among the green rice-shoots.

Your vermilion shanks and feet
no longer wade the paddy pools.
Your pink-lined wings
flash no more across the bamboo glades.

No poet celebrates you now.
No painter spreads your pinions
on the gold-squared sky of screens,
or lets your beak dip
among the sticks of a white fan.

No poet celebrates you now.
How can you be a harbinger of luck,
when your own has been so bad?
—So I shall celebrate you now
in this poem that is your funeral ode. . . .

Once, twelve of you survived.
Japan was your final home,
your nests of snow
on Sado Island's Mount Kokuryu,
on northern winter's
remote peninsula of Noto.

There I saw you once—
a single bird
silently flying the lonely sky
above the cliffs of snow.
Yes, that was where men saw you last. . . .

—For death is now the toki's nest. . . .

James Kirk

THE SPARROW'S SKULL

Memento Mori   *Written at the Fall of France*

The kingdoms fall in sequence, like the waves on the shore.
All save divine and desperate hopes go down, they are no more.
Solitary is our place, the castle in the sea,
And I muse on those I have loved, and on those who have loved me.

I gather up my loves, and keep them all warm,
While above our heads blows the bitter storm:
The blessed natural loves, of life-supporting flame,
And those whose name is Wonder, which have no other name.

The skull is in my hand, the minute cup of bone,
And I remember her, the tame, the loving one,
Who came in at the window, and seemed to have a mind
More towards sorrowful man than to those of her own kind.

She came for a long time, but at length she grew old;
And on her death-day she came, so feeble and so bold;
And all day, as if knowing what the day would bring,
She waited by the window, with her head beneath her wing.

And I will keep the skull, for in the hollow here
Lodged the minute brain that had outgrown a fear;
Transcended an old terror, and found a new love,
And entered a strange life, a world it was not of.

Even so, dread God! even so, my Lord!
The fire is at my feet, and at my breast the sword:
And I must gather up my soul, and clap my wings, and flee
Into the heart of terror, to find myself in thee.

Ruth Pitter

WHAT THE BIRD SAID EARLY IN THE YEAR

I heard in Addison's Walk a bird sing clear
'This year the summer will come true. This year. This year.

'Winds will not strip the blossom from the apple trees
This year, nor want of rain destroy the peas.

'This year time's nature will no more defeat you,
Nor all the promised moments in their passing cheat you.

'This time they will not lead you round and back
To Autumn, one year older, by the well-worn track.

'This year, this year, as all these flowers foretell,
We shall escape the circle and undo the spell.

'Often deceived, yet open once again your heart,
Quick, quick, quick, quick!—the gates are drawn apart.'

C. S. Lewi

Part 4

Faith in God the Redeemer

1. Light in Darkness
2. The Redeemer
3. His Cross and Resurrection

"The Author and Finisher of Our Faith."

St. Paul

1.
Light in Darkness

The people who walked in darkness
have seen a great light:
light has dawned upon them,
    dwellers in a land as dark as death.

For a boy has been born for us, a son given to us
    to bear the symbol of dominion on his shoulder;
        and he shall be called
        in purpose wonderful, in battle God-like,
        Father of all time, Prince of peace.
Great shall the dominion be,
    and boundless the peace
bestowed on David's throne and on his kingdom,
to establish it and sustain it
    with justice and righteousness
    from now and for evermore.
The zeal of the LORD of Hosts shall do this.

The Book of Isaiah
The New English Bible

ANNUNCIATION

Tilted, the unreflecting glass
throws on its back
one corner of the room.

107

In a vase, a long lily,
out of true, does not falter.
A marble does not roll.

The spirit level
still centres its bead
of air. Out of plumb,

the abandoned body of
the floorboards is outflung,
parallels of dust converging on

infinity, a mousehole.
Those deranged bedclothes,
old snows of crumpled news.

Overhead, a slanted window
stabs her with shaft on shaft of sun,
leans its lightweight hard on her—

angel of glass whose pinions,
still billowing with the winds of flight,
are checked curtains signalling

like rally flags
news of a triumph to
devastated streets.

James Kirkup

FOR THE BIRTH OF A GOD

Wherever now you are, and whoever you may be,
In countryside or city, in the mountains or at sea;
Dark with the vigour of the wave that bears our age,
Or fair and impossible as my own lost image:
    You through the furnaces of all disaster
Shall surely walk, and through the deserts of our day.
    Through the spirit's night, the mind's bright master
You shall prove, and through the body's golden clay
Shall breathe the soul, and draw the precious veins of stone

That burn to speech the dumbness of our flesh and bone.
   You, at the last, great saviour, shall arrive, and be
The one our insecurity confesses and awaits.
   For you alone can come, and take us seriously,
With a gay abandon, we who at the gates
Of nothing live with lust, and pride, and vanity and war.

May I, too, prince, now recognize for what you are
   You with the unknown face and the familiar eyes
   Whose voice is all men's, and whose love is wise.

James Kirkup

THE NATIVITY AT NIGHT

After the Painting of Little Gerard of Harlem

He who is our day
Is born at night.
Laid on the winter hay,
A summer's king.
With his own light
He shines on everything.

Though he is bare,
He is not cold,
But burns the air
Of night to noon,
With heat more bold
Than any sun.

His mother's face
Upon him bends
Its wondering grace;
She kneels before,
Joining her hands
In curious prayer.

For what is He,
This Babe she bore,
That angels fly

109

To welcome him?
The ass at the door
And the ox gaze in

With furred eyes
And lifted ears,
While in the skies
To shepherds and to kings
An angel-star appears
And to them sings:

'O, have no fear
Of dark, or of
The news you hear
From me: this night
Is born the Child of Love,
The Prince of Light.

Here for you all
His life is laid
In an ox's stall
He, born of man
And virgin maid
Is God's own Son.

Go, worship Him
With gift and prayer,
He who without sin
Bids you with loving kindness take
Pity on one another, for
His dear sake.

That in His sunny paradise above
You, too, may know His Mercy, Peace and
Love.'

James Kirkup

Night called
and a star broke
the cedars hushed, the hills
rang like bells.

110

We were not there
we did not wake
nor did we see God denied
his crucifixion prophesied.

It was too dark
our eyes were closed
no one had told us
—were we deaf—
or did we merely sleep, unborn?

He was so small
a flake of snow
that blanched the mountains
with its glow.

He was so bright
a flame, whose fire
may reach us yet
vivify us with its heat.

Sister Mary Agnes, Order of Poor Clares

Lord let me come near this year,
And see and hear and sing
The mystery of God's self-emptying.

God's will, it is no grandiose thing
It is the little service that we bring
The open eye, the open ear—
To see—to hear
The insignificant and small
The heart of love to care, to share
A brother's need
That smile that takes the strife from dreary daily life.

God's will
It is the light of love, warmth
That lets the flower of faith

From tiny seed—tight bud—burst forth
Glorious in its simplicity.

111

There as a babe he lies—and cries
This tiny thing
Sent by the will of God
To let men know by way of manger and of cross
God gives—Emptying Himself upon the earth.

Man grasps and makes a name—seeks fame.
God gives Himself away and takes the lowest place.
Takes on Himself the helplessness that every love must know.
God's will for men? Self-emptying.
Pouring out all their love.
And so bestow
Healing of heart and mind. . . . Sight to the blind.
Let me come near this coming year
To see and hear and sing,
The mystery of God's self-emptying.

R. M., A nun of Burnham Abbey

THE ANGEL'S MESSAGE

Stoop down
    Adore, and let
The light of Glory pour
Upon thee.
Come, see,
    For he is seeking thee.
So small and yet so wise
Creator of the world, He lies.

Oh, let thyself be found. . . .
    And joy abound.

R.M., A nun of Burnham Abbey

CHRISTMAS EVE

Is there any difference between birth and death?
The breaking of the womb when life with trembling starts

And the tomb's slaking when with steps of stealth
Spirit forsakes time's old familiar loom and parts?

The one is coming, the other going
Beginning one and end the other;
But who can say we have not been here before
And birth which seems from nothing sprung
Is rather corridor-opening of a door;
We have forgotten what that side was sung
And none can this side ask another.

They said that Christ was born, and drank their ale,
But I knew Christ was dead, the gospel stale,
All hope forlorn, until I kindling thought
His birth and death were one, the difference nought,
For as I at His manger laid my head
I was by nail-pierced hand with wafers fed.

S. L. Henderson Smith

AT CHRISTMAS

Always
in the dark centre
of this season
the birth occurs
noiseless and marvellous;
the seers
move on their journey,
there are gestures
of wonder, and at midnight
a resting star.
Always
it is amazing
that the mountains
do not relinquish
their momentary grandeur,
bend to the stable,
let the ermine tremble
there

113

where the oxen
and the angels are.

Jean Kenward

A BLIND CHILD'S CHRISTMAS CAROL

One day I shall behold the Rose
That blooms beyond the sky,
And the eternal Lily, whose
Perfection cannot die.
I shall behold the Lamb of Love,
And in the living Tree
The burning plumage of the Dove,
The Holy Spirit, see.

I shall behold in Paradise,
After my second birth,
The loveliest and most loving Eyes
That ever dawned on earth.
I shall be like those kings of old
Who journeyed through the night
With myrrh, and frankincense, and gold,
To where the Star was bright.

To where the new-born Face Divine
Dawned like the day on them
Who sought by faith their Light and mine
In far-off Bethlehem.

Ruth Pitt

ST. STEPHEN'S DAY

Yesterday the gentle
Story: the summoning star,
Shepherd and beast and King
In their enchanted ring,
The moment still with awe.

114

Shepherd and beast and King
Wince at a cry:
It is no newborn cry
For He is asleep,
But a cry alerting night.

Who saw the hanging star
Shudder and fall?
I, Stephen, saw
Fragments of hot stone
Whistle down, smite the earth.

Stones thud on flesh,
The bestial mob howls,
No Kings are here to witness.
Yesterday birth blood,
Today pulped flesh and death blood

Streaming from broken eyes:
Yet the triumphant cry,
I see my God.
So was the first day
After the gentle birth.

Patric Dickinson

JESUS AT SCHOOL

The wise Zacharias said
   "This lad is wonderful
And he'd be a hundred times better
   If he went to school."

Jesus went with Zacharias
   Who wished to teach him to read;
"Here's the alphabet, boy. Say A."
   The all-knowing head

Refused. Zacharias used the stick.
   Jesus then said

115

"Strike an anvil, what is the lesson?
    The anvil teaches the man."

Quietly then the boy
    Proved that his words were true,
Speaking to old Zacharias
    More than Zacharias knew.

Said the wise Zacharias then
    "Take the boy from me now,
I can't give any answer,
    Leave me with what I know."

Brendan Kennel

A POEM FOR CHRISTMAS

He waits beside the music-stand, and guides
his magic properties, aloof and faintly sad, but smiling
at the darkened whiteness of our faces: once he pulled
confetti, cards or ribbon from the hair that lies
like fans on his enchanted, heart-shaped brow.

This, surely, is the conjurer we all desired
at birthdays. He weighed us gently down
with wreaths of paper or
a cardboard crown, and made the shy one
suddenly victorious.

His twisted face is pale, and not
exactly like an uncle's: yet there is
that something in him like a relative,
a friendly cousin from the colonies, whom they
all knew, but we had never met before.

Look how he stands up stiffly in his black
performing clothes. Upon the guéridon
the gilded cone, the wizard's wand, the gloves,

the tumbler and the opera-hat repose.
We wonder why he never moves.
We wait, and look towards him for
the miracle, a dove.

James Kirkup

2.

The Redeemer

Behold, a king shall reign in righteousness
　　and his rulers rule with justice,
　　and a man shall be a refuge from the wind
　　　and a shelter from the tempest,
　　　　or like runnels of water in dry ground,
like the shadow of a great rock in a thirsty land.
　　The eyes that can see will not be clouded,
　　and the ears that can hear will listen;
　　　the anxious heart will understand and know,
and the man who stammers will at once speak plain.

The Book of Isai
The New English Bib

THE DUMB SPIRIT

　　Eyes see
　　The shine and smother
　　Of world and otherworld—
　　The Dumb spirit
　　Stifles the breath.

　　Ears hear
　　Clamour and song
　　Flung off the fly-wheel of the straining year—
　　The dumb spirit
　　Knots up the tongue.

Hands feel
The braille of creatures'
Meeting and mesh—
The dumb spirit
Dams the flow of the flesh.

Cast out the dumb,
Lord.
Touch ears.
Let spittle un-numb the tongue.
Let there be no impediment on lung or larynx,
And let the breath
Speak plain again.

Norman Nicholson

THE DWELLING PLACE

Then Jesus turned, and saw them following, and saith unto them,
what seek ye? They said unto him, Rabbi, (which is to say, being interpreted, Master,) where dwellest thou? He saith unto them, Come and
see. They came and saw where he dwelt, and abode with him that day:
for it was about the tenth hour.

Saint John's Gospel

What happy, secret fountain,
Fair shade, or mountain,
Whose undiscover'd virgin glory
Boasts it this day, though not in story
Was then thy dwelling? did some cloud
Fix'd to a Tent, descend and shroud
My distrest Lord? or did a star
Beckon'd by thee, though high and far,
In sparkling smiles haste gladly down
To lodge light, and increase her own?
My dear, dear God! I do not know
What lodg'd thee then, nor where, nor how;
But I am sure, thou dost now come

119

Oft to a narrow, homely room,
Where thou too hast but the least part
My God, I mean *my sinful heart.*

Henry Vaughan

IESU

Iesu is in my heart, his sacred name
  Is deeply carved there. But th'other week
A great affliction broke the little frame.
  Ev'n all to pieces; which I went to seek.
And first I found the corner where was *I*,
  After where *ES*, and next where *U* was graved.
When I had got these parcels, instantly
  I sat me down to spell them; and perceived
That to my broken heart he was *I ease you,*
  And to my whole is IESU.

George Herbert

CHRIST'S BOUNTY

I pray you, Christ, to change my heart,
            To make it whole;
Once you took on flesh like mine,
            Now take my soul.

Ignominy and pain you knew,
            The lash, the scourge,
You, the perfect molten metal
            Of my darkened forge.

You make the bright sun bless my head,
            Put ice beneath my feet,
Send salmon swarming in the tides,
            Give crops of wheat.

When Eve's wild children come to you
            With prayerful words,

120

You crowd the rivers with fine fish,
                    The sky with birds.

You make the small flowers thrive
                    In the wholesome air,
You spread sweetness through the world.
                    What miracle can compare?

Brendan Kennelly

A HYMNE TO GOD THE FATHER

Heare mee, O God!
    A broken heart,
    Is my best part:
Use still thy rod,
    That I may prove
    Therein, thy Love.

If thou hadst not
    Been stern to mee,
    But left me free,
I had forgot
    My selfe and thee.

For sin's so sweet,
    As minds ill bent
    Rarely repent,
Until they meet
    Their punishment.

Who more can crave
    Than thou hast done:
    That gav'st a Sonne
To free a slave?
    First made of nought;
    With All since bought.

Sinne, Death, and Hell,
    His glorious Name
    Quite overcame,

121

Yet I rebel,
    And slight the same.

But, I'll come in,
    Before my losse,
    Me farther tosse,
As sure to win
    Under his Crosse.

Ben Jonson

,

3.

His Cross and Resurrection

He grew up before the LORD like a young plant
    whose roots are in parched ground;
he had no beauty, no majesty to draw our eyes,
    no grace to make us delight in him;
his form, disfigured, lost all the likeness of a man,
    his beauty changed beyond human semblance.
He was despised, he shrank from the sight of men,
    tormented and humbled by suffering;
    we despised him, we held him of no account,
    a thing from which men turn away their eyes.
Yet on himself he bore our sufferings,
    our torments he endured,
    while we counted him smitten by God,
    struck down by disease and misery;
but he was pierced for our transgressions,
    tortured for our iniquities;
the chastisement he bore in health for us
    and by his scourging we are healed.
We had all strayed like sheep,
each of us had gone his own way;
but the LORD laid upon him
    the guilt of us all.
He was afflicted, he submitted to be struck down
    and did not open his mouth;
he was led like a sheep to the slaughter,
like a ewe that is dumb before the shearers.
Without protection, without justice, he was taken away;
    and who gave a thought to his fate,
    how he was cut off from the world of living men,

stricken to the death for my people's transgression?
He was assigned a grave with the wicked,
a burial-place among the refuse of mankind,
though he had done no violence
    and spoken no word of treachery.
Yet the LORD took thought for his tortured servant
and healed him who had made himself a sacrifice for sin;
so shall he enjoy long life and see his children's children,
    and in his hand the LORD's cause shall prosper.
After all his pains he shall be bathed in light,
after his disgrace he shall be fully vindicated;
so shall he, my servant, vindicate many,
    himself bearing the penalty of their guilt.
Therefore I will allot him a portion with the great,
    and he shall share the spoil with the mighty
because he exposed himself to face death
    and was reckoned among transgressors,
because he bore the sin of many
    and interceded for their transgressions.

The Book of Isaiah
The New English Bible

CHRIST COSMONAUT

Out of nothing
with no name
out of a flame
out of a bend
in sound
his comet came
his fiery frame
a neon cross
bones nailed and bound
and found
our gain his loss.

He who was a star
bringing a new light
a love from afar
our brother of the night

a man whose grace
is from other space
yet of this place
and time—as bright
as we are dark, our fall
earth's flying spark—
out of nothing, all.

James Kirkup

THE GREAT AND TERRIBLE DREAM

Dark valley, or dark street: arches or trees
Or rocks? Shadow of evening, or of cloud?
Fear in the air, and a profound unease;
Then panic-driven feet, and from a shroud
Of dust or darkness, ravings as of men
Running in horror from some sight so dire
That the flesh cannot stay, or turn again,
But mindless flees, as hand is snatched from fire.
Fixed in pure terror, horribly afraid,
I listened to that frenzied multitude;
And a calm solemn voice behind me said,
In answer to my thought, *They fear the blood.*
Then in the dream my heart within my breast
Struck hugely stroke on stroke, driving me on
As a ship's engine drives her to the east
Against the eastern gale: Love was alone
And in extremity! Into the crowd
I hurled myself, and fought against the stream
As frantic mothers fight, who hear a loud
Scream from a burning house, an infant's scream.
Men plunged and hurtled by me, without mind,
Ants from a broken anthill, all infused
With one atrocious instinct, fierce and blind.
And wounded, naked, trampled, torn and bruised
I fought against them for a weary time,
Willing to die before my heart should break;
I thought them murderers fleeing from their crime,
And what they feared so madly, I must seek.

Then it was over: then there were no more
Opposing, then the tumult of those men
Ceased, as when sound is cut off by a door
Closing; and all but darkness filled the glen,
Or street, or vaulted place; so silence fell.
And the voice spoke again as solemnly
Behind me; calmly the invisible
Said, *He is there. Look on Him. That is He.*

The fear of death came on me. (Long ago
I saw men carrying a coffin by;
They stumbled, the lid moved; and horror so
Wrung me, that I fell without a cry,
But blackness roared upon me; but in vain,
The shell was empty.) Torn with love and awe,
I saw the Face, the plaited thorns, the stain
Of blood descending to the beard I saw;
And felt the power of life conquering death,
More dread than death, for death is vincible.
It struck me down. It stopped the very breath
Itself had given. But the dream was well:

O well is me, and happy shall I be!
Look! He is there. Look on Him. That is He.

Ruth Pitter

THE BURNING GLASS

No map shows my Jerusalem,
  No history my Christ;
Another language tells of them,
  A hidden evangelist.

Words may create rare images
  Within their narrow bound;
'Twas speechless childhood brought me these,
  As music may, in sound.

Yet not the loveliest song that ever
  Died on the evening air

126

Could from my inmost heart dissever
   What life had hidden there.

It is the blest reminder of
   What earth in shuddering bliss
Nailed on a cross—that deathless Love—
   Through all the eternities.

I am the Judas whose perfidy
   Sold what no eye hath seen,
The rabble in dark Gethsemane,
   And Mary Magdalene.

To very God who day and night
   Tells me my sands out-run,
I cry in misery infinite,
   'I am thy long-lost son.'

Walter de la Mare

THE AIRY CHRIST

After reading Dr. Rieu's translation of St. Mark's Gospel

Who is this that comes in grandeur, coming from the blazing East?
This is he we had not thought of, this is he the airy Christ.

Airy, in an airy manner in an airy parkland walking,
Others take him by the hand, lead him, do the talking.

But the Form, the airy One, frowns an airy frown,
What they say he knows must be, but he looks aloofly down,

Looks aloofly at his feet, looks aloofly at his hands,
Knows they must, as prophets say, nailéd be to wooden bands.

As he knows the words he sings, that he sings so happily
Must be changed to working laws, yet sings he ceaselessly.

Those who truly hear the voice, the words, the happy song,
Never shall need working laws to keep from doing wrong.

Deaf men will pretend sometimes they hear the song, the words,
And make excuse to sin extremely; this will be absurd.

Heed it not. Whatever foolish men may do the song is cried
For those who hear, and the sweet singer doesn't care that he
    was crucified.

For he does not wish that men should love him more than anything
Because he died; he only wishes they would hear him sing.

Stevie Smith

LORD OF THE DANCE

I danced in the morning when the world was begun,
And I danced in the moon and the stars and the sun;
And I came down from heaven and I danced on the earth,
At Bethlehem I had my birth:

> *Dance then, wherever you may be;*
> *I am the Lord of the Dance, said he;*
> *And I'll lead you all wherever you may be,*
> *And I'll lead you all in the Dance, said he.*

I danced for the scribe and the pharisee,
But they would not dance and they wouldn't follow me.
I danced for the fishermen, for James and John—
They came with me and the dance went on:

I danced on the Sabbath and I cured the lame;
The holy people said it was a shame.
They whipped and they stripped and they hung me on high;
And they left me there on a Cross to die:

I danced on a Friday when the sky turned black;
It's hard to dance with the devil on your back.
They buried my body and they thought I'd gone;
But I am the dance and I still go on:

They cut me down and I leapt up high,
I am the life that'll never, never die;

I'll live in you if you'll live in me;
I am the Lord of the Dance, said he:

ONE MORE STEP

One more step along the world I go,
One more step along the world I go.
From the old things to the new,
Keep me travelling along with you.
  And it's from the old I travel to the new.
  Keep me travelling along with you.

Round the corners of the world I turn,
More and more about the world I learn.
All the new things that I see
You'll be looking at along with me.
  And it's from the old I travel to the new.
  Keep me travelling along with you.

As I travel through the bad and good
Keep me travelling the way I should.
Where I see no way to go
You'll be telling me the way, I know.
  And it's from the old I travel to the new.
  Keep me travelling along with you.

Give me courage when the world is rough,
Keep me loving though the world is tough.
Leap and sing in all I do,
Keep me travelling along with you.
  And it's from the old I travel to the new.
  Keep me travelling along with you.

You are older than the world can be,
You are younger than the life in me.
Ever old and ever new,
Keep me travelling along with you.

And it's from the old I travel to the new.
Keep me travelling along with you.

Sydney Carter

BALLAD OF THE BREAD MAN

Mary stood in the kitchen
Baking a loaf of bread.
An angel flew in through the window.
We've a job for you, he said.

God in his big gold heaven,
Sitting in his big blue chair,
Wanted a mother for his little son.
Suddenly saw you there.

Mary shook and trembled,
It isn't true what you say.
Don't say that, said the angel.
The baby's on its way.

Joseph was in the workshop
Planing a piece of wood.
The old man's past it, the neighbours said
The girl's been up to no good.

And who was that elegant feller,
They said, in the shiny gear?
The things they said about Gabriel
Were hardly fit to hear.

Mary never answered.
Mary never replied.
She kept the information,
Like the baby, safe inside.

It was election winter.
They went to vote in town.
When Mary found her time had come
The hotels let her down.

130

The baby was born in an annex
Next to the local pub.
At the midnight, a delegation
Turned up from the Farmers' Club.

They talked about an explosion
That cracked a hole in the sky,
Said they'd been sent to the Lamb & Flag
To see God come down from on high.

A few days later a bishop
And a five-star general were seen
With the head of an African country
In a bullet-proof limousine.

We've come, they said, with tokens
For the little boy to choose,
Told the tale about war and peace
In the television news.

After them came the soldiers
With rifle and bomb and gun,
Looking for enemies of the state
The family had packed and gone.

When they got back to the village
The neighbours said, to a man,
That boy will never be one of us.
Though he does what he blessed well can.

He went round to all the people
A paper crown on his head.
Here is some bread from my father.
Take, eat, he said.

Nobody seemed very hungry.
Nobody seemed to care.
Nobody saw the God in himself
Quietly standing there.

He finished up in the papers.
He came to a very bad end.

He was charged with bringing the living to life.
No man was that prisoner's friend.

There's only one kind of punishment
To fit that kind of crime.
They rigged a trial and shot him dead.
They were only just in time.

They lifted the young man by the leg,
They lifted him by the arm,
They locked him in a cathedral
In case he came to harm.

They stored him safe as water
Under seven rocks.
One Sunday morning he burst out
Like a jack-in-the-box.

Through the town he went walking.
He showed them the holes in his head.
Now do you want any loaves? he cried.
Not today, they said.

Charles Causley

One afternoon I took the bus to the University, and walked out towards the Mount of Olives. In the convent at the top Russian nuns were singing a service. I climbed the tower and watched the sun set and the sky go red. The three-thousand-foot decline, the Dead Sea and the sand beyond the Jordan stretched into the distance. To the west all Jerusalem within its walls could be seen. As I climbed down in the growing darkness I was overwhelmed by a sense of God's power, and that power in me. As I walked down the hill I could see his resurrected self coming to meet me.

When asked why I am a Christian, I sometimes jump all the other arguments and just describe that moment on the Mount of Olives.

At that age, twenty-one, I passionately needed a dramatic revelation and God in his mercy gave it to me. Some find God in King's College Chapel, others in St. Peter's, Rome. God knows those places as he knows others, and if you want to see him he won't hide for ever.

Donald Swan

EASTER

No human eye was by
To witness Christ arise,
But I, this morning heard
The Resurrection of the Word.

It sprang through night, opaque,
A note so pure and clear,
I felt my spirit wake—
It flooded everywhere.

I know that it has been;
There is a vision new.
I see the universe
Divinely bathed in dew.

Sister Mary Agnes, Order of Poor Clares

THE REVIVAL

Unfold, unfold! take in his light,
Who makes thy cares more short than night.
The joys, which with his day-star rise,
He deals to all, but drowsy eyes:
And what the men of this world miss,
Some drops and dews of future bliss.
   Hark' how his winds have chang'd their note,
And with warm whispers call thee out.
The frosts are past, the storms are gone:
And backward life at last comes on.
The lofty groves in express joys
Reply unto the turtle's voice,
And here in dust and dirt, O here
The lilies of his love appear!

Henry Vaughan

ROCK DAFFODILS

Not till I saw rock daffodils
Diminutive, in spurred and fluted gold,

133

Did these eyes magnify God's holy hills;
Was all my joy in Easter told.

NICODEMUS

                    O risen Lord,
I do not ask you to forgive me now;
There is no need.
I came to-night to speak to your dead body,
To touch it with my hands and say 'Forgive,'
For though I knew it could not speak to me
Or even hear, yet it was once yourself;
It is dissolved and risen like a dew,
And now I know,
As dawn forgives the night, as spring the winter,
You have forgiven me. It is enough.
Why do I kneel before your empty tomb?
You are not here, for you are everywhere;
The grass, the trees, the air, the wind, the sky,
Nothing can now refuse to be your home;
Nor I. Lord, live in me and I shall live.
This is the word you spoke,
The whole earth hears it, for the whole earth cries,
I AM THE RESURRECTION, AND THE LIFE: HE THAT BELIEVETH
IN ME THOUGH HE WERE DEAD, YET SHALL HE LIVE: AND
WHOSOEVER LIVETH AND BELIEVETH IN ME SHALL NEVER DIE

Andrew Young

LAMMAS

THE SONG OF THE REAPERS

We know a field.
A sheltered, fertile ground,
Well-favoured by the sun.
    There the first yield

Of corn is reaped and bound
Before the harvest is begun.

It is a sheaf
Of whitest gold, the green
Half-fainted from the stem.
Upon the leaf
Spring's last veins are seen.
Each ear is a Jerusalem.

Now from this first
Pure sheaf the bread is baked.
And offered, fragrant, fresh,
To God.—Who thirst
And hunger shall be slaked
By holy wine, fed by this flesh.

For when we eat
This bread that is new-made
We take into our blood
His grace, our meat.
By faith, the earth is fed
And by His love we have our bread.

James Kirkup

Here is my servant, whom I uphold,
my chosen one in whom I delight,
I have bestowed my spirit upon him,
and he will make justice shine on the nations.
He will not call out or lift his voice on high,
or make himself heard in the open street.
He will not break a bruised reed,
or snuff out a smouldering wick;
he will make justice shine on every race,
never faltering, never breaking down,
he will plant justice on earth,
while coasts and islands wait for his teaching.

Thus speaks the LORD who is God,
he who created the skies and stretched them out,

who fashioned the earth and all that grows in it,
who gave breath to its people,
the breath of life to all who walk upon it:
I, the LORD, have called you with righteous purpose
and taken you by the hand:
I have formed you, and appointed you
to be a light to all peoples,
a beacon for the nations,
to open eyes that are blind,
to bring captives out of prison,
out of the dungeons where they lie in darkness.

The Book of Isaiah
The New English Bible

'Look forward to the coming of your shepherd, and he will give you everlasting rest; for he who is to come at the end of the world is close at hand. Be ready to receive the rewards of the kingdom; for light perpetual will shine upon you for ever and ever. Flee from the shadow of this world, and receive the joy and splendour that await you. I bear witness openly to my Saviour. It is he whom the Lord has appointed; receive him and be joyful, giving thanks to the One who has summoned you to the heavenly realms. Rise, stand up, and see the whole company of those who bear the Lord's mark and sit at his table. They have moved out of the shadow of this world and have received shining robes from the Lord. Receive, O Zion, your full number, and close the roll of those arrayed in white who have faithfully kept the law of the Lord. The number of your sons whom you so long desired is now complete. Pray that the Lord's kingdom may come, so that your people, whom I summoned when the world began, may be set apart as his own.'

I, Ezra, saw on Mount Zion a crowd too large to count, all singing hymns of praise to the Lord. In the middle stood a very tall young man, taller than all the rest, who was setting a crown on the head of each one of them; he stood out above them all. I was enthralled at the sight, and asked the angel, 'Sir, who are these?' He replied, 'They are those who have laid aside their mortal dress and put on the immortal, those who acknowledged the name of God. Now they are being given crowns and palms.' And I asked again, 'Who is the young man setting crowns on their heads and giving them palms?' and the angel replied, 'He is the Son of God, whom they acknowledged in this mortal life.' I began praise those who had stood so valiantly for the Lord's name. Then the angel said to me: 'Go and tell my people all the great and wonderful acts of the Lord God that you have seen.'

The Book of Esdras
Apocrypha

Part 5

Not Only the Saints and Heroes, But the Men and Women Who Day by Day Illumine Life for the Rest of Us, Are Too Great for Any Destination Except the One Faith Sees for Them. They Travel to the Light of God's Eternity

1. The Worth of Men to God and Each Other
2. The Holy, the Great and the Good
3. Remembering Our Friends
4. In Memoriam

"My Son's Brothers; they are my children;
I am their Father."

Charles Péguy

1.

The Worth of Men to God and Each Other

They are my Son's brothers; they are my children; I am their father.
Our *Father which art in Heaven,* my Son taught them that prayer. *Sic
  ergo vos orabitis. Therefore you shall pray thus.*
Our *Father which art in Heaven,* that day he knew very well what he
  was doing, my Son who loved them so much.
Who lived among them, who was like one of them.
Who went about like them, who spoke like them, who lived like them.
Who suffered.
Who suffered like them, who died like them.
And who loves them so much, having known them.
Who has brought back to Heaven, a kind of flavour of man, a kind of
  flavour of earth.
My Son who loved them so much, who loves them eternally in Heav-
  en.
He knew very well what he was doing on that day, my Son who loves
  them so much.
When he put that barrier between them and me, *Our Father which art
  in Heaven,* those three or four words.
That barrier which my anger and perhaps my justice will never pass.
Happy is he who sleeps under the protection of the vanguard of those
  three or four words.
Those words which go before every prayer as the hands of a supplicant
  before his face.
As the two hands of a supplicant advance joined together before his
  face and the tears on his face.
Those three or four words which conquer me, me the unconquerable.
And which they send in front of their misery like two invincible hands
  joined together.
Those three or four words which advance like a stong prow in front of a
  weak ship,

And which cleave the wave of my anger.
And when the prow has passed, the ship passes and all the fleet behind
it.
Nowadays, God says, that is how I see them;
And during my eternity, eternally, God says,
By the contrivance of my Son, it is thus that I must eternally see
them. . . .

Charles Péguy

God's beloved, tattered humanity, will bring Evil at last to despair

THE COMBAT

It was not meant for human eyes,
That combat on the shabby patch
Of clods and trampled turf that lies
Somewhere beneath the sodden skies
For eye of toad or adder to catch.

And having seen it I accuse
The crested animal in his pride,
Arrayed in all the royal hues
Which hide the claws he well can use
To tear the heart out of the side.

Body of leopard, eagle's head
And whetted beak, and lion's mane,
And frost-grey hedge of feathers spread
Behind—he seemed of all things bred.
I shall not see his like again.

As for his enemy, there came in
A soft round beast as brown as clay;
All rent and patched his wretched skin;
A battered bag he might have been,
Some old used thing to throw away.

Yet he awaited face to face
The furious beast and the swift attack.

Soon over and done. That was no place
Or time for chivalry or for grace.
The fury had him on his back.

The two small paws like hands flew out
To right and left as the trees stood by.
One would have said beyond a doubt
This was the very end of the bout,
But that the creature would not die.

For ere the death-stroke he was gone,
Writhed, whirled, huddled into his den,
Safe somehow there. The fight was done,
And he had lost who had all but won.
But oh his deadly fury then.

A while the place lay blank, forlorn,
Drowsing as in relief from pain.
The cricket chirped, the grating thorn
Stirred, and a little sound was born.
The champions took their posts again.

And all began. The stealthy paw
Slashed out and in. Could nothing save
These rags and tatters from the claw?
Nothing. And yet I never saw
A beast so helpless and so brave.

And now, while the trees stand watching still
The unequal battle rages there.
The killing beast that cannot kill
Swells and swells in his fury till
You'd almost think it was despair.

Edwin Muir

Man is only a reed—the weakest thing in nature. But he is a reed that
thinks. It is not necessary for the whole universe to arm itself to crush
him: a mist, a drop of water, is enough to kill him. But if the universe
crushes him, man will still be nobler than that which kills him, since
he knows he is dying, knows of the power of the universe over him, of
which the universe knows nothing. In thought, then, our entire dignity

consists. It is on this we must draw and not on the conquest of space and time, with which we should not know how to cope. Let us, then, work at thinking straight; that is the foundation of conduct.

Blaise Pascal

Indeed, unless and until *each man* is prepared to beg the skill of others to help him be complete, he is not a whole man.

This pattern applies in every area of life. Each man of faith has to ask other men of faith what insight they have about God. The man with great scientific skill in laboratories must ask the native of the desert about the skills he has learnt in the open wastes. The sophisticated painter of Europe can learn from the Tongan craftswoman about the making of *tapa* cloth from beaten bark (stuck together with semolina, what's more!). Those who are rich lose the art of being poor, and can learn that art from the poor around them. The lessons are endless, and this learning should never cease. The reason is that God exists in *all* men, and therefore to know God fully we would have to know all men: and not only all men but all things and all animals. The extinction of an animal species diminishes all of us. The death of each man diminishes all of us. But we are not *diminished* but *hurt* when any man, woman or child ceases to learn and considers himself self-sufficient, be it in skill, in wealth or in power. That person breaks the chain of learning, and interferes with those who are continuing. He is a destroyer.

The true politics of the world start only when each living soul is learning from all the others. Nations exist only as artificial structures created by men primarily to divide themselves from one another, and create an artificial and precarious security, which is regularly shattered by war and disaster. The only true relationship is that of brother to brother, sister to brother and brother to sister. All the rest is vanity, and the world's talk.

Donald Swann

MEETING WITH A STRANGER

You, through whose face
all lovely faces look,
and are resolved for ever

in your soul's true mirror:
you, in whose unspoken words
the irrevocable voices speak again,
making in this less divided moment
the remembered music that the heart accords.

O you who are myself and yet another,
who are the world, and the unknown
through which the town, the river,
the familiar gardens and the fountain shines;
here is my hand, and with it let all hands
be given, and be held, in yours and mine.

James Kirkup

THESE TWO

ALL PEOPLE ARE WORTH LOVING

But the man who goes down to the shore
and tries to weave a rope
from grains of sand, so that—throwing it
round the Moon's neck as she surfaces
from the waves—he can rise in the sky;
and the man who, bent over a golden
river, spends all his life modelling it
into the form of the figureless wind,
to give this world a new courage;
—these two above all others have the right
to live in the tent of my shadow.

When I am absent, know that they are at home.

Stefan Doinas

2.
The Holy, the Great and the Good

THE HOLY MAN

A trapped bird
A wrecked ship
An empty cup
A withered tree
Is he
Who scorns the will of the King above.

Pure gold
Bright sun
Filled wine-cup
Happy beautiful holy
Is he
Who does the will of the King of love.

Brendan Kennelly

SAINT, BIRD, ANGEL

Saint Anfaidh walked alone
    Where a thin stream was flowing
And there he saw a little bird
    Sorrowing.

"God" he thought, "what's happening?
    I cannot think;
But till I understand, I shall not
    Eat or drink."

An angel stood beside him
    And quietly said,
"Mo Lua, gentle son of Ocha,
    Has just died.

All living things lament him,
    He was loved by all,
He never killed a living thing
    Great or small.

The beast laments him with his cry,
    Man with a tender word,
And look, beside you, grieving stands
    A little bird."

Brendan Kennelly

When the truth shines out in the soul, and the soul sees itself in the truth, there is nothing brighter than that light or more impressive than that testimony. And when the splendour of this beauty fills the entire heart, it naturally becomes visible, just as a lamp under a bowl or a light in darkness are not there to be hidden. Shining out like rays upon the body, it makes it a mirror of itself so that its beauty appears in a man's every action, his speech, his looks, his movements and his smile.

St. Bernard

THE HEROES

When these in all their bravery took the knock
And like obedient children swaddled and bound
Were borne to sleep within the chambered rock,

A splendour broke from that impervious ground,
Which they would never know. Whence came that greatness?
No fiery chariot whirled them heavenwards, they
Saw no Elysium opening, but the straitness
Of full submission bound them where they lay.

What could that greatness be? It was not fame.
Yet now they seemed to grow as they grew less.
And where they lay were more than where they had stood.
They did not go to any beatitude.
They were stripped clean of feature, presence, name,
When that strange glory broke from namelessness.

Edwin Muir

ELEGY FOR DEAD COSMONAUTS

The earth, walled in by stars,
sent us spinning against the sacrificial block,
the infinitely curving monolith
of space, and nailed us there
for many days and nights, a rhythm of orbits
soaring, sinking with the centrifugal force of time.

We three left earth no more alive
than dead. We three returned
less dead than many left alive:
dead to the world, but not to space
that we have finally surrendered to
and made our home from home.

Death took our breath away
but rewarded us with vaster aspirations,
revelations. Too late, now, we know
what you do wrong, why countdowns end in nothing.
—And why you cannot see a certain truth,
beyond science, staring us in the face.

James Kirku,

DUNS SCOTUS'S OXFORD

Towery city and branchy between towers;
Cuckoo-echoing, bell-swarmèd, lark-charmèd, rook-racked,
    river-rounded;
The dapple-eared lily below thee; country and town did
Once encounter in, here coped and poisèd powers;

Thou hast a base and brickish skirt there, sours
That neighbour-nature thy grey beauty is grounded
Best in; graceless growth, thou hast confounded
Rural rural keeping—folk, flocks and flowers.

Yet ah! this air I gather and I release
He lived on; these weeds and waters, these walls are what
He haunted who of all men most sways my spirits to peace;

Of reality the rarest-veined unraveller; a not
Rivalled insight, be rival Italy or Greece;
Who fired France for Mary without spot.

Gerard Manley Hopkins

SHAKESPEARE ROAD, S. E. 24

Not marble. Yet low down
Under the windows of this corner shop
A multicoloured frieze,
Crazy patchwork of little bits,
Hand-made, one man's defiance.
No picture postcards and no statuettes;
No call for them here
As in that other place
Where now they look for him,
His absence is bought and sold.

Grassily quiet now
In orchards walled or hedged
Sweeten mutations of his leathercoat,
Pomewater, costard, codling, applejohn,
Russetting too, the rare, the dying savours.

Blackbird and thrush and linnet, the same, the same,
Sing to no ear quite open,
No eye quite open dares nor lens can follow
Business the winds and clouds transact
With light, green light, half-sunbeams with the leaves.

Here, then. Look for him here
Where boys ride bicycles over rubble, skirting
A grey van gutted of its engine, dumped
Outside the Council Works;
Down a long row
Of dingy terrace houses
And, facing it, a barred and spiked embankment
Of willow herb and refuse, depots and railway sidings,

His road, and anyone's,
With relics of a sort,
The rag and bone man's horse,
The rag and bone man's wares,
Perhaps his book, patched and passed on,
Lived in, moved through.

Michael Hamburger

Epitaph: ON SIR WALTER RAWLEIGH AT HIS EXECUTION

Great heart, who taught thee so to dye?
Death yielding thee the victory?
Where took'st thou leave of life? if there,
How couldst thou be so freed from feare?
But sure thou dy'st and quit'st the state
Of flesh and blood before thy fate.
Else what a miracle were wrought,
To triumph both in flesh and thought?
I saw in every stander by,
Pale death, life onely in thine eye:
Th'example that thou left'st was then,
We look for when thou dy'st agen.
  Farewell, truth shall thy story say,
  We dy'ed, thou onely liv'dst that day.

Anonymous

VAN GOGH

Your turbulent intensity
Painted the poor with truth and pity:
Age-old griefs, the prisoners' slouching round,
The near starving, the lonely wife, and love's ripe zones,
But also the bony knees, drooped anguished dugs.
You painted too new ploughed ripe purple fields,
The shining airy grace May orchard yields
Candescent blossom dancing to greet sweet cloud
Prancing branches, with the buff visiting moth.

In Vincent's room you proved how matter lives,
With barely static bed, floor, table, chairs.
At night in Arles your stars were Catherine-wheels,
The café figures warmed in southern trance.

The Sun both angel and devil was
A murderous mirror, but vision's glass:
Sunflowers have eyes, jagged hair of flame,
Cornfields are gold that has yet no name
Where the quivering lark goes, cypress upward flows.

When from the dire storm-wrack a flock of crows
Swept blackly down on the yellow wheat,
You shot yourself. Death's stroke was feat:
A giver of beauty, you stand afar.
It takes Death to reach a star.

Joseph Braddock

THE STRANGER

Careless how it struck those nearest to him,
whose inquiring he'd no longer brook,
once more he departed; lost, forsook.—
For such nights of travel always drew him
stronglier than any lover's night.
How he'd watched in slumberless delight
out beneath the shining stars all yonder
circumscribed horizons roll asunder,
ever-changing like a changing fight;

others, with their moon-bright hamlets tendered
like some booty they had seized, surrendered
peacefully, or through tall trees would shed
glimpses of far-stretching parks, containing
grey ancestral houses that with craning
head a moment he inhabited,
knowing more deeply one could never bide;
then, already round the next curve speeding,
other highways, bridges, landscapes, leading
on to cities darkness magnified.

And to let all this, without all craving,
slip behind him meant beyond compare
more to him than pleasure, goods, or fame.
Though the well-steps in some foreign square,
daily hollowed by the drawers there,
seemed at times like something he could claim.

Rainer Maria Rilke

3.

Remembering Our Friends

THE GOOD

(For Eavan)

The good are vulnerable
As any bird in flight.
They do not think of safety,
Are blind to possible extinction
And when most vulnerable
Are most themselves.
The good are real as the sun,
Are best perceived through clouds
Of casual corruption
That cannot kill the luminous sufficiency
That shines on city, sea and wilderness,
Fastidiously revealing
One man to another,
Who yet will not accept
Responsibilities of light.
The good incline to praise,
To have the knack of seeing that
The best is not destroyed
Although forever threatened.
The good go naked in all weathers,
And by their nakedness rebuke
The small protective sanities
That hide men from themselves.
The good are difficult to see
Though open, rare, destructible.

Always, they retain a kind of youth,
The vulnerable grace
Of any bird in flight,
Content to be itself,
Accomplished master and potential victim,
Accepting what the earth or sky intends.
I think that I know one or two
Among my friends.

Brendan Kennelly

THE ARCHBISHOP OF SENS SUGGESTS
A VISIT TO HIS OLD FRIEND, ALCUIN: ALCUIN REPLIES

'There's a sorry little scrub that is servant unto me,
And at the statutory hours he feeds me every day.
He's my seneschal and butler,
He's the cook and the hostler,
And the laundryman and kitchen man and bootboy too.
But if I send him out on an errand down the street,
I know not how it is—but he never will come back . . .
Every man jack I have goes the selfsame way.

'It's hunger thins my household and scatters my poor men,
Like a rascal tax collector that can never fill his wame.
So let you stay at Sens, my good bishop, where you still
Can keep your men about you and can let them eat their fill:
And let no fond hopes delude you to the sweet fields of the Sauer;
Believe me, my lord bishop, you are better where you are.
For whatever drink is to be drunk or meat upon a bone,
Believe me, my lord bishop, we can finish it at home.
You've the Yonne and the Saône to fill you full of fish,
And the vineyards of Sens, and sometimes to your dish,
Comes a good horned wether to get your blessing on it.
And all your hungry household can be let loose upon it,
To carve it up and eat it up and then sing grace.
So be mindful of poor Alcuin, you sitting snug and warm
In your own chimney corner—and the Lord bless you, Sam!'

Taken from 'Poetry in the Dark Ages
A lecture delivered by Helen Wadde

ALCUIN WRITES TO HIS FRIEND,
ARNO OF SALZBURG, MANY LEAGUES AWAY

No mountain and no forest, land nor sea,
Shall block love's road, deny the way to thee . . .
Yet why must love that's sweet
So bitter tears beget,
Honey and gall in one same goblet set?
Even so, O world, the feet
Of sorrow follow hard upon delight,
Joy breaketh in a cry,
And all sweet things are changed to bitterness.
They will not stay for me: yea, all things haste to die.

Wherefore, O world,
So soon to die,
From us depart,
And thou, my heart,
Make haste to fly
Where is delight that fades not,
The unchanging shore,
The happy house where friend from friend divides not,
And what he loves, he hath for ever more.
Take me, beloved, in thy prayer with thee,
Where shall be no estranging thee and me.

Taken from 'Poetry in the Dark Ages,'
A lecture delivered by Helen Waddell

SONNET 26

Lord of my love, to whom in vassalage
Thy merit hath my duty strongly knit,
To thee I send this written embassage,
To witness duty, not to show my wit:
Duty so great, which wit so poor as mine
May make seem bare, in wanting words to show it,
But that I hope some good conceit of thine
In thy soul's thought, all naked, will bestow it;
Till whatsoever star that guides my moving,
Points on me graciously with fair aspect,

And puts apparel on my tatter'd loving,
To show me worthy of thy sweet respect:
    Then may I dare to boast how I do love thee:
    Till then not show my head where thou mayst prove me.

Shakespear

A TIME TO TALK

When a friend calls to me from the road
And slows his horse to a meaning walk,
I don't stand still and look around
On all the hills I haven't hoed,
And shout from where I am, "What is it?"
No, not as there is a time to talk.
I thrust my hoe in the mellow ground,
Blade-end up and five feet tall,
And plod: I go up to the stone wall
For a friendly visit.

Robert Fro

SUNDAY VISIT

We finally found him
curled up in the chair like a many-wrinkled shell
staring blindly out at nothing
among a gathering of imbecilic fossils
his one good eye fastening fiercely onto life
the hair still sturdy though silver under the old cloth cap.

We finally found him
through all that terrible labyrinth of grey concrete cells
quietly rounding out his days
alone in a morass of moronic camaraderie
his doomed cell mates snoozing and snoring all around
and he with his one good eye defying the shadows.

156

The tears came then
not soft, but real
the tears of a real man broken by life
groping wildly with gnarled fingers at the straws of life
in that awful room of no life
and the television set blaring forth its banalities
drowning whatever words of comfort our futile tongues could offer.

I had no words for him
no words to span the heartbreak of years
when Samson-like he had stood between us and chaos
bringing to us the small rare trinkets of his love.
I had for him only whiskey
the old bitter gift
the poor tribute of one poorer in spirit
than that jaded near-blind half-deaf soul reclining so tamely
in a wicker chair
in a ward of fearful paralysing resignation
a ward full of already dead people
sleeping as the television blared.

Yet the hand that gripped mine spelled out love
and the raw lovely courage of that old landscaped face
put my feeble pity to shame.

Christy Brown

THE THATCHER

He whittled scallops for a hardy thatch,
His palm and fingers hard as the bog oak.
You'd see him of an evening, crouched
Under a tree, testing a branch. If it broke
He grunted in contempt and flung it away,
But if it stood the stretch, his sunken blue
Eyes briefly smiled. Then with his long knife he
Chipped, slashed, pointed. The pile of scallops grew.

Astride a house on a promised day,
He rammed and patted scallops into place

157

Though wind cut his eyes till he seemed to weep.
Like a god after making a world, his face
Grave with the secret, he'd stare and say—
"Let the wind rip and the rain pelt. This'll keep."

Brendan Kennell

In Memoriam

LOUIS MACNEICE
September 2, 1963

I turned on the transistor:
By luck, for your sorrel,
Your *Vol de Nuit*,
It was Haydn.

Black and diffident man
Of the bog and the stoa
Whose rush of love
Was rejected,

Whose wolfhound
Bent round my table,
Who are no longer around
In your Chinese

Garden of poems.
Where one is of water,
On which tea-yellow
Leaves of another

Are falling, always
Are falling, this one
Is a stone by itself,
On which you inscribe

With invisible legible letters
That unrest of the soul
Which you found
So wryly appalling.

You have gone: will
No longer arrange
In sunlight with wit
Your aloneness.

But, classical quizzical
One, whose scent is
Sharp in the centre,
Your garden is open.

Geoffrey Grigson

LIGHT DYING

In Memoriam: Frank O'Connor (Michael O'Donovan)

Climbing the last steps to your house, I knew
That I would find you in your chair,
Watching the light die along the canal,
Recalling the glad creators, all
Who'd played a part in the miracle.
A silver-haired remembering king, superb there
In dying light, all ghosts being at your beck and call,
You made them speak as only you could do.

Of generosity or loneliness or love
Because, you said, all men are voices, heard
In the pure air of the imagination.
I hear you now, your rich voice deep and kind,
Rescuing a poem from time, bringing to mind
Lost centuries with a summoning word,
Lavishing on us who need much more of
What you gave, glimpses of heroic vision.

So you were angry at the pulling down
Of what recalled a finer age: you tried
To show how certain things destroyed, ignored,

Neglected was a crime against the past,
Impoverished the present. Some midland town
Attracted you, you stood in the waste
Places of an old church and, profoundly stirred,
Pondered how you could save what time had sorely tried.

Or else you cried in rage against the force
That would reduce to barren silence all
Who would articulate dark Ireland's soul;
You knew the evil of the pious curse,
The hearts that make God pitifully small
Until He seems the God of little fear
And not the God that you desired at all;
And yet you had the heart to do and dare.

I see you standing at your window,
Lifting a glass, watching the dying light
Along the quiet canal bank come and go
Until the time has come to say good-night.
You see me to the door; you lift a hand
Half-shyly, awkwardly, while I remark
Your soul's fine courtesy, my friend, and
Walk outside, alone, suddenly in the dark.

But in the dark or no, I realise
Your life's transcendent dignity,
A thing more wonderful than April skies
Emerging in compelling majesty,
Leaving mad March behind and making bloom
Each flower outstripping every weed and thorn.
Life rises from the crowded clay of doom.
Light dying promises the light re-born.

Brendan Kennelly

IN MEMORIAM: BERTRAND RUSSELL

another February, on a Sunday afternoon eight years ago
wept for you, and for a world that could reject your voice,

You were so frail, so ancient; yet stronger than us all.
You stood beside me on a platform in Trafalgar Square
among the toothless lions of a tyrannous imperial pride,
under the shadow of Nelson strutting in the falling snow.

Your head was bare, and your wild white hair
blazed like your mind in the wind of whirling flakes.
Your face, the mask of a tragic hawk,
was sad and bitter as you cried your warnings and defiance
at the armed forces of error, the police of Britain,
the criminal politicians, the priests of power, the insane
manufacturers of arms and poison gas and atom bombs,
inhuman profiteers all, sucking the blood of human misery.

You stood alone before the gathered heads of microphones
tilted intelligently, raised like vipers, cobras, about to strike.
—But like a saint, or like Apollo, god of poetry and music,
you charmed them into peace. You won their love with love,
with the fearless beauty of your mind, your noble voice.

Dear man, I remember your friendship for the lost and helpless,
and the grasp of your withered hand in mine that February day,
delicate but strong. I remember the wise humour of your smile,
twisted yet pure; the sparkle in your hooded, sombre eyes;
the deep lines in your cheeks, the nose like a mountain peak,
—And O, that great and simple brow—so vast, so calm, so full!

Most of all, I remember how you taught me to have courage
to defy world in solitude; how to disarm
the dangerous stupidity of man, using weapons not of this world—
intellect with love; wit with pity; candour with compassion.

Now, in a foreign snow, my tears are falling for you,
and for the world, that did not heed your warning cries.

Tokyo, February 3, 19.
James Kirk

VISITING THE GRAVES IN ZOSHIGAYA CEMETERY

It is a fine Sunday morning,
an autumn in December.

162

Here, in hard and stony Tokyo
there is a place of peace and gentleness.
There are trees and bushes
that cast moving leaf-shadows
over memorial stones
and tablets in which the shadowed names
are deeply cut by winter sun.

At the gardener's cottage
one can borrow a simple home-made broom—
bamboo twigs of "mosodake"—
and an old water-bucket made of faded wood
in which a water-ladle
leans like an everlasting flower.

It is like a small city here.
The stone monuments and steps and little walls
are like houses, villas, castles for souls.

But it is a city of silence.
There are only gardeners in the streets,
and birds.
Joined now by
the shadows of our shades.

Here and there are white posts
and signboards on which black characters
are barely brushed.
They point in the direction of
the graves we are to visit.

The paths of earth
that a long night frosted
begin to thaw, but
they are fringed still with ice.

Here is the grave
of Koizumi Yakumo.
A few withered flowers
stand in the stone holders.
We put fresh water in,
and a few new flowers—red
chrysanthemums, and yellow,
and a few small narcissi.

With the broom
we sweep your grave, and tidy the weeds.

Then we light a small bonfire
of dead maple leaves and
the paper wrappings from
bundles of dark-green incense sticks,
which we kindle in the flames
and place before your stone,
the stone of your wife,
the stone of your family—
Three stones that are more than stone.

These stones are severe and calm,
but they are not hard like the streets of Tokyo.
Surrounded by trees and plants—
dwarf azaleas, a Chinese pine,
a jasmine or a gardenia,
a large shady tree, and a hedge
of spindle bushes within
a low bamboo fence.

The stones live among the leaves'
shifting shadows, and
seem to move a little
when a faint breeze stirs the branches.
For these are not just stones.
They are the memories of men. . . .

James Kirku

POEM FOR SEAN COLLIS

You who went so innocently before us
do not forget us in that green-gold world of yours.
You the gay laugh upon the Wicklow wind
smiling boy upon a rainbow
galloping over the morning of your life
blessedly unmet with crippling remembrances
shaming us with your enthusiasms.

Spare us now a thought of quiet love
in all your fourteen-year-old wisdom
you whom death has so dismally failed to possess.

You will always enter through the farmhouse door
laden with clean-cut turf for the fire
bearing warmth of the young heart
bearing tokens rare beyond your knowing
for those who knew you too briefly
and loved you too well for jealous time to suffer
yet had unkillable joy in that knowledge.

Gather still turf for that unending fire
from your brighter side of the river
joining us all so improbably as one
over a candle-lit table far from last supper
bridging lives once stellar in distance
through the firefly flaming of your youth
and its dark tongueless ending.

I did not know you well, knowing only your eyes.
And knowing your eyes, knew you.
In some other better time boy on rainbow
beyond the brittle dimensions of now
sup with me again at the same table
and crumble between us the bread of brothers.

Sean of light gentleness and boyish wayward ways
the cloud that darkens your last green hour
hangs over us all.

Christy Brown

EPITAPH FOR ONE DEAD AT RONCEVALLES

'Buried in this low grave his pale limbs lie
Whose spirit climbs the starry steep of heaven.
Born of a famous stock, of the blood of France,
All gifts of gentleness and noble living
Were his but yesterday.

The down of manhood on his rosy cheek
Scarce fledged: alas, so youth and beauty died . . .
The day King Charlemagne spurned under foot
The soil of Spain, that day he died to the world,
And now, where'er he be, he lives to God . . .

Go with him, now, O Vincent, mighty martyr,
Plead for him, blessed one, with the Most High.
Here in his grave-mound though his body lie,
He climbs the shining road, stands in God's House.

And all ye Christian folk that cross the threshold
Of this holy place, plead for him with the Son
Begotten of the Father's heart, and say
'God in Thy mercy'—say ye all together—
'Redeem Thy servant Eghard from his sins.'

Taken from 'Poetry in the Dark Ages,
A lecture delivered by Helen Waddel

A NINTH CENTURY REQUIEM
FOR THE ABBESS OF GANDESHEIM
WHO DIED YOUNG

Thou hast come safe to port
   I still at sea,
The light is on thy head,
   Darkness in me.

Pluck thou in heaven's field
   Violet and rose,
While I strew flowers that will thy vigil keep
Where thou dost sleep,
Love, in thy last repose.

Taken from 'Poetry in the Dark Ages,
A lecture delivered by Helen Waddel

EPITAPH

We who are left behind—weep
for us the long drawn night
holds in its dark no sleep
for us no peace.

You who have gone from us—sleep
wrapped in the final peace
lying where none may weep
wrapped in all night.

We shall not see you wake—who weep
our eyes are closed
We see your eyes are shut—who sleep
whilst you awake.

Anne Lewis-Smith

THE GOD-DAUGHTER

Hers was the lamb shy early spring
the gentle bud half opening
but now unpetalled.
>   The primrose smile, the fairy ring
>   of laughter light about her lips.

Hers was the youth of little things
warm trust in all small feathered wings
but now enfolded.
>   Wide eyed as loving hands made strings
>   of daisies for her soft hairs crown.

Hers was springtime magic, bringing
music with pale harebells ringing
now an elegy.
>   Hers the endless summer singing
>   ours the winter of her going.

Anne Lewis-Smith

THE SAINTS

The angels stand, the mighty angels stand
and bear, and you don't know what they are bearing.
The Saints, the Saints though, through whose shining band
we pass, are ours, immeasurably sharing
in all we've been and all we have on hand.

They gathered up their life from far and wide:
He only took it to restore it all
to earthliness it made more glorified:
to winds, to beasts, to the gay coronal
of bound-up things. Beside beside Beside.

Whence all's now radiant and monstrantial,
and when we lift it we are sanctified.

Rainer Maria Rilke

Part 6

The Children and the Lovers Keep Faith Alive in Us. The Freshness and Light of Spring Is in Children and Lovers Alike. They Are Mysterious Creatures, Appearing to Live for a Short While Outside Time. From Mystery Wonder Grows, and from Wonder Faith

"We receive more than we can ever give; we receive it from the past, on which we draw with every breath, but also—and this is a point of faith—from the source of the mystery itself, by the means which religious people call Grace."

Edwin Muir

1.
The Children

GOD SPEAKS OF THE CHILDREN

Nothing is so beautiful as a child who falls asleep while saying its
  prayers, God says.
I tell you there is nothing so beautiful in the world.
I have never seen anything so beautiful in the world.
And yet I have seen some beauty in the world
And I am a judge of it. My Creation overflows with beauty.
My Creation overflows with marvels.
There are so many one doesn't know where to put them.
I have seen millions and millions of stars rolling at my feet like the
  sands of the sea.
I have seen days blazing like flames.
Summer days in June, in July, in August.
I have seen winter evenings laid down like a cloak.
I have seen summer evenings as calm and gentle as the descent of
  paradise
All sprinkled with stars.
I have seen the slopes of the Meuse and the churches which are my
  own houses.
And Paris and Rheims and Rouen and the cathedrals which are my
  own palaces and my own castles.
So beautiful that I shall keep them in Heaven.
I have seen the capital of the kingdom and Rome the capital of
  Christendom.
I have heard the singing of the Mass and of triumphant Vespers.
And I have seen those plains and valleys of France
Which are more beautiful than anything.

I have seen the dark, deep sea, and the dark, deep forest, and the dark,
   deep heart of man.
I have seen hearts devoured by love
Throughout a life -time
Lost in charity.
Burning like flames.
I have seen martyrs inspired by faith
Holding firm as a rock on the torturer's frame
Between the iron teeth.
(Like a soldier holding firm all alone all his life
Through faith
In his General [apparently] absent).
I have seen martyrs flaming like torches
Earning palms forever green,
And I have seen gathering beneath the iron claws
Drops of blood which glittered like diamonds.
And I have seen the dropping of many tears of love
Which will endure longer than the stars of the sky.
And I have seen faces of prayer, faces of tenderness
Lost in charity.
Which will shine eternally through endless nights.
And I have seen whole lives from birth to death,
From baptism to the Viaticum,
Unroll like a fair skein of wool.
Well, I tell you, God says, I know nothing so beautiful in all the world
As a little child who falls asleep while saying his prayers
Under the wing of his Guardian Angel
And who laughs to the angels as he goes to sleep.
And who is already confusing everything and understanding nothin
   more
And who stuffs the words of the *Our Father* all awry, pell-mell into th
   words of the *Hail Mary*
While a veil is already dropping on his eyelids
The veil of night on his face and his voice.
I have seen the greatest Saints, God says. Yet I say to you,
I have never seen anything so funny and in consequence I kno
   nothing so beautiful in the world
As the child who falls asleep saying his prayers
(As the little creature who falls asleep confidently)
and who jumbles his *Our Father* with his *Hail Mary*.
Nothing is so beautiful and it is even a point
On which the Blessed Virgin is of my opinion
About it.

And I can truly say it is the only point on which we are of the same
    opinion. For generally we are of contrary opinions.
Because she is in favour of mercy.
While it is necessary that I should be in favour of justice.

*   *   *   *

As for you men (God says), just try to invent a child's saying.
You know very well that you cannot.
And not only that you cannot invent one
Not even one, but when they are uttered
You cannot even remember them. When a child's saying breaks forth
    among you
You cry out, you break forth yourselves in a wonder
Which is sincere and profound and which will redeem you and to
    which I do justice.
And you say, the whole of you says,
You say with your eyes, you say with your voice,
You laugh, you say to yourselves and you say aloud at the table:
That's good, that is, I must remember it. And you swear to yourselves
To share it with your friends, to tell it to everybody,
You have so much pride in your children (I don't blame you for it, God
    says,
It is what is best in you and it is what will redeem you).
You think that you can easily relate it.
You realise that you no longer remember it.
And not only that, but you cannot find it again, it has vanished from
    your memory.
It is too pure a water and has fled from your muddy memory, your
    stained memory.
And it wanted to flee, it did not want to remain.

*   *   *   *

When a child's saying is uttered in the family circle,
When a child's saying
Falls
Among the confusion of the day,
Among the noise of the day,
(In the sudden silence),
In the sudden recollection
At the family table.
O men and women seated at that table suddenly bowing your heads,

173

you listen to the passing-by
Of your former soul.

*　　*　　*　　*

Charles Péguy

TO A CHILD BEFORE BIRTH

This summer is your perfect summer. Never will the skies
So stretched and strident be with blue
As these you do not see; never will the birds surprise
With such light flukes the ferns and fences
As these you do not hear. This year the may
Smells like rum-butter, and day by day
The petals slip from the cups like lovers' hands,
Tender and tired and satisfied. This year the haws
Will form as your fingers form, and when in August
The sun first stings your eyes,
The fruit will be red as brick and free to the throstles.
Oh but next year the may
Will have its old smell of plague about it; next year
The songs of the birds be selfish, the skies have rain;
Next year the apples will be tart again.
But do not always grieve
For the unseen summer. Perfection is not the land you leave,
It is the pole you measure from; it gives
Geography to your ways and wanderings.
What is your perfection is another's pain;
And because she in impossible season loves
So in her blood for you the bright bird sings.

Norman Nicholson

A CHILD ACCEPTS

"Later," his mother said; and still those little hands
Clawed air to clutch the object of their need,
Abandoned as birds to winds or fishes to tide,
Pure time that is timeless, time untenanted.

174

"Later," she said; and the word was cold with death,
Opposing space to his time, intersecting his will,
He summoned the cry of a wounded animal,
Mindless Adam whose world lies crushed by the Fall,

But suddenly mended his face and far from tears
Grew radiant, relaxed, letting his hands drop down.
"Later," he sang, and was human, fallen again,
Received into mind, his dubious, his true demesne.

"Later," he played with the word, and later will envy
The freedom of birds and fishes for ever lost,
When, migrant in mind whom wind and water resist,
Here he must winter in body, bound to the coast;

Or, not all his "laters" past, perhaps he'll know
That the last releases: reversed, his needs will throng
Homewards to nest in his head and breed among
Those hidden rocks that wrecked him into song.

Michael Hamburger

FOR A FAMILY ALBUM

Four heads in one lamp's light
And each head bowed into peculiar darkness,
Reading, drawing, alone.
A camera would have caught them, held them there
Half-lit in the room's warm halflight,
Left them, refused to tell
How long till that lamp was broken,
Your hair pinned up or cut or tinted or waved.

I cannot even describe them, caught no more
Than a flash of light that ripped open
The walls of our half-lit room;
Or the negative—a black wedge
Rammed into light so white that it hurt to look.

Leave this page blank.
You'd neither like nor believe
The picture no lens could have taken:

Tied to my rooted bones
In your chairs you were flying, flying.

Michael Hamburger

ADVICE TO YOUNG CHILDREN

'Children who paddle where the ocean bed shelves steeply
Must take great care they do not
Paddle too deeply.'

Thus spake the awful ageing couple
Whose heart the years had turned to rubble.

But the little children, to save any bother,
Let it in at one ear and out at the other.

Stevie Smith

THE MERRY-GO-ROUND

JARDIN DU LUXEMBOURG

With roof and shadow for a while careers
the stud of horses, variously bright,
all from that land that long remains in sight
before it ultimately disappears.
Several indeed pull carriages, with tight-
held rein, but all have boldness in their bearing;
with them a wicked scarlet lion's faring
and now and then an elephant all white.

Just as in woods, a stag comes into view,
save that it has a saddle and tied fast
thereon a little maiden all in blue.

And on the lion a little boy is going,
whose small hot hands hold on with all his might,
while raging lion's tongue and teeth are showing.

176

And now and then an elephant all white.

And on the horses they come riding past,
girls too, bright-skirted, whom the horses-jumps here
scarce now preoccupy: in full career
elsewhither, hitherwards, a glance they cast—

And now and then an elephant all white.

And this keeps passing by until it's ended,
and hastens aimlessly until it's done.
A red, a green, a grey is apprehended,
a little profile, scarcely yet begun.—
And now and then a smile, for us intended,
blissfully happy, dazzlingly expended
upon this breathless, blindly followed fun . . .

Rainer Maria Rilke

THE SITE OF THE FIRE

Shunned by the autumn morning, which had got
mistrustful, lay behind the sooty-stemmed
lime trees by which the heath-house had been hemmed
a newness, emptiness. Just one more spot

where children, whence they'd come a mystery,
snatched after rags and filled the air with screams.
But all of them grew quiet whenever he,
the son from here, out of hot, half-charred beams,

with manage of a long forked bough, was trying
to rescue kettles and bent cooking-ware,—
till, looking at them as if he were lying,
he'd bring the others to believe what there,

upon that very spot, once used to stand.
It seemed so strange now it had ceased to be:
fantasticer than Pharaoh seemed. And he
was also different. As from some far land.

Rainer Maria Rilke

COMPREHENDING IT NOT

December, 1921. Seven years of age
And my mother dead—the house in mourning,
The shop shut up for Christmas—I
Was fobbed off to my Grandma's with my Christmas Tree
Bundled under my arm. Out
In the brown packed streets the lamplight drizzled down
On squirming pavements; the after-smell of war
Clung like a fungus to wall and windowsill.
And the backyards reeked of poverty. Boys,
Their big toes squirting through their boots,
Growled out *While Shepherds Watched* to deaf door-knobs,
And the Salvation Army—euphoniums, slung, un-playing—
Stumped the length of the town at the thump of a drum
To cracked Hallelujahs in the Market Square.

I edged past muttering entries, sidled inside the lobby,
And slammed the door on the dark. My Grandma
Banged the floor with her stick to greet me,
Tossed me a humbug and turned again to the goose,
Spluttering on the kitchen range. My four rough uncles
Barged jokily around in flannel shirtsleeves:
Challenged to comic fisticuffs or gripped me
With a wrestler's grip and hyped me and cross-buddocked
In Cumberland-and-Westmoreland style—till puffed, at last, and wear
Of horse-play and of me, they ripped my Christmas
Tree from its wrapper, unfolded its gaunt
Umbrella frame of branches, stuck candles in the green raffia,
And stood it on the dresser, well out of my reach.

I crouched down by the fire, crunching my humbug,
And scissoring holly and bells from coloured card.
The huff of the smoke brought water to my eyes;
The smell of the goose made me retch. Then suddenly,
The gas plopped out and the house was doused in darkness—
A break in the main and not a chance of repair
Till the day after Boxing Day. Matches rattled;
A twist of paper torn from *The Daily Mail*
Relayed the flame from grate to candle,
And soon, high on the dresser, my Christmas Tree,
Ignited like a gorse-bush, pollened the room with light.

Proud as a proselyte,
I stuffed white wax in the mouth of a medicine bottle,
Pioneered the wild lobby and the attic stairs
And dared the heathen flagstones of the yard,
Bearing my gleam of a gospel. At the scratch of a match,
Christmas crackled up between winter walls,
And Grandma's house was home, her sharp voice called in kindness,
And the fists no longer frightened. Tickled at the trick of it,
I "Merry-Christmas-ed" gas-pipe, gas and gas-men,
"God-blessed" the darkness and pulled crackers with the cold—
Scarcely aware what it was that I rejoiced in:
Whether the black-out or the candles,
Whether the light or the dark.

Norman Nicholson

MASTERS OF CERTAIN ARTS

Looking for things which were fun,
  Hanging round on the way,
When I was young they complained
  I was late, again day after day.

When they caught me they beat me,
  Late again, Grigson III, they would say.
But the boot has changed feet and I see
  It grows late in the day.

You'll never learn, they insisted,
  Be late for your funeral, they'd say.
Late again for parade, and for prep. and for prayers,
  I admit, now it's late in the day.

I was always behind, but I ask them
  If they can honestly say
Their breakfast of worm was so good
  For them, day after day.

Geoffrey Grigson

Three Modern Psalms Written by Schoolboys

WITHOUT HIS HAND

O God, O God,
Who built strong buildings
And makes them perfect and straight,
What would a building be without a hand from God?

O God, O God,
Who has given us earth to live upon,
To plant seeds which give us food,
And green grass to play upon,
What would they be without life from God?

O God, my God,
Who has given us a strong kick for kicking footballs,
And strong hands to catch them with.
And has given us a brain to think,
And lips that we might tell the answer,
What would I be without You?

E. Whiteloc

SOMETHING TO LOVE

Lord on high,
Lord above
Please give us something
That we can love.
Our love grows longer,
Our hearts grow stronger;
Can we live, any longer?

O give us a car,
Or maybe a cow,
A lion, an ox,
Or even a plough:
Something to love,

Not full of anger,
Something that we can
Protect from danger.

T. Church

GOD OF TWIST, ROCK AND TRAD

God made man;
He also made birds.
Is there a God that is to prove
He stands like a mountain impossible to move?
There must be a God like night and day.
He helps us to work; also to play.
Is there an after life
After we are dead?
Or do we rot in a grave or a bed?

According to adults teenagers are bad,
Because of the Twist, or Rock or just Trad.
Why should they judge us by that alone?
Think of the hours women waste on the phone!

John Odell

Three Hymns for Children

HONESTY

I
I have a house, the house of prayer,
  (No spy beneath my eaves)
And purring gratitude is there,
  And he that frights the thieves.

II
If I of honesty suspend
  My judgment, making doubt,
I have a good domestic friend,
  That soon shall point it out.

III

'Tis to be faithful to my charge,
   And thankful for my place,
And pray that God my pow'rs enlarge,
   To act with greater grace.

IV

To give my brother more than due,
   In talent or in name;
Nor e'en mine enemy pursue,
   To hurt or to defame.

V

Nay more, to bless him and to pray,
   Mine anger to controul;
And give the wages of the day
   To him that hunts my soul.

MIRTH

I

If you are merry sing away,
   And touch the organs sweet;
This is the Lord's triumphant day,
Ye children in the gall'ries gay,
   Shout from each goodly seat.

II

It shall be May to-morrow's morn,
   A field then let us run,
And deck us in the blooming thorn,
Soon as the cock begins to warn,
   And long before the sun.

III

I give the praise to Christ alone,
   My pinks already show;
And my streak'd roses fully blown,
The sweetness of the Lord make known,
   And to his glory grow.

IV

Ye little prattlers that repair
  For cowslips in the mead,
Of those exulting colts beware,
But blythe security is there,
  Where skipping lambkins feed.

V

With white and crimson laughs the sky,
  With birds the hedge-rows ring;
To give praise to God most high,
And all the sulky fiends defy,
  Is a most joyful thing.

FOR SATURDAY

I

NOW's the time for mirth and play,
Saturday's an holiday;
Praise to heav'n unceasing yield,
I've found a lark's nest in the field.

II

A lark's nest, then your play-mate begs
You'd spare herself and speckled eggs;
Soon she shall ascend and sing
Your praises to th'eternal King.

Christopher Smart

SONNET 143
MOTHER AND CHILD

Lo, as a careful housewife runs to catch
One of her feather'd creatures broke away,
Sets down her babe, and makes all swift dispatch
In pursuit of the thing she would have stay;
While her neglected child holds her in chase,
Cries to catch her whose busy care is bent
To follow that which flies before her face,

Not prizing her poor infant's discontent:
So runn'st thou after that which flies from thee,
Whilst I thy babe chase thee afar behind;
But if thou catch thy hope, turn back to me,
And play the mother's part, kiss me, be kind:
    So will I pray that thou mayst have thy 'Will,'
    If thou turn back and my loud crying still.

Shakespeare

TO A MOTHER

Know, I am never far from you, I bear you
inwardly as you bore me—as intimately too
and as my flesh is of your own
and our early mesh, woven one
so you are still my own
and everything about you, home,
the features, eyes, the hands, your entire form
are the past, present and to come,
the familiarity, the ease
of my living, and my peace.

Sister Mary Agnes, Order of Poor Clare

CHILD

I am your laughing, crying,
possibility:
I keep on coming as
I did before,

hoping and hungering
and with no visible
means of support
whatever.

Naked need is
all I offer:

my extremity is
your opportunity,

my Bethlehem
is where you can be born.
And will you be
King Herod to yourself?

Look in the mirror of
my cradle, see
your laughing, crying,
possibility,

hoping and hungering
and with no visible
means of support
whatever.

Sydney Carter

2.
The Lovers

SONNET 18

Shall I compare thee to a summer's day?
Thou art more lovely and more temperate:
Rough winds do shake the darling buds of May,
And summer's lease hath all too short a date:
Sometime too hot the eye of heaven shines,
And often is his gold complexion dimm'd;
And every fair from fair sometime declines,
By chance or nature's changing course untrimm'd;
But thy eternal summer shall not fade,
Nor lose possession of that fair thou owest;
Nor shall Death brag thou wander'st in his shade,
When in eternal lines to time thou grow'st:
    So long as men can breathe, or eyes can see,
    So long lives this, and this gives life to thee.

Shakespear

SONNET 109

O, never say that I was false of heart,
Though absence seem'd my flame to qualify.
As easy might I from myself depart
As from my soul, which in thy breast doth lie:
That is my home of love: if I have ranged,
Like him that travels, I return again;

Just to the time, not with the time exchanged,
So that myself bring water for my stain.
Never believe, though in my nature reign'd
All frailties that besiege all kinds of blood,
That it could so preposterously be stain'd,
To leave for nothing all thy sum of good;
    For nothing this wide universe I call,
    Save thou, my rose; in it thou art my all.

Shakespeare

Be then ever your self, and let no woe
Win on your health, your youth, your beauty: so
Declare your self base Fortune's Enemy,
No less by your contempt than constancy:
That I may grow enamoured on your mind,
When my own thoughts I there reflected find.
For this to th' comfort of my Dear I vow,
My Deeds shall still be what my words are now;
The Poles shall move to teach me ere I start;
And when I change my Love, I'll change my heart;
Nay, if I wax but cold in my desire,
Think, heaven hath motion lost, and the world, fire:
Much more I could, but many words have made
That, oft, suspected which men would perswade;
Take therefore all in this: I love so true,
As I will never look for less in you.

John Donne

SONG

    Sweetest love, I do not goe,
      For weariness of thee,
    Nor in hope the world can show
      A fitter Love for mee;
        But since that I
    Must dye at last, 'tis best,
    To use my selfe in jest
      Thus by fain'd deaths to dye;

Yesternight the Sunne went hence
    And yet is here to day,
He hath no desire nor sense,
    Nor halfe so short a way:
        Then feare not mee.
But beleeve that I shall make
Speedier journeys, since I take
    More wings and spurres than hee.

O how feeble is mans power,
    That if good fortune fall,
Cannot add another houre,
    Nor a lost houre recall!
        But come bad chance,
And wee joyne to'it our strength,
And wee teach it art and length,
    It selfe o'er us to'advance.

When thou sigh'st, thou sigh'st not winde,
    But sigh'st my soule away,
When thou weep'st, unkindly kinde,
    My lifes blood doth decay.
        It cannot bee
That thou lov'st mee, as thou say'st,
If in thine my life thou waste,
    That art the best of mee.

Let not thy divining heart
    Forthinke mee any ill,
Destiny may take thy part,
    And may thy feares fulfill;
        But thinke that wee
Are but turn'd aside to sleepe;
They who one another keepe
    Alive, ne'er parted bee.

John Don.

        Out upon it, I have lov'd,
        Three whole days together;
        And am like to love three more,
        If it prove fair weather.

Time shall moult away his wings
Ere he shall discover
In the whole wide world agen
Such a constant Lover.

But the spite on't is, no praise
Is due at all to me:
Love with me had made no staies,
Had it any been but she,

Had it any been but she
And that very Face,
There had been at least ere this
A dozen dozen in her place.

Sir John Suckling

HOW GLAD ARE THE SMALL BIRDS

How glad are the small birds
    That rise and sing on one bough,
How near to each other! How far
    Is my love from me now!

White as new milk, sweet as the fiddle,
    Bright as the summer sun
Is she. Dear God in heaven,
    Free me from pain!

Brendan Kennelly

LOVERS WHO MEET IN CHURCHES

Mary Godwin's letter to Shelley, October 25, 1814

Lovers who meet in churches
And sit there indifferent to God,
Or dead. Priests, this is a charity
You most unwillingly provide,
This privacy. You cannot hear
Her pagan heart by the chill

Tomb-chest pounding. Her words,
O my own one be happy
O my love, my dear.

Geoffrey Grigson

UPON THE DEATH OF SIR ALBERT MORTON'S WIFE

He first deceas'd; She for a little tri'd
To live without him: lik'd it not, and di'd.

Sir Henry Wotton

BELOVED, LOST TO BEGIN WITH

Beloved,
lost to begin with, never greeted,
I do not know what tones most please you.
No more when the future's wave hangs poised is it you
I try to discern there. All the greatest
images in me, far-off experienced landscape,
towers and towns and bridges and unsuspected
turns of the way,
and the power of those lands once intertwined
with the life of the gods:
mount up within me to mean
you, who forever elude.

Oh, you are the gardens!
Oh, with such yearning
hope I watched them! An open window
in a country house, and you almost stepped out
thoughtfully to meet me. Streets I discovered,—
you had just walked down them,
and sometimes in dealers' shops the mirrors,
still dizzy with you, returned with a stare
my too-sudden image.— Who knows whether the
self-same bird didn't ring through each of us,
separately, yesterday evening?

Rainer Maria Rilke

THERE IS A LADY SWEET AND KIND

There is a Lady sweet and kind,
Was never face so pleas'd my mind;
I did but see her passing by,
And yet I love her till I die.

Her gesture, motion and her smiles,
Her wit, her voyce, my heart beguiles,
Beguiles my heart, I know not why,
And yet I love her till I die.

Her free behaviour, winning lookes,
Will make a Lawyer burne his bookes.
I touched her not, alas, not I,
And yet I love her till I die.

Had I her fast betwixt mine armes,
Judge you that thinke such sports were harmes,
Wer't any harm? no, no, fie, fie!
For I will love her till I die.

Should I remaine confined there,
So long as Phebus in his sphere,
I to request, she to denie,
Yet would I love her till I die.

Cupid is winged and doth range,
Her countrie so my love doth change,
But change she earth, or change she skie,
Yet will I love her till I die.

Thomas Ford

SONNET

Inadequate of words! They are but noises
Harsh or musical, mellow or slow or strong!
Why, all the breathing air is full of voices,
For every touch and every thought's a song.
Oh, words! By words I cannot say I love you:

These letters of the alphabet, this grammar,
This cadence of coarse art—can these things move you?
Words? When in wooing Shakespeare did but stammer?
Hush! While I move within thoughts reach of you,
Or far more fortunate, far more, even nearer,
Not in vain words the world makes speech of you;
Nor I whom words betray, nor you, the hearer,
Have need, just then, of ears or lips or eyes:
The waters woo for me, the night replies.

Frank Kendon

LINES FOR LIOBA

ON HER FIRST VISIT

I

The small flowers you brought
the morning of your leaving
are a week of age this morning
yet they fill my room still
most sweetly, most eloquently
and bring to my saddened mind
your gentleness strong as flowers
breathing out of your silences.

II

Your hands stirred then;
delicate white petals in your lap
against the soft leaf-brown dress.

III

Your gentleness disarmed me;
pointless my arrows fell
in the clear path of your gaze.

IV

You said little;
we broke from the net of words
the black forest of chosen language
free and familiar upon the bright strand

of our understanding
happy and wise as only we can be
who demand nothing of each other;
we looked with eyes not in our heads
and were not dismayed.

V

The small truth you brought with the flowers
grows strong-rooted in crevices of my heart;
not now forever can you escape into unremembrance;
not now forever can knowledge of you be lost
in a trap of time;
as a flower in my mind you shall grow
and time is kind to flowers.

Christy Brown

OCTOBER LOVE

Was nothing there? No resin smelling pine,
no mushrooms, moss, or fingers touching mine,
no empty cottage, no one there to play
the broken old piano in the shed?
—and did I dream I turned to walk away
but hands caressed me, lips on my lips said
no one was watching, why then should I go?
Was I alone when suddenly I found
the soft mimosa gold where none should grow,
and was there no one wrapped their arms around
me crying 'celebrate?' Was there no kiss?
Ah love, there is no truth in this.
It was all there, kisses, mimosa tree,
but things as these are not for all to see.

Anne Lewis-Smith

REMEMBRANCE

If I should leave you in the days to come—
God grant that may not be—

But yet if so,
Your love for me must fade I know.
You will remember—and you will forget.
But oh! imperishable—strong
My love for you shall burn and glow
Deep in your heart—your whole life long,
Unknown, unseen, but living still in bliss
So you shall bear me with you all the days.
Forget then what you will.
I died—but not my love for you,
That lives for aye—though dumb,
Remember this
If I should leave you in the days to come.

Agatha Christi

3.

Mystery

When we talk of our development I fancy we mean little more than
that we have changed with the changing world; and if we are writers or
intellectuals, that our ideas have changed with the changing fashions
of thought, and therefore not always for the better. I think that if any of
us examines his life, he will find that most good has come to him from
the few loyalties, and a few discoveries made many generations before
he was born, which must always be made anew. These too may sometimes appear to come by chance, but in the infinite web of things and
events chance must be something different from what we think it to
be. To comprehend that is not given to us, and to think of it is to recognize a mystery, and to acknowledge the necessity of faith. As I look
back on the part of the mystery which is my own life, my own fable,
what I am most aware of is that we receive more than we can ever give;
we receive it from the past, on which we draw with every breath, but
also—and this is a point of faith—from the Source of the mystery itself,
by the means which religious people call Grace.

Edwin Muir

Yet in this journey back
If I should reach the end, if end there was
Before the ever-running roads began
And race and track and runner all were there
Suddenly, always, the great revolving way
Deep in its trance;—if there was ever a place
Where one might say, 'Here is the starting-point,'
And yet not say it, or say it as in a dream,

In idle speculation, imagination,
Reclined at ease, dreaming a life, a way,
And then awaken in the hurtling track,
The great race in full swing far from the start,
No memory of beginning, sign of the end,
And I the dreamer there, a frenzied runner:—
If I should reach that place, how could I come
To where I am but by that deafening road,
Life-wide, world-wide, by which all come to all,
The strong with the weak, the swift with the stationary,
For mountain and man, hunter and quarry there
In tarrying do not tarry, nor hastening hasten,
But all with no division strongly come
For ever to their steady mark, the moment,
And the tumultuous world slips softly home
To its perpetual end and flawless bourne.
How could we be if all were not in all?
Borne hither on all and carried hence with all,
We and the world and that unending thought
Which has elsewhere its end and is for us
Begotten in a dream deep in this dream
Beyond the place of getting and spending.
There's no prize in this race; the prize is elsewhere,
Here only to be run for. There's no harvest,
Though all around the fields are white with harvest.
There is our journey's ground; we pass unseeing.
But we have watched against the evening sky,
Tranquil and bright, the golden harvester.

Edwin Mu

THE EVE OF CHRISTMAS

It was the evening before the night
That Jesus turned from dark to light.

Joseph was walking round and round
And yet he moved not on the ground.

He looked into the heavens, and saw
The pole stood silent, star on star.

196

He looked into the forest: there
The leaves hung dead upon the air.

He looked into the sea, and found
It frozen, and the lively fishes bound.

And in the sky, the birds that sang
Not in feathered clouds did hang.

Said Joseph: 'What is this silence all?'
An angel spoke: 'It is no thrall,

But is a sign of great delight:
The Prince of Love is born this night.'

And Joseph said: 'Where may I find
This wonder?'—'He is all mankind,

Look, he is both farthest, nearest,
Highest and lowest, of all men the dearest.'

Then Joseph moved, and found the stars
Moved with him, and the evergreen airs,

The birds went flying, and the main
Flowed with its fishes once again.

And everywhere they went, they cried:
'Love lives, when all had died!'

In Excelsis Gloria!

James Kirkup

PILGRIM'S PROBLEM

By now I should be entering on the supreme stage
Of the whole walk, reserved for the late afternoon.
The heat was to be over now; the anxious mountains,
The airless valleys and the sun-baked rocks, behind me.

Now, or soon now, if all is well, come the majestic
Rivers of foamless charity that glide beneath

Forests of contemplation. In the grassy clearings
Humility with liquid eyes and damp, cool nose
Should come, half-tame, to eat bread from my hermit hand.
If storms arose, then in my tower of fortitude—
It ought to have been in sight by this—I would take refuge;
But I expected rather a pale mackerel sky,
Feather-like, perhaps shaking from a lower cloud
Light drops of silver temperance, and clovery earth
Sending up mists of chastity, a country smell,
Till earnest stars blaze out in the established sky
Rigid with justice; the streams audible; my rest secure.
I can see nothing like all this. Was the map wrong?
Maps can be wrong. But the experienced walker knows
That the other explanation is more often true.

C. S. Lewi

NEW YEAR'S EVE

All our perceiving is a memory.
The flood-waters of the senses back sluggishly up the nerves,
And when the waves clamber on the rocks, the upper pools
Are still as goldfish bowls, the weed spread wide on the floor;
But brine chills the blood of the stream, the cool
Frill of foam pushes among the rushes
When the tide is already ebbing from the shore.

The glance is seen
Only when the glance has been;
The touch is felt
Only when the hand is gone;
The word is heard
Only when the word is spoken;
And only when the silence is broken
Is the silence heard or felt or even known.

All our memory is a perceiving.
Only in memory are the seven words
Linked from lip to ear at the heart's call;
Only in memory are the seven notes
Strung on the thread of a tune;

198

Only in memory are the smile, and all
The accessories of greeting and of parting,
The flush, the wind-unravelled curl,
The round of breast and thigh,
The blue of a dress, the angle of an eye,
The unasked, unintended pressure of the turn of a knee,
Fleshed and embodied as a girl.

To know is to accept that understanding
Is beyond our hands and away from our eyes.
Even a tree is a thought, a girl's hair
Is a creed, a need is a prayer.
Life is faith, seeing is believing:
All our memory is a perceiving.

Norman Nicholson

On this tree is a bird: it dances in the
    joy of life.
None knows where it is: and who
    knows what the burden of its
    music may be?
Where the branches throw a deep
    shade, there does it have its nest:
    and it comes in the evening and
    flies away in the morning, and says
    not a word of that which it means.
None tells me of this bird that sings
    within me.
It is neither coloured nor colourless:
    it has neither form nor outline:
It sits in the shadow of love.
It dwells within the Unattainable, the
    Infinite, and the Eternal; and no
    one marks when it comes and goes.
Kabir says: 'O brother Sadhu!
    deep is the mystery. Let wise men
    seek to know where rests that bird.'

Rabindranath Tagore

BROAD DAYLIGHT

ON NOT UNDERSTANDING, WHICH IS ZEN

Out of all the world
take this forest.

Out of all the forest
take this tree.

Out of all the tree
take this branch.

Out of all the branch
take this leaf.

And on this leaf
that is like no other

observe this drop of rain
that is like no other.

And in this single drop
observe the reflection

of leaves and branches,
of the entire tree,

of the forest
of all the world—

Then only
will you see

the stars beyond
the light of day.

James Kirku

THE WOOD

When we entered the wood that bright spring morning
The fairy beckoned, the bluebell danced.

We paid no heed to the old crone's warning,
But wandered as our footsteps chanced.
The air was sweet, the day had just begun—
So beautiful it was, we would have stayed
And played, but from a distant glade
"Further," the bird called, "further, further on."

By noon, our steps were somewhat slower,
For the groves were dense and heavy with heat.
Many a green bower
Invited us to cool retreat,
Many a gay exotic flower
Said "Pluck" and many a fruit cried "Eat."
We would have rested in the afternoon,
But still the bird sang "Further, further on."

Now the trees are few and bare,
The wood is thinning out—and where
Is the promised land, the city of the sun?
"Further," the bird cries. "Further. Further on."

Francis Newbold

COME IN

As I came to the edge of the woods,
Thrush music—hark!
Now if it was dusk outside,
Inside it was dark.

Too dark in the woods for a bird
By sleight of wing
To better its perch for the night,
Though it still could sing.

The last of the light of the sun
That had died in the west
Still lived for one song more
In a thrush's breast.

Far in the pillared dark
Thrush music went—

Almost like a call to come in
To the dark and lament.

But no, I was out for stars:
I would not come in.
I meant not even if asked,
And I hadn't been.

Robert Frost

STOPPING BY WOODS
ON A SNOWY EVENING

Whose woods these are I think I know.
His house is in the village, though;
He will not see me stopping here
To watch his woods fill up with snow.

My little horse must think it queer
To stop without a farmhouse near
Between the woods and frozen lake
The darkest evening of the year.

He gives his harness bells a shake
To ask if there is some mistake.
The only other sound's the sweep
Of easy wind and downy flake.

The woods are lovely, dark, and deep,
But I have promises to keep,
And miles to go before I sleep,
And miles to go before I sleep.

Robert Fros

NEITHER OUT FAR NOR IN DEEP

The people along the sand
All turn and look one way.

They turn their back on the land.
They look at the sea all day.

As long as it takes to pass
A ship keeps raising its hull;
The wetter ground like glass
Reflects a standing gull.

The land may vary more;
But whatever the truth may be—
The water comes ashore,
And the people look at the sea.

They cannot look out far.
They cannot look in deep.
But when was that ever a bar
To any watch they keep?

Robert Frost

SHADOWS IN THE WATER

In unexperienc'd Infancy
Many a sweet Mistake doth ly:
Mistake the false, intending true;
A *Seeming* somewhat more than *View*,
   That doth instruct the Mind
   In Things that lie behind,
And many Secrets to us show
Which afterwards we come to know.

Thus did I by the Water's brink
Another World beneath me think:
And while the lofty spacious Skies
Reversed there abus'd mine Eyes,
   I fancy'd other Feet
   Came mine to touch or meet;
As by some Puddle I did play
Another World within it lay.

Beneath the Water people drown'd,
Yet with another Heav'n crown'd,
In spacious Regions seem'd to go

As freely moving to and fro:
   In bright and open Space
   I saw their very face;
Eyes, Hands, and Feet they had like mine;
Another Sun did with them shine.

'Twas strange that People there should walk,
And yet I could not hear them talk:
That through a little wat'ry Chink,
Which one dry Ox or Horse might drink,
   We other Worlds should see,
   Yet not admitted be;
And other Confines there behold
Of Light and Darkness, Heat and Cold.

I call'd them oft, but call'd in vain;
No Speeches we could entertain:
Yet did I there expect to find
Some other World, to please my Mind.
   I plainly saw by these
   A new *Antipodes,*
Whom, tho they were so plainly seen,
A Film kept off that stood between.

By walking Men's reversed Feet
I chanc'd another World to meet;
Tho it Did not to View exceed
A Phantasm, 'tis a World indeed,
   Where Skies beneath us shine,
   And Earth by Art divine
Another Face presents below
Where People's Feet against Ours go.

Within the Regions of the Air,
Compass'd about with Heav'ns fair,
Great Tracts of Land there may be found
Enricht with Fields and fertile Ground;
   Where many num'rous Hosts
   In those far distant Coasts,
For other great and glorious Ends,
Inhabit, my yet unknown Friends.

O ye that stand upon the Brink,
Whom I so near me, through the Chink

With Wonder see: What Faces there,
Whose Feet, whose Bodies, do ye wear?
  I my Companions see
  In You, another Me.
They seemed Others, but are We;
Our second Selves those Shadows be.

Look how far off those lower Skies
Extend themselves! Scarce with mine Eyes
I can reach, O ye my Friends,
What *Secret* borders on those Ends?
  Are lofty Heavens hurl'd
  'Bout your Inferior World?
Are ye the Representatives
Of other People's distant Lives?

Of all the Play-mates which I knew
That here I do the Image view
In other Selves; what can it mean?
But that below the purling Stream
  Some unknown Joys there be
  Laid up in Store for me;
To which I shall, when that thin Skin
Is broken, be admitted in.

Thomas Traherne

A GHOSTING

In Memoriam: Richard Mundy, Miller

'Who be it calls me from my long whoam
Mid deep mosses and loam?'

'I call, old miller, from distant view.
I'm as ghostly as you.'

'What fine housen be this we'm come tew,
Wide winders fettled new, lady?'

'It's what they made out of our old mill
After we'd gone down hill.'

'My o'd mill were an innocent place
Niver lackin i' grace, lady.'

'In my time too. It was dignified,
Simple and unified.'

'Wheer's the ripe smell o' granary meal
Solid enough to feel, lady?'

'Gone with the stones and the waterwheel
They tore out with such zeal.'

'Wheer's the sound o' small water fallin'
Like an o'd friend callin', lady?'

'Silenced this long time and forever.
Their scheme was too clever.'

'An' the sough o' the sluice open wide
Wi' its powerful pride, lady?'

'Gone with the white-webbed hopper and chute,
Every wove-hum mute.'

'The bright chain-hoist that ran through my hold
An' the full sacks o' gold, lady?'

'All gone, though still whole in our heart-dreams
With the memoried streams.'

'An' th' kitchen-place, my beer pot-hole,
Bread oven, rakin' pole, lady?'

'Turned to this white-sterile box of glaze
That never kindled blaze.'

'An' the close bed-chamber, feather bed
To rest my work-mazed head, lady?'

'Become this rich carpeted expanse
Grand enough for a dance.'

'Wheer's my Lizzie's geranium pot
That bloomed all summer hot, lady?'

'Gone with the currant-bush bleaching cloths
And woodbine, full of moths.'

'Cowslips that th' hedge drew up so tall,
Fern by the waterfall, lady?'

'All gone now—but the water's still here—
See the great pond shine clear!'

'Aye—how it glosses the glimmin' sky
An' us ghosts grievin' by, lady.'

'Only the ancient water's unchanged
Though all else be estranged.'

'Why did ye lure me to view this wrack?
I'd be fain gettin' back, lady.'

'To restore faith in what is, not seems.
See how the water gleams.'

Pitt Clark

FAFNIR AND THE KNIGHTS

In the quiet waters
Of the forest pool
Fafnir the dragon
His tongue will cool

His tongue will cool
And his muzzle dip
Until the soft waters lave
His muzzle tip

Happy simple creature
In his coat of mail
With a mild bright eye
And a waving tail

Happy the dragon
In the days expended
Before the time had come for dragons
To be hounded

Delivered in their simplicity
To the Knights of the Advancing Band
Who seeing the simple dragon
Must kill him out of hand

The time has not come yet
But must come soon
Meanwhile happy Fafnir
Take thy rest in the afternoon

Take thy rest
Fafnir while thou mayest
In the long grass
Where thou liest

Happy knowing not
In thy simplicity
That the knights have come
To do away with thee.

When thy body shall be torn
And thy lofty spirit
Broken into pieces
For a knight's merit

When thy lifeblood shall be spilt
And thy Being mild
In torment and dismay
To death beguiled

Fafnir, I shall say then,
Thou art better dead
For the knights have burnt thy grass
And thou couldst not have fed.

Stevie Smith

THE UNICORN

This is the creature there has never been.
They never knew it, and yet, none the less,

they loved the way it moved, its suppleness,
its neck, its very gaze, mild and serene.

Not there, because they loved it, it behaved
as though it were. They always left some space.
And in that clear unpeopled space they saved
it lightly reared its head, with scarce a trace

of not being there. They fed it, not with corn,
but only with the possibility
of being. And that was able to confer

such strength, its brow put forth a horn. One horn.
Whitely it stole up to a maid, — to *be*
within the silver mirror and in her.

Rainer Maria Rilke

Where, in what ever-blissfully watered gardens, upon what trees,
out of, oh, what gently dispetalled flower-cups do these
so strange-looking fruits of consolation mature?
Delicious, when, now and then, you pick one up in the poor

trampled field of your poverty. Time and again you find
yourself lost in wonder over the size of the fruit,
over its wholesomeness, over its smooth, soft rind,
and that neither the heedless bird above nor jealous worm at the root

has been before you. Are there, then, trees where angels will congre-
    gate,
trees invisible leisurely gardeners so curiously cultivate,
that, without being ours, they bear for us fruits like those?

Have we, then, never been able, we shadows and shades,
with our doing that ripens too early and then as suddenly fades,
to disturb that even-tempered summer's repose?

Rainer Maria Rilke

Part 7
Faith, Hope and Charity

"I am, God says, the Lord of the Virtues."

1.
Faith and Doubt

THE THREE VIRTUES

I am, God says, Master of the Three Virtues. . . .

It is Faith who holds fast through century after century.
It is Charity who gives herself through centuries of centuries,
But it is my little hope
Who gets up every morning. . . .

It is Faith who watches through centuries of centuries.
It is Charity who watches through centuries of centuries.
But it is my little hope
who lies down every evening
and gets up every morning
and really has very good nights. . . .

Faith is a great tree, an oak rooted in the heart of France,
And under the wings of that tree, Charity, my daughter Charity
  shelters all the distress of the world.
And my little hope is only that little promise of a bud which
  shows itself at the very beginning of April. . . .

Charles Péguy

FAITH AS OBEDIENCE

"If ye have faith and doubt not, if ye shall say unto this mountain, Be
ᥒou removed and cast into the sea, it shall be done." Good peo-

213

ple . . . have been tempted to tempt the Lord their God upon the strength of this saying. . . . Happily for such, the assurance to which they would give the name of faith generally fails them in time. Faith is that which, knowing the Lord's will, goes and does it; or, not knowing it, stands and waits. . . . But to put God to the question in any other way than by saying, "What wilt thou have me to do?" is an attempt to compel God to declare Himself, or to hasten His work. . . . The man is therein dissociating himself from God so far that, instead of acting by the divine will from within, he acts in God's face, as it were, to see what He will do. Man's first business is, "What does God want me to do?"—not "What will God do if I do so and so?" . . .

Do you ask, "What is faith in Him?" I answer, the leaving of your way, your objects, your self, and the taking of His and Him; the leaving of your trust in men, in money, in opinion, in character, in atonement itself, *and doing as He tells you.* I can find no words strong enough to serve for the weight of this obedience. . . .

Instead of asking yourself whether you believe or not, ask yourself whether you have this day done one thing because He said, *Do it,* or once abstained because He said, *Do not do it.* It is simply absurd to say you believe, or even want to believe, in Him, if you do not do anything He tells you. . . .

Oh the folly of any mind that would explain God before obeying Him! That would map out the character of God instead of crying, Lord what wouldst thou have me to do! . . .

George Macdonald

FAITH AND DOUBT

To deny the existence of God may . . . involve less unbelief than the smallest yielding to doubt of His goodness. I say *yielding;* for a man may be haunted with doubts, and only grow thereby in faith. Doubts are the messengers of the Living One to the honest. They are the first knock at our door of things that are not yet, but have to be, understood. . . . Doubts must precede every deeper assurance; for uncertainties are what we first see when we look into a region hitherto unknown, unexplored, unannexed.

George Macdonald

'Faith' is often used by agnostics as a term of abuse. That is to say, it
s taken to refer to the blind credulity which accepts all kinds of dog-
mas and creeds without question, repeating parrot-like what it has
been taught, and closing its ears to doubt and reason. Such 'faith'
should certainly be attacked. It is compounded of laziness, obstinacy,
ignorance and fear. Because it is rigid and unyielding it can quite easily
be shaken and altogether destroyed.

But this is not the true faith—the faith which is recommended by Pa-
anjali. True faith is provisional, flexible, undogmatic, open to doubt
and reason. True faith is not like a picture frame, a permanently limited area of acceptance. It is like a plant which keeps on throwing forth
shoots and growing.

Swami Prabharananda and Christopher Isherwood

Basically I am like St. Thomas, in that I desire to touch and see. The
thing wrong with St. Thomas is not that he could not believe what the
disciples said, but that he was not bold enough to trust the only kind of
real evidence that faith could ask for: the only kind of evidence which,
at the present time, it is likely to obtain. Faith must be prepared to
trust the reality of its desire: to lean on something which, in time and
place, may not be there—not yet, at any rate. That is what the artist
does. His faith is in the picture or the poem or the table or the chair,
which is not created yet, but which is pushing to be born. Faith is creation, and creation faith. If we are in fact created in the image of our
creator, then we are created to create.

St. Thomas was right to question hearsay evidence. He was wrong in
not trusting, as Jesus did, the evidence he was born with. So was I. That
what Jesus was telling him, I believe, in the story related in the Gospel of St. John. Can I accept that story, as true history? I do not know.
But I can trust it as a parable, for the truth of parable is always in the
present tense. It is by the parable, not by the history, that we are saved,
even though the history be true. You can believe the history and not be
saved. "The devils believe also, and tremble," Jesus said. They believed, but lacked the faith.

I am in no position to blame St. Thomas. It is hard to be as tough as
Jesus was: to have the faith that Jesus had; to create as boldly as Jesus
did. It is hard even to believe that Jesus wanted us to do this. I was not
encouraged to believe it, but I do now begin to.

Sydney Carter

Wherever faith is, the abyss of possible doubt is opened up. Our faith
is always a search for something that is not there. Thus it is perfectly
understandable that Augustine should speak of the "hands of faith,"
reaching out into the dark. It is genuinely not easy to live and to lift
ourselves up into something that is greater than ourselves. A mature
person believes, not because it is easier to believe, but in spite of the
fact that it is more difficult. . . .

We are constantly lifting ourselves up beyond our present state. Our
desire exceeds again and again what our own heart can conceive of.
That which lays its unconditional claim upon us, at the same time
vanishes away from us into the hidden, undefined region of the "wholly other" in which it belongs. . . .

God seems to have closed his doors and sealed them with an everlasting indifference. Our own relationship to God is like a nightmare:
we are running towards something unattainable; the more we run, the
further the road stretches in front of our feet. Our God is constantly
there, except when we most desperately need him. Events take their
course, as though our fervent supplications were never heard. Troubles
are not averted, the shadowy figures of destiny remain in the shadow,
the helpless receive no lasting relief, the sorrowful have to wait a long
time for comfort. We have to endure the sight of people whom we love
deeply and for whom we pray in faith, cast about on a sea of pain, fear,
horror and confusion. A Christian is often able to overcome this "em-
bitterment of faith" only in a love that does not seek knowledge. In an
ultimate silence before God, he then falls, without asking his questions, into the arms of God who is inscrutable, unimaginable and immeasurable, into the arms of God who is silent. This conquest of the
heart, bringing an end to lamentation and imposing silence, is something holy. It is the final culmination of a life of faith, and becomes a
confident trust that resists any impulse to rebel. This is the most perfect gift that someone who is disappointed and "weary for God" can
offer to his God. Without this vacillation between certainty and doubt,
between security and revolt, this ultimate perfection of faith would be
unthinkable. If someone, still persevering in faithful self-giving,
should sink to the point where he experiences at their most painful the
existential consequences both of security in God and of revolt, he is
touching on something that is neither security nor revolt, but an attentive silence full of understanding, which comes into being when God
silences the questions that are on our lips with his love.

Ladislaus Boros

The courage to be myself eludes me,
A shadow of what might be I remain,
And all the while in other lives I see
The wholeness that I lack and can't attain.

The freedom to be myself eludes me,
For freedom itself does not liberate;
To be free to serve is the key to love
That can make of life a meaningful state.

The challenge of loving faith includes me,
I hear this call and can never stay out,
For love without faith is but sentiment
And faith is the courage to live in doubt.

E.M., A nun of Burnham Abbey

MY BELIEVING BONES

Swung by the rhythm of
a yes and no
between the living and
the dead I go.
The dance is in my bones
and though I see
that every dancing bone
will cease to be
I will believe my bones
and learn to trust
my living and my dying,
for I must.

Coming and going by
the dance, I see
that what I am not is
a part of me.
Dancing is all that I
can ever trust,
the dance is all I am,
the rest is dust.

I will believe my bones
and live by what
will go on dancing when
my bones are not.

SITTING BY A BUSH IN BROAD SUNLIGHT

When I spread out my hand here today,
I catch no more than a ray
To feel of between thumb and fingers;
No lasting effect of it lingers.

There was one time and only the one
When dust really took in the sun;
And from that one intake of fire
All creatures still warmly suspire.

And if men have watched a long time
And never seen sun-smitten slime
Again come to life and crawl off,
We must not be too ready to scoff.

God once declared He was true
And then took the veil and withdrew,
And remember how final a hush
Then descended of old on the bush.

God once spoke to people by name.
The sun once imparted its flame.
One impulse persists as our breath;
The other persists as our faith.

Robert Fro

218

2.
Love and Joy

I.

The Joy of the Love Between God and Man

God, out of Whom we be all come, in Whom we be all enclosed, into Whom we shall all wend. . . . For ere that He made us He loved us, and when we were made we loved Him.

OUR MAKER LOVETH US

For our soul is so specially loved of Him that is highest, that it overpasseth the knowing of all creatures: that is to say, there is no creature that is made that may fully know how much and how sweetly and how tenderly our Maker loveth us. And therefore we may with grace and His help stand in spiritual beholding, with everlasting marvel of this high, overpassing, inestimable Love that Almighty God hath to us of His Goodness. And therefore we may ask of our Lover with reverence all that we will.

For our natural Will is to have God, and the Good Will of God is to have us; and we may never cease from willing nor from longing till we have Him in fullness of joy: and then may we no more desire.

Truth seeth God, and Wisdom beholdeth God, and of these two cometh the third: that is, a holy marvellous delight in God; which is Love. Where Truth and Wisdom are verily, there is Love verily, coming of them both. And all God's making: for He is endless sovereign Truth, endless sovereign Wisdom, endless sovereign Love, unmade; and man's Soul is a creature in God which hath the same properties *made,* and evermore it doeth that it was made for: it seeth God, it beholdeth God, and it loveth God. Whereof God enjoyeth in the creature; and the creature in God, endlessly marvelling.

In which marvelling he seeth his God, his Lord, his Maker so high, so great, and so good, in comparison with him that is made, that scarcely the creature seemeth ought to the self. But the clarity and the clearness of Truth and Wisdom maketh him to see and to bear witness that he is made for Love: in which God endlessly keepeth him.

Julian, Anchoress of Norwich

AND THUS I SAW HIM, AND SOUGHT HIM; AND I HAD HIM, I WANTED HIM

And because of this great, endless love that God hath to all Mankind He maketh no disparting in love between the blessed Soul of Christ and the least soul that shall be saved. For it is full easy to believe and to trust that the dwelling of the blessed Soul of Christ is full high in the glorious Godhead, and verily, as I understand in our Lord's signifying where the blessed Soul of Christ is, there is the Substance of all the souls that shall be saved by Christ.

Highly ought we to rejoice that God dwelleth in our soul, and much more highly ought we to rejoice that our soul dwelleth in God.

Thus it fareth with our Lord Jesus and with us. For verily it is the most joy that may be, as to my sight, that He that is highest and mightiest, noblest and worthiest, is lowest and meekest, homeliest and most courteous: and truly and verily this marvellous joy shall be shewn us all when we see Him.

And this willeth our Lord that we seek for and trust to, joy and delight in, comforting us and solacing us, as we may with His grace and with His help, unto the time that we see it verily. For the most fulness of joy that we shall have, as to my sight, is the marvellous courtesy and homeliness of our Father, that is our Maker, in our Lord Jesus Christ that is our Brother and our Saviour.

For it is God's will that we have true enjoying with Him in our salvation, and therein He willeth that we be mightily comforted and strengthened; and thus willeth He that merrily with His grace our soul be occupied. For we are His bliss: for in us He enjoyeth without end and so shall we in Him, with His grace.

Julian, Anchoress of Norwich

OUR SALVATION

And I saw full surely that it behoveth needs to be that we should be in longing and in penance unto the time that we be led so deep into

God that we verily and truly know our own Soul. And truly I saw that into this high deepness our good Lord Himself leadeth us in the same love that He made us, and in the same love that he bought us by Mercy and Grace through virtue of His blessed Passion. And notwithstanding all this, we may never come to full knowing of God till we know first clearly our own Soul.

I saw our Lord Jesus. . . . The oneing with the Godhead gave strength to the manhood for love to suffer more than all men might suffer. . . . For He that is highest and worthiest was most fully made nought and most utterly despised.

For as much as He was most tender and pure, right so He was most strong and mighty to suffer.

And for every man's sin that shall be saved He suffered: and every man's sorrow and desolation He saw, and sorrowed for Kindness and love.

And I, beholding all this by His grace, saw that the Love of Him was so strong which He hath to our soul that willingly He chose it with great desire, and mildly He suffered it with well-pleasing.

For the soul that beholdeth it thus, when it is touched by grace, it shall verily see that the pains of Christ's Passion pass all pains: all pains that is to say, which shall be turned into everlasting, o'erpassing joys by the virtue of Christ's Passion.

Then said our good Lord Jesus Christ: *Art thou well pleased that I suffered for thee?* I said: *Yea, good Lord, I thank Thee; Yea, good Lord, blessed mayst Thou be.* Then said Jesus, our kind Lord: *If thou are pleased. I am pleased: it is a joy, a bliss, an endless satisfying to me that ever suffered I Passion for thee; and if I might suffer more, I would suffer more.*

And also, for more understanding, this blessed word was said: *Lo, how I loved thee! Behold and see that I loved thee so much ere I died for thee that I would die for thee; and now I have died for thee and suffered willingly that which I may. And now is all my bitter pain and all my hard travail turned to endless joy and bliss to me and to thee. How should it now be that thou shouldst anything pray that pleaseth me but that I should full gladly grant it thee? For my pleasing is thy holiness and thine endless joy and bliss with me.*

This is the understanding, simply as I can say it, of this blessed word: *Lo, how I loved thee.* This shewed our good Lord for to make us glad and merry.

Julian, Anchoress of Norwich

The Joy of Loving Each Other

THE FAITH THAT "LIVING IS GIVING"

The birds grew silent, because their history laid hold on them, compelling them to turn their words into deeds, and keep eggs warm, and hunt for worms.

George Macdonald

THREE FEMININE THINGS

Female Yew-tree, shedding condensed drops of transpired water

See how my yew-tree
In utter drought and heat
Breeds kindness in blindness,
Drops dew about her feet;
How she in beauty,
She in her ancient calm,
Stands sleeping, stands weeping
Her penitential balm.

Like that poor widow
Who gave her livelihood,
Since living is giving,
She sheds her stainless blood;
From holy shadow,
Dark mourning that she wears,
Comes coolness in fulness,
Come drops as warm as tears.

Poor young woman

Sorrow and weakness
Lie heavy on this maid;
Small earnings, great yearnings—
She loves, but is afraid;

Here she in meekness,
She in poor attire,
Sits sewing, unknowing
The end of her desire.

But that poor rapture,
Like a thin eager root,
Could flourish, could nourish
Some blessed leaf or shoot;
Or tower to the capture,
Like eagle in the air,
And singing, come bringing
An angel by the hair.

Evening Star

The last vermilion
Smoulders along the west
Horizon, to blazon
The dead day's arms and crest
On that pavilion,
Clear-hung with lucent green,
Where growing, where glowing,
The Planet stands, the queen.
Pearl in the hollow
Height of the sun's void throne,
Fast sinking, but linking
The eye to splendour gone;
Faithfully follow,
Bearing a blessed name;
Still turning, still burning
With white reflected flame.

Ruth Pitter

Is not this what I require of you as a fast:
    to loose the fetters of injustice,
    to untie the knots of the yoke,
        to snap every yoke
    and set free those who have been crushed?
Is it not sharing your food with the hungry,
taking the homeless poor into your house,
    clothing the naked when you meet them

and never evading a duty to your kinsfolk?
Then shall your light break forth like the dawn
and soon you will grow healthy like a wound newly healed;
    your own righteousness shall be your vanguard
        and the glory of the LORD your rearguard.
Then, if you call, the LORD will answer;
    if you cry to him, he will say, 'Here I am.'
If you cease to pervert justice,
to point the accusing finger and lay false charges,
    if you feed the hungry from your own plenty
        and satisfy the needs of the wretched,
    then your light will rise like dawn out of darkness
        and your dusk be like noonday;
    the LORD will be your guide continually
    and will satisfy your needs in the shimmering heat;
        he will give you strength of limb;
    you will be like a well-watered garden,
like a spring whose waters never fail.
The ancient ruins will be restored by your own kindred
    and you will build once more on ancestral foundations;
you shall be called Rebuilder of broken walls,
    Restorer of houses in ruins.

The Book of Isaia
The New English Bib

PRAYER OF MOTHER TERESA OF CALCUTTA

Make us worthy, Lord, to serve our fellow men throughout the wor
who live and die in poverty and hunger.
    Give them through our hands this day their daily bread, and by o
understanding love, give peace and joy.

THE LUMINOUS LIGHT OF LOVE AND THE JOY OF IT

Mother Teresa's Home for the Dying is overflowing with love, as o
senses immediately on entering it. This love is luminous, like t
haloes artists have seen and made visible round the heads of the sain·
I find it not at all surprising that the luminosity should register or

photographic film. The supernatural is only an infinite projection of the natural, as the furthest horizon is an image of eternity. Jesus put mud on a blind man's eyes and made him see. It was a beautiful gesture, showing that he could bring out even in mud its innate power to heal and enrich. All the wonder and glory of mud—year by year giving creatures their food, and our eyes the delight of flowers and trees and blossoms—was crystallized to restore sight to unseeing eyes.

One thing everyone who has seen the film seems to be agreed about is that the light in the Home for the Dying is quite exceptionally lovely. That is, from every point of view, highly appropriate. Dying derelicts from the streets might normally be supposed to be somewhat repellant, giving off stenches, emitting strange groans. Actually, if the Home for the Dying were piled high with flowers and resounding with musical chants—as it may well have been in its Kali days—it could not be more restful and serene. So, the light conveys perfectly what the place is really like; an outward and visible luminosity manifesting God's inward and invisible omnipresent love. This is precisely what miracles are for—to reveal the inner reality of God's outward creation. I am personally persuaded that Ken recorded the first authentic photographic miracle. . . .

Their life is tough and austere by worldly standards, certainly; yet I never met such delightful, happy women, or such an atmosphere of joy as they create. Mother Teresa, as she is fond of explaining, attaches the utmost importance to this joyousness. The poor, she says, deserve not just service and dedication, but also the joy that belongs to human love. This is what the Sisters give them abundantly. . . .

As the whole story of Christendom shows, if everything is asked for, everything—and more—will be accorded; if little, then nothing. It is curious, when this is so obvious, that nowadays the contrary proposition should seem the more acceptable, and endeavour be directed towards softening the austerities of the service of Christ and reducing its hazards with a view to attracting people into it. After all, it was in kissing a leper's hideous sores that St. Francis found the gaiety to captivate the world and gather round him some of the most audacious spirits of the age, to whom he offered only the glory of being naked on the naked earth for Christ's sake. If the demands had been less, so would the response have been. I should never have believed it possible, knowing India as I do over a number of years, to induce Indian girls of good family to tend outcasts and untouchables brought in from Calcutta streets, yet this, precisely, is the very first task that Mother Teresa gives them to do when they come to her as postulants. They do it, not just in obedience, but cheerfully and ardently, and gather round her in ever greater numbers for the privilege of doing it.

Accompanying Mother Teresa, as we did, to these different activities for the purpose of filming them—to the Home for the Dying, to the lepers and unwanted children—I found I went through three phases. The first was horror mixed with pity, the second compassion pure and simple, and the third, reaching far beyond compassion, something I had never experienced before—an awareness that these dying and derelict men and women, these lepers with stumps instead of hands, these unwanted children, were not pitiable, repulsive or forlorn, but rather dear and delightful; as it might be, friends of long standing, brothers and sisters. How is it to be explained—the very heart and mystery of the Christian faith? To soothe those battered old heads, to grasp those poor stumps, to take in one's arms those children consigned to dustbins, because it is his head, as they are his stumps and his children, of whom he said that whosoever received one such child in his name received him. . . .

The Christian religion finds expression thus, in the love of those who love Christ, more comprehensibly and accessibly than in metaphysical or ethical statements. It is an experience rather than a conclusion, a way of life rather than an ideology; grasped through the imagination rather than understood through the mind, belonging to the realm of spiritual rather than intellectual perception; reaching quite beyond the dimension of words and ideas. As St. Augustine found on that wonderful occasion at Ostia with his mother shortly before she died, when they were carried together to somewhere near the very presence of God, and then, returning, found words as clumsy instruments as a surgeon might find a hacksaw, or an artist a house-painter's brush—'And while we spoke of the eternal Wisdom, longing for it and straining for it with all the strength of our hearts, for one fleeting instant we reached out and touched it. Then, with a sigh, leaving our spiritual harvest bound to it, we returned to the sound of our own speech, in which each word has a beginning and an ending—far, far different from your Word, our Lord, who abides in Himself for ever, yet never grows old and gives new life to all things.'

As it is so beautifully put in the opening chapter of the Fourth Gospel: *And the Word was made flesh, and dwelt among us, full of grace and truth.* The Christian story is simply an endless presentation of this process of the Word becoming flesh and dwelling gracefully and truthfully among us. Whether in the ultimate silence of the mystic, such as befell St. Augustine and his mother—a silence that comprehends all that ever has been, will be and can be said and understood and sensed from before the beginning of time to beyond its ending. Or in a Mother Teresa and her Missionaries of Charity going about the world and shining their light in its darkest places. Or in the splendour of artistic crea-

226

ion; in the great cathedrals climbing into the sky to God's greater glo-
y; in the glowing words, the sentient stone and paint, the swelling
sounds of music. Or in the solitary soul questing for truth, in the tiniest mechanisms of our mortal existence, as in the universe's illimit-
able reaches. Or in the beatific soap opera of worship, with its monoto-
nously repeated pleas, confessions and expectations, its *glorias* and its
misereres, its plainsong and hallelujah choruses; eyes piously down-
cast, and knees piously kneeling on the world's cold stone. In each and
every manifestation of our mortal seeking the immortal, or our tempo-
al seeking the eternal, or our imperfect seeking the perfect. Of men
reaching up to God, and God in love and compassion bending down to
man. . . .

Malcolm Muggeridge

MOTHER TERESA

No revolution will come in time
    to alter this man's life
    except the one
    surprise of being loved.

It is too late to talk of Civil Rights,
    neo-Marxism,
    psychiatry
    or any kind of sex.

He has only twelve more hours to live.
    Forget about
    a cure for cancer, smoking, leprosy
    or osteo-arthritis.

Over this dead loss to society
    you pour your precious ointment,
    wash the feet
    that will not walk tomorrow.

Mother Teresa, Mary Magdalene,
    your love is dangerous, your levity
    would contradict
    our local gravity.

But if love cannot do it, then I see
   no future for this dying man or me.
   So blow the world to glory,
   crack the clock. Let love be dangerous.

Sydney Carter

CRISIS FACE

"One cup of rice is all we can allow."
The eyes look back in hunger and in pain.
Wide, deep brown eyes sunken beneath the brow
Pulled taut by famine in a world insane.

The rip of water tearing through the plain
Leaves goats and people islanded on hills:
They come to fear the never-ending rain
And curse the Lord who will not pay their bills.

Too rapidly the face of earth now fills
With myriad faces, each demanding "Why
Do I not count?" Enormous crisis kills
Our understanding; need defeats supply.

The Buddha smiles; in him no tears I trace.
Stay with us Christ, we need your crisis face.

Bernard Thorogoc

A human being loves another, because he is who and what he is; h
seeks the other's own self; he seeks what makes the other this particu
lar individual person. To love means to say: it is good that you are yo
it is very good. Why?

Before he began to love, it was as though he were not himself. It is a
though all that he "was" was the parts that he had to play before th
world and before himself. But once he loves, he is. He loves, and there
fore he is. And the other person has the same experience with him. Th
other person "is" himself with a newly-achieved assurance from th
moment they love each other. This signifies something of inestimab
value: each receives his own self from the other as a mutual gift. Bo

"are" by being involved in each other, by being "we." Their existence is one existence in common.

Love does not exist, then, until two people can say "we" because that is what they are. This word "we" contains a full and binding pledge: I want to be "with you," and I also wish that you should be "with me." From this moment on I belong to you, and am at your disposal. From now on you will never be alone; even when we are separated, and even when death itself parts us, I shall remain with you. Everything that I have and am will be at your disposal, and I know that I shall always remain in you and that my own person will be kept safer in your hands than in mine.

When two people say "we" because love has made them we in very reality, a new sphere of existence is created. The whole world takes on another dimension, a new depth. This new sphere of existence is not simply "already there"; it comes into existence as a function of the free self-giving of one person to another. It comes from the intention and the attempt not to treat the other person as a possession, as a thing. The banner under which love comes to fulfilment reads: "I make no claim." Love renounces any possessiveness, and flees from every urge to enslave another. On the contrary, it makes an offer. And what love offers is not one thing or another, but "itself"; basically, love gives neither the body, nor talents, nor qualities, nor riches, nor any other possessions"; it gives the very essence of a person, his own self. In this act of pure giving it is the giver himself who becomes the gift. The other opens himself to receive the gift, gives himself in the same way, and this is an act of grace. For each one knows that he can never deserve this giving, in which the other gives him what is most his own. And this is the glorious and marvellous thing about love. The gift that is given in love is ultimately always the giver himself. All the other gifts which may be received in love are shot through with the splendour of this self-giving. The real giving in love takes place, not on the lowly level of what I have and what I possess, but on the exalted plane of what I am. The very being of some other person comes towards us in the form of gifts, however small these may be; love transfigures these gifts and turns them into a means of sharing personal existence; the gifts of self-giving flow towards us like a torrent from the person who loves. Through this, someone who loves, even in circumstances where love seems least at home, experiences joy, a new and brighter life in his existence. This joy, this light, is a phenomenon that accompanies love, and is at the same time a revelation of the fact that someone who loves has come close to the origin of all being.

Ladislaus Boros

THE THING CALLED LOVE

Yes, I have experienced it now,
The thing called love.
Not in consuming passion of desire, but in near-far fire;
Not in the voice, but in the ear.
It is a steeling of the heart to bear
The pain where I in sympathy depart to share
Another's sphere.
Where all I thought I cared about, I lose
Without care.
Eager to be where only my love is
And find Him there.

Sister Mary Agnes, Order of Poor Clare

HOSPITALITY IN ANCIENT IRELAND

God in Heaven!
The door of my house will always be
Open to every traveller.
May Christ open His to me!

If you have a guest
And deny him anything in the house,
It's not the guest you hurt.
It's Christ you refuse.

Brendan Kennel

GIVING AND TAKING

Take as a gift
A love all freely given.
A great Lord commends your thrift.
Keep as His gift
This hope of heaven.

To take is hard
For minds narrowed by living.

But open your breath to a word.
     To take is hard,
     When it is giving.

          Let breath increase
     Within your heart and spirit.
Your gain is His, His gain your lease
     Of breath's increase
          That gives life credit.

          Faith is His bond
     Love's capital assures.
Such grace does more than lend.
     Faith is your bond.
          Give. It is yours.

          Give as a gift
     A love all freely given.
A great word reveals its drift.
     Treasure the gift
          Of spendthrift heaven.

James Kirkup

BIRTH

I don't know if I shall be
Speaking or silent, laughing or crying,
When it comes to me

Out of its own distant place
To shine at the window, rustle the curtains,
Brush my face

More lightly than gossamer,
So inspiring and fragile
I shall not dare to stir

Or hardly breathe until I sense
In my heart and mind
Its delicate omnipotence.

I may know then
The price and value of stillness
Commonly ignored by men

And be content to feel
It possess me,
Steal

Through my remotest countries
And establish its rule
Where, my bravest days,

I would not dare to venture.
Then, if I find courage enough,
I may speak in a manner

Befitting this thing.
God help me the moment
My heart starts opening

To comprehend and give.
I will be born in that hour of grace.
I will begin to live.

Brendan Kennell

A GIVING

Here in this room, this December day,
Listening to the year die on the warfields
And in the voices of children
Who laugh in the indecisive light
At the throes that but rehearse their own
I take the mystery of giving in my hands
And pass it on to you.

I give thanks
To the giver of images,
The reticent God who goes about his work
Determined to hold on to nothing.
Embarrassed at the prospect of possession

He distributes leaves to the wind
And lets them pitch and leap like boys
Capering out of their skin.
Pictures are thrown behind hedges,
Poems skitter backwards over cliffs,
There is a loaf of bread on Derek's threshold
And we will never know who put it there.

For such things
And bearing in mind
The midnight hurt, the shot bride,
The famine in the heart,
The demented soldier, the terrified cities
Rising out of their own rubble.

I give thanks.

I listen to the sound of doors
Opening and closing in the street.
They are like the heartbeats of this creator
Who gives everything away.
I do not understand
Such constant evacuation of the heart,
Such striving towards emptiness.
Thinking, however, of the intrepid skeleton,
The feared definition,
I grasp a little of the giving
And hold it close as my own flesh.

It is this little
That I give you.
And now I want to walk out and witness
The shadow of some ungraspable sweetness
Passing over the measureless squalor of man
Like a child's hand over my own face
Or the exodus of swallows across the land.

And I know it does not matter
That I do not understand.

Brendan Kennelly

3.
Hope

The final thing that men are striving for in all these different aspects of hope is their "homecoming." This lies in the background of all day-dreams, illusions, Utopias, systems of thought and forms of art.

Man's self is still in front of him, his true self lies in looking for himself; what he is, is hope. Man is to be understood not so much from his past as from the future he dreams of.

Before the present day it was Christianity which took "man the dreamer" most seriously. One of the finest expressions of the completely transcendent final fulfilment is found in St. Paul's statement of the basis of the Christian understanding of existence: "What no eye has seen, nor ear heard, nor the heart of man conceived, what God has prepared for those who love him" (1 Cor. 2:9). One can sum up the whole of Christianity, adapting an expression used by Karl Rahner, as follows: It is a hope in which God so surpasses human longings, that the wildest and most immoderate dreams of mankind seem to be of a timid and almost animal stupidity. Even from this single point of view, Christianity would be the religion which most corresponded to the inner constitution of the being of man. That is why Christians feel a sense of solidarity with every sort of hope. They see a brother in everyone who uses the language of hope. A Christian can go about with a gentle smile amongst men who reflect their single great dreams in the day-dreams of everyday life, in cut-price sales, in pamphleteering and dressing up, in Utopias and wish-fulfilment entertainment, and in everything that men have ever contrived in art and philosophy; and he might well think that in the depth of their soul these people are Christians, and that they are dreaming, often without knowing it, of the resurrection and ascension, of a completely "saved" world, and of heaven. The idea of heaven is the legacy of the most radical and most central hope. Heaven is the central and innermost significance of everything that man has ever hoped.

Ladislaus Boros

THE ARTIST IS THE TRADESMAN OF HOPE

This led me to speculate on the artist or writer as the tradesman of hope. I'd put it like this: the artist's faith in the blank page, his joy in creating and looking forward to something entirely new, is a form of Christian hope, the blank canvas or manuscript paper being his highest excitement and his inspiration. As the last work he wrote becomes tasteless to him, so his appetite for the next grows, and he foresees it with acute pleasure; in this way he is not only a tradesman of hope, but of faith also. I wonder if it was the sight of all that vast void that gave God the hunger to create the wonderful world in which we live.

Donald Swann

ON A SMALL FIGURE, FASHIONED OUT OF CHALK

This creature takes shape from my mind
Where the gulls are always calling seaward
And in the slippery dark lodges a nest of stars.

Dough-shape, I will put it by itself to prove.
Let it become warm as a bird's breast and hard
Like the rock I hold to under the plunge of the seas.

This is what is shaped in your heart.
Will it be leavened with your own dark?
It may be wet with the blood of afterbirth.

My being fashions this; it is not mine.
It shall be shared for the showing forth of love;
Invoked from the dust of stars, it shall breathe praise.

L.M., A nun of Burnham Abbey

THE NEW SONG

Be faithful to the new song
thrusting through your
earth like a daffodil.
Be flexible
and travel with the rhythm.

Let your mind
be bent by what is coming:
making is
a way of being made
and giving birth

a way of being born.
You are the child
and father of a carol,
you are not
the only maker present.

How you make
is how you will be made.
Be gentle to
the otherness you carry,
broken by

the truth you cannot tell yet.
Mother and be
mothered by your burden.
Trust, and learn
to travel with the music.

Sydney Carter

NOWHERE AND NEVER

Dig, Michelangelo,
Down in the marble,
A wonder is waiting
That no one can see.
Nowhere and never

And now and for ever
I look for a thing
That is looking for me.

Over the water I
Sail, like a fisherman,
Casting my net in
The dark of the sea.
Nowhere and never
And now and for ever
I look for a thing
That is looking for me.

Faith is a digger
And hope is a diver
And down in the marble
Or under the sea
Nowhere and never
And now and for ever
I look for a thing
That is looking for me.

Nowhere and never
And now and for ever
Loving and labour
Will bring it to be
Nowhere and never
And now and for ever
I look for a thing
That is looking for me.

Songs of Sydney Carter

THE GOD OF THE VIRTUES SPEAKS OF ETERNITY ITSELF

Shall it be said that there will be eyes so extinguished, eyes so dimmed
That no spark will ever light them more.
And that there will be voices so exhausted, and souls so dull
That no emotion will ever stir them more.
And that there will be souls so exhausted

By trials, by sorrow,
By tears, by prayer, by toil.
And by having seen what they have seen. And from having suffered
what they have suffered,
And by having gone through what they have gone through. And from
knowing what they know.

That they will have had enough of it.
Enough of it for eternity, and all they will ask is to be left alone—in
peace.
Dona eis, Domine, pacem,
Et requiem aeternam. Peace and eternal rest.
Because they will have learnt certain things about life on earth.
And do not want to hear of anything except a place of rest,
To lie down and sleep in.
To sleep, to sleep at last.
And all that they will be able to bear and all that I can do
And bring
(The man I take in his earthly sleep is fortunate, and it's a good sign,
my children)
As the desperately ill and the desperately wounded cannot endure
life any more or the remedy or even the idea of a cure,
But only the balm on the wound.
And no longer have any taste for health.
So shall it be said that on so many wounds,
They will only endure the freshness of balm,
Like a wounded man in a fever.
And that they will no longer have any taste for my Paradise
And for my Eternal Life.
And all that I shall be able to put on so many wounds;
On so many scars and so many sacrifices;
And on the bitterness of so many chalices
And on the thanklessness of so much malice
And on the pricks of so many penances
And on the racked bones of the tortured;

And on the stains of so much blood;

* * * *

Will be to send down like the balm of evening,
As after the burns of a scorching midday the great descent of a fine
summer's evening,
The slow fall of an eternal night.
O Night, shall it be said I created you last,

And that my Paradise and that my Beatitude
Will be nothing but a great night of clarity,
A great eternal night.
And that the crown of my Judgement and the beginning of
    Paradise and of my Beatitude will be
The sunset of an eternal summer.

And so it would be, God says.
And all I could put on the open mouths
Of the martyrs' wounds
Would be balm and oblivion and night.
And all would finish in lassitude,
That tremendous adventure,
As after a burning harvest
The slow descent of a great summer's evening.
If there were not my little Hope,
For it is through my little Hope alone that Eternity shall be,
And Beatitude shall be,
And Paradise shall be. And Heaven and everything.
For she alone, just as she alone in the days of this Earth
Makes a new morrow spring from an old yesterday.
So from the relics of Judgement Day and from the ruins and the rubble
    of Time
She alone will bring forth new eternity.

I am, God says, the Lord of the Virtues.
Faith is the Sanctuary-lamp,
Which burns eternally.
Charity is that great fire of wood
Which you light on your hearth
So that my children the poor can come and warm themselves on win-
    ter evenings.
And around Faith I see all my faithful
Kneeling together in the same attitudes and with the same voice
And the same prayer.
And around Charity I see all my poor
Sitting in a circle before the fire.
And holding out their palms to the warmth of the hearth.
But my Hope is the flower and the fruit and the leaf and the branch
And the sprig and the growth and the bud and the flower
Of Eternity itself.

                        *   *   *   *

Charles Péguy

Part 8

Men and Women of Faith Speak to Us of Other Gifts of the Spirit, Given to Our Giving

1. Truth
2. Humility and Penitence
3. Mercy
4. Prayer and Silence
5. Courage

"Self-giving renders our being open to receive gifts. To give oneself, ） receive what is given and give oneself again—this is, as it were, the reathing of the spirit. This is the foundation of spiritual greatness in ²an."

Ladislaus Boros

1.
Truth

This day is dear to me above all other
    days, for to-day the Beloved Lord
    is a guest in my house;
My chamber and my courtyard are
    beautiful with His presence.
My longings sing His Name, and they
    are become lost in His great beauty:
I wash His feet, and I look upon His
    Face; and I lay before Him as an
    offering, my body, my mind, and
    all that I have.
What a day of gladness is that day
    in which my Beloved, who is my
    treasure, comes to my house!
All evils fly from my heart when I see
    my Lord.
'My Love has touched Him; my
    heart is longing for the Name
    which is Truth.'
Thus sings Kabir, the servant of all
    servants.

Rabindranath Tagore

Here in this little bay,
Full of tumultuous life and great repose,
Where twice a day,
The purposeless glad ocean comes and goes,
Under high cliffs, and far from the huge town,

243

I sit me down.
For want of me the world's course will not fail;
When all its work is done, the lie shall rot;
The truth is great and shall prevail,
When none cares whether it prevail or not.

Coventry Patmor

There is therefore a catholic spirit, a communion of saints in th
love of God and all goodness, which no one can learn from that whic
is called orthodoxy in particular churches, but is only to be had by a t
tal dying to all worldly views, by a pure love of God, and by such a
unction from above as delivers the mind from all selfishness an
makes it love truth and goodness with an equality of affection in ever
man, whether he is Christian, Jew or Gentile. He that would obtai
this divine and catholic spirit in this disordered, divided state of thing
and live in a divided part of the church without partaking of its div
sion, must have these three truths deeply fixed in his mind. First, th
universal love, which gives the whole strength of the heart to God, an
makes us love every man as we love ourselves, is the noblest, the mo
divine, the Godlike state of the soul, and is the utmost perfection
which the most perfect religion can raise us; and that no religion do
any man any good but so far as it brings this perfection of love in
him. This truth will show us that true orthodoxy can nowhere l
found but in a pure disinterested love of God and our neighbour. Se
ond, that in this present divided state of the church, truth itself is to
and divided asunder; and that, therefore, he can be the only true cath
lic who has more of truth and less of error than is hedged in by any c
vided part. The truth will enable us to live in a divided part unhurt l
its division, and keep us in true liberty and fitness to be edified and a
sisted by all the good that we hear or see in any other part of t
church. . . . Thirdly, he must always have in mind this great trut
that it is the glory of the Divine Justice to have no respect of parties
persons, but to stand equally disposed to that which is right or wro
as well in the Jew as in the Gentile. He therefore that would like
God likes, and condemn as God condemns, must have neither the ey
of the Papist nor the Protestant; he must like no truth the less becau
Ignatius Loyola or John Bunyan were very zealous for it, nor have t
less aversion to any error, because Dr. Trapp or George Fox had broug
it forth.

William L

244

2.
Humility and Penitence

Humility is the voluntary abdication of power, wherever one's own advantage and one's own self-assertion is involved. Humility is a power which affirms our existence, and regards it as something untouchable and sacred from which one must draw back in reverence. Accordingly, true humility is a creative power. Only a great love, with no intention but to give itself, not measuring its own value by the reaction it causes, laying its hand to the plough and not turning back, only such a love can lift other men up, release them from their poverty and bestow on them a new quality of being.

Since every being longs for consummation and transfiguration, every corner of the world cries out for our selfless submissiveness, our humility. If we do not hear this call, it can lead to our hardening our hearts, abandoning ourselves to something that is not part of our true self, and to the diminishing of our being. Gabriel Marcel calls this refusal *le refus de l'invocation* (the rejection of the appeal). But if, instead, we affirm again and again our humble self-resignation, if our ear is always attentive to the appeal of creation in its weakness to our humility, the spiritual potentiality of our existence increases, and our power of receiving being itself grows also. Submissiveness and increased receptivity are very closely related in the spiritual life. They are two interwoven strands of humility. What makes us truly spiritual is a receptivity that comes from submissiveness. To be creative means ultimately to have the power to receive. In humility we become more than we already are. Self-giving renders our being open to receive gifts. To give oneself, to receive what is given and give oneself again—this is, as it were, the breathing of the spirit. This is the foundation of spiritual greatness in man.

Ladislaus Boros

When thou feelest that thou mayest in no wise put them (distrac
tions) down, cower then down under as a caitiff and a coward over
come in battle, and think it is but folly to strive any longer with them
and therefore thou yieldest thyself to God in the hands of thine ene
mies. . . . And surely, I think, if this device be truly conceived, it i
nought else but a true knowing and a feeling of thyself as thou art,
wretch and a filthy thing, far worse than nought; the which knowin
and feeling is meekness (humility). And this meekness meriteth t
have God mightily descending to venge thee on thine enemies, so as t
take thee up and cherishingly dry thy ghostly eyes, as the father doth
the child that is at the point to perish under the mouths of wild swin
and mad biting bears.

Cice
Translated by Clifton Wolte

I have but one word to say to you concerning love for your neig
bour, namely that nothing save humility can mould you to it; nothi
but the consciousness of your own weakness can make you indulge
and pitiful to that of others. You will answer, I quite understand th
humility should produce forbearance towards others, but how am
first to acquire humility? Two things combined will bring that abou
you must never separate them. The first is contemplation of the de
gulf, whence God's all-powerful hand has drawn you out, and ov
which He ever holds you, so to say, suspended. The second is the pre
ence of that all-penetrating God. It is only in beholding and loving G
that we can learn forgetfulness of self, measure duly the nothingne
which has dazzled us, and accustom ourselves thankfully to decrea
beneath that great Majesty which absorbs all things. Love God and y
will be humble; Love God and you will throw off the love of self; lo
God and you will love all that He gives you to love for love of Him.

Féne.

AWFUL WARNINGS FOR THOSE WHO LACK HUMILITY

He who has begun to recognize duty and acknowledge the facts
life is but a tottering child on the path of life. He is on the path: he is
wise as at the time he can be; the Father's arms are stretched out to
ceive him; but he is not therefore a wonderful being; not therefor

246

model of wisdom; not at all the admirable creature his largely remaining folly would, in his worst moments (that is, when he feels best) persuade him to think himself; he is just one of God's poor creatures. . . .

Am I going to do a good deed? Then, of all times,—Father, into thy hands: lest the enemy should have me now. . . .

What riches and fancied religion, with the self-sufficiency they generate between them, can make man or woman capable of, is appalling. . . . To many of the religious rich in that day, the great damning revelation will be their behaviour to the poor to whom they thought themselves very kind. . . .

He had a great respect for money and much over-rated its value as a means of doing even what he called good: religious people generally do. . . .

A man may sink by such slow degrees that, long after he is dead, he may go on being a good churchman or a good dissenter and thinking himself a good Christian.

George Macdonald

REPENTANCE

Repentance is *metanoia,* or 'change of mind'; and without it there cannot be even a beginning of the spiritual life—for the life of the spirit is incompatible with the life of that 'old man,' whose acts, whose thoughts, whose very existence are the obstructing evils which have to be repented. This necessary change of mind is normally accompanied by sorrow and self-loathing. But these emotions are not to be persisted in and must never be allowed to become a settled habit of remorse. In Middle English 'remorse' is rendered, with a literalness which to modern readers is at once startling and stimulating, as 'again-bite.' In this cannibalistic encounter, who bites whom? Observation and self-analysis provide the answer: the creditable aspects of the self bite the discreditable and are themselves bitten, receiving wounds that fester with incurable shame and despair. But in Fénelon's words, 'It is mere self-love to be inconsolable at seeing one's own imperfections.' Self-reproach is painful; but the very pain is a reassuring proof that the self is still intact; so long as attention is fixed on the delinquent ego, it cannot be fixed upon God and the ego (which lives upon attention and dies only when that sustenance is withheld) cannot be dissolved in the divine Light.

Aldous Huxley

As the light grows, we see ourselves to be worse than we thought.
We are amazed at our former blindness as we see issuing from our heart
a whole swarm of shameful feelings, like filthy reptiles crawling from
hidden cave. But we must be neither amazed nor disturbed. We are no
worse than we were; on the contrary, we are better. But while our
faults diminish, the light we see them by waxes brighter, and we are
filled with horror. So long as there is no sign of cure, we are unaware of
the depth of our disease; we are in a state of blind presumption and
hardness, the prey of self-delusion. While we go with the stream, we
are unconscious of its rapid course; but when we begin to stem it even
so little, it makes itself felt.

Fénelon

To one of his spiritual children our dear father (St. François de Sales)
said, 'Be patient with everyone, but above all with yourself. I mean, do
not be disheartened by your imperfections, but always rise up with
fresh courage. I am glad you make a fresh beginning daily; there is no
better means of attaining to the spiritual life than by continually beginning again, and never thinking that we have done enough. How are
we to be patient in bearing with our neighbour's faults, if we are impatient in bearing with our own? He who is fretted by his own failings
will not correct them; all profitable correction comes from a calm,
peaceful mind.'

Jean Pierre Camus

He willeth. . . that we endlessly hate the sin and endlessly love the
soul, as God loveth it. Then shall we hate sin as God hateth it, and love
the soul as God loveth it. And this word that He said is an endless comfort: *I keep thee secure.*

Julian, Anchoress of Norwich

3.

Mercy

Mercy is a sweet gracious working in love, mingled with plenteous pity: for mercy worketh in keeping us, and mercy worketh turning to us all things to good. Mercy, by love, suffereth us to fail in measure and in as much as we fail, in so much we fall; and in as much as we fall, in so much we die; for it needs must be that we die in so much as we fail of the sight and feeling of God that is our life. Our failing is dreadful, our falling is shameful, and our dying is sorrowful: but in all this the sweet eye of pity and love is lifted never off us, nor the working of mercy ceaseth.

For I beheld the property of mercy, and I beheld the property of grace: which have two manners of working in one love. Mercy is a pitiful property which belongeth to the Motherhood in tender love; and grace is a worshipful property which belongeth to the royal Lordship in the same love. Mercy worketh: keeping, suffering, quickening, and healing; and all is tenderness of love. And grace worketh: raising, rewarding, endlessly overpassing that which our longing and our travail deserveth, spreading abroad and shewing the high plenteous largess of God's royal Lordship in His marvellous courtesy; and this is of the abundance of love. For grace worketh our dreadful failing into plenteous, endless solace; and grace worketh our shameful falling into high, worshipful rising; and grace worketh our sorrowful dying into holy, blissful life.

For it needeth us to fall, and it needeth us to see it. For if we never fell, we should not know how feeble and how wretched we are of our self, and also we should not fully know that marvellous love of our Maker. For we shall see verily in heaven, without end, that we have grievously sinned in this life, and notwithstanding this, we shall see that we were never hurt in His love, we were never the less of price in His sight. And by the assay of this falling we shall have an high, marvellous knowing of love in God, without end. For strong and marvellous is that love which may not, nor will not, be broken for trespass.

In which Shewing I saw that sin is most contrary,—so far forth that as long as we be meddling with any part of sin, we shall never see clearly the Blissful Cheer of our Lord. And the more horrible and grievous that our sins be, the deeper are we for that time from this blissful sight. And therefore it seemeth to us oftentimes as we were in peril of death, in a part of hell, for the sorrow and pain that the sin is to us. And thus we are dead for the time from the very sight of our blissful life. But in all this I saw soothfastly that we be not dead in the sight of God, nor He passeth never from us. But He shall never have His full bliss in us till we have our full bliss in Him, verily seeing His fair Blissful Cheer. For we are ordained thereto in nature, and get thereto by grace. Thus I saw how sin is deadly for a short time in the blessed creatures of endless life.

And ever the more clearly that the soul seeth this Blissful Cheer by grace of loving, the more it longeth to see it in fulness. For notwithstanding that our Lord God dwelleth in us and is here with us, and albeit He claspeth us and encloseth us for tender love that He may never leave us, and is more near to us than tongue can tell or heart think, yet may we never stint of moaning nor of weeping nor of longing till when we see Him clearly in His Blissful Countenance. For in that precious blissful sight there may be no woe abide, nor any weal fail.

Flee we to our Lord and we shall be comforted, touch we Him and we shall be made clean, cleave we to Him and we shall be sure, and safe from all manner of peril.

For our courteous Lord willeth that we should be as homely with Him as heart may think or soul may desire. But let us beware that we take not so recklessly this homeliness as to leave courtesy. For our Lord Himself is sovereign homeliness, and as homely as He is, so courteous He is: for He is very courteous. And the blessed creatures that shall be in heaven with Him without end, He will have them like to Himself in all things. And to be like our Lord perfectly, it is our very salvation and our full bliss.

Julian, Anchoress of Norwich

MERCY

Mercy is one of the greatest acts the human heart is capable of. It source is love. If love has become really deep rooted in a person, that is

250

if it has taken possession of his body and soul and of his whole being, then at the same time it has made him liable to suffer. People are astonishingly quick to notice the unselfish and generous heart. From selfless love, they seek help and above all the warmth of human affection: the hungry seek food, the thirsty ask for a drink, the naked for clothing, the stranger for a home, the captive for release; the sick ask to be cared for and the dying ask for comfort, the unrighteous desire patience, the ignorant ask to be taught, the sorrowful seek consolation, and all men, the living and the dead, call for prayer. It is customary to speak of the seven works of mercy. They are a visible expression of all the misery of human existence.

To take this misery upon ourselves brings suffering with it, sometimes unbearable suffering. The distress of others takes more out of us than does our own suffering. Our existence is threatened more by the frailty of others than by our own weakness. The helplessness of someone who is suffering is often too much for us. Someone comes to us with his face drawn with his suffering, and we are powerless and unable to help. There still remains one final work of mercy, that cannot simply be equated with the other seven, because it is the basis of all mercy. When suffering goes really deep, one can often only help by "sympathizing," sharing in the suffering. The only thing one is still able to do is to open one's heart, let the suffering of the other person pour in, and persevere in sharing in his suffering, until he finds that his suffering is relieved because someone who loves him is sharing the burden. Anyone who thinks it is easy to persevere in love to the bitter end in this way, so that this becomes the most characteristic act of our life, does not yet know the profundity of human love.

Ladislaus Boros

THE MERCY OF JESUS

The God-Man is our Redeemer. But as our Redeemer his task was not to take our suffering away, however much he may have wished to do, but to share in our suffering himself, to sanctify it, and to make it a means of redemption for each of us. Redemption does not mean magic, but the opening up of a new possibility at the point where what is human has come to an end, the opening up of a new dimension and not the removal of reality. What is human must persist with all its darkness. But into this darkness there comes the call of redemption, a call to live out our wretched existence in a new way, on the basis of new principles and promises. This is redemption. Anything else would be magic. But let no one deceive himself: to endure this was a heart-breaking act even for one who was God and man. What an immense tension he had to endure! On the one hand, his mercy urged him irresistibly to give his help, while at the same time his hands were bound by the very nature of his divine task. His soul was martyred throughout his life. At this point an abyss opens before us, and the longer we gaze into it, the more we are seized by a holy trembling at the sight of Jesus.

Ladislaus Boros

4.
Prayer and Silence

The brothers asked Abba Agatho: 'Father, which virtue in our way of life needs most effort to acquire?' And he said to them: 'Forgive me, I think nothing needs so much effort as prayer to God. If a man is wanting to pray, the demons infest him in the attempt to interrupt prayer, or they know that prayer is the only thing that hinders them. All the other efforts of a religious life, whether they are made vehemently or gently, have room for a measure of rest. But we need to pray till we breathe out our dying breath. That is the great struggle.'

Aelred Squire

The man who links together his prayer with deeds of duty and fits seemly actions with his prayer is the man who prays without ceasing, for his virtuous deeds or the commandments he has fulfilled are taken up as part of his prayer. For only in this way can we take the saying 'pray without ceasing' as being possible, if we can say that the whole life of the saint is one mighty integrated prayer.

Origen

SPECTRUM

A little window, eastward, low, obscure,
A flask of water on the vestry press,

253

A ray of sunshine through a fretted door,
And myself kneeling in live quietness:

Heaven's brightness was then gathered in the glass,
Marshalled and analysed, as one by one
In terms of fire I saw the colours pass,
Each in its proper beauty, while the sun

Made his dear daughter Light sing her own praise,
(As Wisdom may, who is a mode of light),
Counting her seven great jewels; then those rays
Remerged in the whole diamond, total sight.

This globe revolved subservient: that just star
Whirled in his place; water and glass obeyed
The laws appointed: with them, yet how far
From their perfection, I still knelt and prayed.

Ruth Pitte

When you say your prayers, you must go into your private room
and shut the door, and say your prayers to your Father who is in se-
cret. And your Father, who sees what is done in secret, will give yo
your reward in full. For, when the door is shut, someone prays in hi
private room when, while his mouth is silent, he pours forth the affec
tion of his heart in the sight of the heavenly pity. And the voice i
heard in secret, when it cries out in silence with the holy desires.

St. Gregory the Gre

The continuous interior Prayer of Jesus is a constant uninterrupte
calling upon the divine Name of Jesus with the lips, in the spirit, in th
heart; while forming a mental picture of his constant presence, and in
ploring his grace, during every occupation, at all times, in all place
even during sleep. The appeal is couched in these terms, 'Lord Jesu
Christ, have mercy on me.' One who accustoms himself to this appe
experiences as a result so deep a consolation and so great a need to off
the prayer always, that he can no longer live without it, and it will co
tinue to voice itself within him of its own accord.

Many so-called enlightened people regard this frequent offering of ne and the same prayer as useless and even trifling, calling it me-hanical and a thoughtless occupation of simple people. But unfortu-ately they do not know the secret which is revealed as a result of this 1echanical exercise, they do not know how this frequent service of the ps imperceptibly becomes a genuine appeal of the heart, sinks down 1to the inward life, becomes a delight, becomes as it were, natural to 1e soul, bringing it light and nourishment and leading on to union 'ith God.

St. John Chrysostom, in his teaching about prayer, speaks as follows: Jo one should give the answer that it is impossible for a man occupied 'ith worldly cares, and who is unable to go to church, to pray always. verywhere, wherever you may find yourself, you can set up an altar to od in your mind by means of prayer. And so it is fitting to pray at)ur trade, on a journey, standing at the counter or sitting at your andicraft. . . . In such an order of life all his actions, by the power of 1e invocation of the Name of God, would be signalized by success, 1d finally he would train himself to the uninterrupted prayerful in-)cation of the Name of Jesus Christ. He would soon come to know)m experience that frequency of prayer, this sole means of salvation, a possibility for the will of man, that it is possible to pray at all mes, in all circumstances and in every place, and easily to rise from equent vocal prayer to prayer of the mind and from that to prayer of e heart, which opens up the Kingdom of God within us.'

Translated from the Russian by R.M. French

THE SECRET

I bless the hand that once held mine,
   The lips that said:
'No heart, though kiss were Circe's wine,
   Can long be comforted.'

Ay, though we talked the long day out
   Of all life marvels at,
One thing the soul can utter not,
   Or self to self relate.

We gazed, enravished, you and I,
   Like children at a flower;

But speechless stayed, past even a sigh . . .
　　Not even Babel Tower

Heard language strange and close enough
　　To tell that moment's peace,
Where broods the Phoenix, timeless Love,
　　And divine silence is.

Walter de la M

SILENCE

True experience always comes about in withdrawal "from t
crowd." The original, true and proper attitude of the mind is—as He
clitus says—that of "listening to the truth of things," the avoidance
the pressure of falsehoods, half-measures, mediocrity and gossip. C
journey into the territory of being should be made in silence, wi
wondering, wide-open eyes. The fullness of truth and reality is
vealed only to someone who attains to a silence which covers every
pect of his being, or who, in other words, makes his basic attitude
wards the whole of being one of delicate and reserved courtesy.

Silence and withdrawal (or, more exactly, "reserve") set things fi
to manifest their true being; they cause things to shine with their ov
inner light. That is why the injunction in the Old Testament is so tr
for man: "Make balances and scales for your words, and make a dc
and a bolt for your mouth" (Ecclus. 28:25). We loquacious human I
ings once again have an inner need of silence. If it were only absolut
still for a moment; if everything accidental, fortuitous and compl
were silent; if the sound made by our senses ceased; then perhaps
could appreciate reality to the full, and love it with an undivided hea

For anyone who wishes to hear what is true and real, every vo
must for once be still. Silence, however, is not merely the absence
speech. It is not something negative; it is "something" in itself. It i
depth, a fullness, a peaceful flow of hidden life. Everything true a
great grows in silence. Without silence we fall short of reality and ca
not plumb the depths of being. Kierkegaard, who was acutely aware
this, once made the profoundly true statement: "Silences are the or
scrap of Christianity we still have left."

Ladislaus Bo

THE SILENCE OF JESUS

We have only to read and meditate on the accounts of the passion to be struck by the singular silence and composure of Jesus in his suffering. Before the judge, before the frenzy of the crowd, he stood calm, surrounded by a wonderful silence. The storms of hatred, the frenzy and the turmoil did not penetrate his soul. By his mere presence, by the concentrated power of his being, he was more than all the others who stood there yelling at him, and who, as Luke says, "vehemently accused him." He was a man with knowledge in the midst of the blind. It is only behind this silence that is to be found the true, the great, the wonderful. It signifies wealth and happiness, even in suffering. It is a recollected presence, a holy readiness, an inner calm. What has he to do with those who are dishonourable, who consider themselves righteous, who wish to pass judgement on everything, who have never experienced desperation or dumb suffering? What can he say to them? Nothing! And therefore he says nothing. He just lets what is happening ride over him. He never became "pathetic" in his suffering, and gave no shattering answers; nothing disturbed his composure. These men had condemned themselves, not him. Jesus had nothing to do with cunning and force. That, nevertheless, he could remain silent in the face of everything, goes beyond all human ability.

Was not this the silence of *God*, the silence of him who is an infinite distance above us, and who, for that very reason, is infinitely close to us?

Here is a man mighty in speech and mightier still in silence, the second person of the Trinity, the incomprehensible God who became a suffering human being, infinitely distant and at the same time infinitely near, quiet, silent and yet an intimate friend to us all, who lives in inaccessible light and is yet kind and compassionate. In the crucified Lord we recognize ourselves completely; in the resurrected Lord we have our hope. This is what our God is like. This is he whom we worship; we weep and rejoice before him who has created and redeemed us, before Jesus the silent, before the Lord of all goodness and kindness.

Ladislaus Boros

It is better to keep silence and to be, than to talk and not to be. It is a fine thing to teach, if the speaker practises what he preaches. Now there is only one teacher who *spoke and it came to pass*, and the things which he did in silence are worthy of the Father. He that truly possesses the word of Jesus is able also to listen to his silence. Nothing is hidden from the Lord, but our own secrets are near him. Let us therefore do everything, knowing that he dwells in us, so that we may be his temples and he himself be in us as our God.

St. Ignatius

5.
Courage

ENCOURAGEMENT, ON A LEAF

Written on a gold leaf in Greek
    Take Courage—
and we who survived placed the leaf
under your hands, so that without
all loss of hope you might meet indifferent
Charon, and cross the cold Styx.

Friend, things have changed. Charon we meet,
the cold river flows through our lives. If,
as we shut you away, if
you could pass out to ourselves in your grey
claw from your peace
the gold leaf on which
Take Courage is written.

Geoffrey Grigson

Part 9

Faith Maintained in Darkness and Tribulation

1. God Is Faithful
2. Dark Times and Dark Moods
3. Men in Prison
4. Acceptance and Courage in Storm and Darkness
5. Merciful Night
6. Songs of Deliverance

God is faithful, who will not suffer you to be tempted above that ye are able; but will with the temptation also make a way to escape, that ye may be able to bear it.

St. Paul

1.
God Is Faithful

THE BLIND BOY

Alone, in the unseeing crowd, he walks with eyes
half-closed against night's inner radiance, a candle-beam
less insupportable than the darkness of a day.
With lifted face he wanders through the city of his dream.
   His smile seems to enjoy
in open secrecy a flower invisible to all
who are shut out from gardens only by a wall.

A voice hints at the kindness that a touch confirms.
For him all distance is a sum of measured steps
that must be counted faultlessly, or else a strange
town is entered, where a compass in the brain
   swings in no charted field.
Here nothing counts for him, to whom a faith
in his condition is the surest light,

   and trust in the complete
creation of his heart the only hope of sight.

James Kirkup

THE BLIND POET

Thus with the Year
Seasons return, but not to me returns
Day, or the sweet approach of Ev'n or Morn,

Or sight of vernal bloom, or Summers Rose,
Or flocks, or herds, or human face divine;
But cloud in stead, and ever-during dark
Surrounds me, from the chearful wayes of men
Cut off, and for the Book of knowledge fair
Presented with a Universal blank
Of Natures works to mee expung'd and ras'd,
And wisdome at one entrance quite shut out.
So much the rather thou Celestial light
Shine inward, and the mind through all her powers
Irradiate, there plant eyes, all mist from thence
Purge and disperse, that I may see and tell
Of things invisible to mortal sight.

John Milton

The hands of a man touch the hands of the Creator in all that he has made.

TO A BLIND FRIEND

To you who cannot see save with your hands
I dedicate the surfaces of stones;
Worn fibres of old woods; the flesh of leaves,
And all the overtones and undertones
Responsive to the touch and blind to sight
Guiding your hands through their perceptive night.
May you be blessed with essences more rare
(For memory's sake) than what is merely seen
And soon forgotten by the ranging eye,
Whose wide perspectives often miss
That which the more discriminating hands will hold
For recollection and for future love:
The narratives of shells and historied coins;
Memories stroked through wood and weathered stone;
The flow of water underneath the hands;
The flow of wind like water through the grass,
And all the tactile treasures of the dark.
To you whom blindness has made more aware
Of those less salient features of the world

That come within the compass of your hands
To harvest more than sight,
I consecrate the darkness that must lie
Outside the sun-filled orbit of the eye
That is not dark to you, but is a day
Richer for unseen bearing where you walk
As magnetized as steel, alert and drawn
To all that is enhanced and magnified,
And is the special province of your hands
Unerringly to touch and recognize.

Eric Barker

FRIENDSHIP

A Poem Written in Time of War

Parting from a friend in the street
Close by a shattered dwelling,
I see life's long deceit,
A vision too subtle for telling;
The long deceit of peace,
Certainty, comfort, ease.
I turn, and look at my friend;
I watch the diminishing figure
Pause at the ruined end
Of the road, as though grief's rigour
Gripped him. I know he is grieving.
Will love never understand?
Shall I, in the moment of leaving,
In the touch of hand by hand,
Bind the wounded soul, and lift
The cup to his lips again,
With all my life in the gift,
My privilege of pain?
Shall I in that privilege share
The death in his heart, the grave
Of hope, the dreadful sojourn there,
Until he stirs and wakes
To the joy of the world once more,
The joy that sometimes breaks
Afresh the wounds which sorrow tore?

At that moment, he may be glad,
When faith reopens his eyes
On a world that is broken and mad,
To find one thing that he had
In the past, one thing to recognize
And greet with a trembling word,
Hooded in fear, unbelieving
Still, denying that he has heard
The summons to leave the dark, grieving
Grave of the soul. I shall have shared
With him, that drink of deadly wine
Which at our birth is prepared,
The dark cup of to-morrow,
The cup of knowledge and sorrow,
That perhaps makes mortal divine.

Richard Church

SONNET 30

When to the sessions of sweet silent thought
I summon up remembrance of things past,
I sigh the lack of many a thing I sought,
And with old woes new wail my dear time's waste:
Then can I drown an eye, unused to flow,
For precious friends hid in death's dateless night,
And weep afresh love's long since cancell'd woe,
And moan the expense of many a vanish'd sight:
Then can I grieve at grievances foregone,
And heavily from woe to woe tell o'er
The sad account of fore-bemoaned moan,
Which I new pay as if not paid before.
     But if the while I think on thee, dear friend,
     All losses are restored and sorrows end.

Shakespeare

There are those who suffer greatly, and yet, through the recognition
that pain can be a thread in the pattern of God's weaving, find the way
to a fundamental joy.

CREATION'S ROBE: A TEILHARDIAN POEM

Suffering is knit into creation,
A thread of seminal deprivation
Conceived at the very heart of matter.
From the first innocence of each being
To the final agony of its dying,
Inconsolably, pain weaves its pattern.

They feel it most who suffer most alone
And see no hope or reason to console
The terrors and the hardness of their fears.
The unendurable may be endured
Only when the experience is shared
And a pattern, in the sharing, appears.

Healing is not the absence of all hurt;
Its pattern is in wholeness only brought
By a painful weaving to completion.
When thread to thread is knit in close embrace
As sorrow leaps to sudden joyfulness
Then suffering is fitting reparation.

E.M., A nun of Burnham Abbey

THE NAME OF THE LORD

'The name of the Lord is a strong tower: the righteous runneth into it and is safe.' This phrase—which at first may sound rather too poetical—comes to have a very real and literal significance in our spiritual life. When the mind is so violently disturbed by pain or fear or the necessities of some physical emergency that it cannot possibly be used for meditation or even rational thought, there is still one thing that you can always do; you can repeat his name, over and over. You can hold fast to that, throughout all the tumult. Once you have really tested and proved the power of the holy Word, you will rely upon it increasingly.

Swami Prabharananda and Christopher Isherwood

2.
Dark Times and Dark Moods

FEAR

How can I shut them out?
With hands on ears I run
While brigand bands of fears
Like over-hanging granite cliffs about my path
Stand stiff in phalanges of wrath to tear
The tissue of the reason's banisters apart,
For fear is like a stair
That is not there
A tension felt within
Dumb as an unformed sin;
Raise your brave barricades of courage as you will,
Sew on brocades of duty, take your fill
Of alcoholic loot of hop and vine,
There is no armour burnished, intertwined
With faith or philosophic mail,
There is no thought, no act, all all will fail
And leave the tarnished brain in agony
Tortured upon the rack, beyond the pale,
To lie and daily cry for breathing's end,
That it may wait beneath time's grass green sod
For God to send
A friend.

S. L. Henderson Smith

DIRGE

From a friend's friend I taste friendship,
From a friend's friend love,

268

My spirit in confusion,
Long years I strove,
But now I know that never
Nearer I shall move,
Than a friend's friend to friendship,
To love than a friend's love.

Into the dark night
Resignedly I go,
I am not so afraid of the dark night
As the friends I do not know,
I do not fear the night above
As I fear the friends below.

Stevie Smith

Fear nothing, for I am with you;
be not afraid, for I am your God.
I strengthen you, I help you,
I support you with my victorious right hand.

I say to you, Do not fear;
it is I who help you,
fear not, Jacob you worm and Israel poor louse.
It is I who help you, says the LORD.

The Book of Isaiah
The New English Bible

RESTLESSNESS

Weighing the stedfastness and state
Of some mean things which here below reside,
Where birds like watchful Clocks the noiseless date
    And Intercourse of times divide,
Where Bees at night get home and hive, and flowrs
    Early, as well as late,
Rise with the Sun, and set in the same bowrs;

    I would (said I) my God would give

269

The staidness of these things to man! for these
To his divine appointments ever cleave,
    And no new business breaks their peace;
The birds nor sow, nor reap, yet sup and dine,
      The flowrs without clothes live,
Yet *Solomon* was never drest so fine.

     Man hath still either toyes, or Care,
He hath no root, nor to one place is ty'd,
But ever restless and Irregular
    About this Earth doth run and ride,
He knows he hath a home, but scarce knows where,
      He sayes it is so far
That he hath quite forgot how to go there.

     He knocks at all doors, strays and roams,
Nay hath not so much wit as some stones have
Which in the darkest nights point to their homes,
    By some hid sense their Maker gave;
Man is the shuttle, to whose winding quest
     And passage through these looms
God order'd motion, but ordain'd no rest.

Henry Vaughan

THE PULLEY

    When God at first made man,
Having a glasse of blessings standing by,
  Let us (said he) poure on him all we can.
Let the world's riches, which dispersed lie,
    Contract into a span.

    So strength first made a way,
Then beautie flowed, then wisdom, honour, pleasure.
  When almost all was out, God made a stay,
Perceiving that alone of all his treasure
    Rest in the bottome lay.

    For if I should (said he)
Bestow this jewell also on my creature,

He would adore my gifts instead of me,
And rest in Nature, not the God of Nature.
So both should losers be.

Yet let him keep the rest,
But keep them with repining restlessness.
Let him be rich and wearie, that at least,
If goodnesse leade him not, yet wearinesse
May tosse him to my breast.

George Herbert

Discontent

SONNET 29

When, in disgrace with fortune and men's eyes,
I all alone beweep my outcast state,
And trouble deaf heaven with my bootless cries,
And look upon myself, and curse my fate,
Wishing me like one more rich in hope,
Featured like him, like him with friends possess'd,
Desiring this man's art and that man's scope,
With what I most enjoy contented least;
Yet in these thoughts myself almost despising,
Haply I think on thee, and then my state,
Like to the lark at break of day arising
From sullen earth, sings hymns at heaven's gate;
    For thy sweet love remember'd such wealth brings
    That then I scorn to change my state with kings.

Shakespeare

Thou art indeed just, Lord, if I contend
With thee; but, sir, so what I plead is just.
Why do sinners' ways prosper? and why must
Disappointment all I endeavour end?
   Wert thou my enemy, O thou my friend,
How wouldst thou worse, I wonder, than thou dost

271

Defeat, thwart me? Oh, the sots and thralls of lust
Do in spare hours more thrive than I that spend,
Sir, life upon thy cause. See, banks and brakes
Now, leavèd how thick! lacèd they are again
With fretty chervil, look, and fresh wind shakes
Them; birds build—but not I build; no, but strain
Time's eunuch, and not breed one work that wakes.
Mine, O thou lord of life, send my roots rain.

Gerard Manley Hopkins

Bereavement

SCAZONS

Passing to-day by a cottage, I shed tears
When I remembered how once I had dwelled there
With my mortal friends who are dead. Years
Little had healed the wound that was laid bare.

Out little spear that stabs. I, fool, believed
I had outgrown the local, unique sting,
I had transmuted away (I was deceived)
Into love universal the lov'd thing.

But Thou, Lord, surely knewest thine own plan
When the angelic indifferences with no bar
Universally loved but Thou gav'st man
The tether and pang of the particular;

Which, like a chemic drop, infinitesimal,
Plashed into pure water, changing the whole,
Embodies and embitters and turns all
Spirit's sweet water to astringent soul.

That we, though small, may quiver with fire's same
Substantial form as Thou—nor reflect merely
As lunar angel back to Thee, cold flame.
Gods we are, Thou has said; and we pay dearly.

C. S. Lewis

ELEGY FOR A DEAD GOD

Leave us alone. Leave us, hope
of our deliverance, leave us alone.
We did not deserve
the wonder in our midst,
for by inexcusable error
that we knew, and did not
know we were committing,
we ignored his nature and his need.

Give us a dead flower, O someone,
a dead leaf, a glass wreath,
give us the telescoping spine
of dim and dimmer-focused dying,
the crack of the dead branch
torn by the gale of earth
from the air's crashing tree,
the shot hare's human crying.

What is our fault, what word
did we utter as if it were untrue?
Give us a dead bird
in the broken nest of our clasping fingers
and let it lie there
under the dead thought of our speaking,
under the dry lips of our inconsolable
weeping, under the dead fright of our eyes.

Wandering all night in the forgotten rain,
we did not know, we knew too well that impermanent
divinity, but all we could think of was the tall
presence inhabiting our loneliness.
Now voices in the afternoon calling from across the street
are always yours, and yours the steps running towards us
at evening, to greet our solitude with words and wishes,
measuring the depths of heaven with a light remark.

Why did you ever speak to us,
O, why did you let us drink
the wines we did not know,

and now will never know?
Why did you teach us smiles
that were not our own, and strange
laughter that we loved, and a loquacity
rich and curious to our startled throats?

For we are an ignorant people: not
omniscient, because we know too much.
What was it killed you?
What careless look, meaningless clutch
of dying hands towards the never-dying,
what unspoken tenderness too much
in our unbroken silences? And yet,
what god were you, who did not understand our sentences?

Love begets love, so they said.
It was not love that begot ours,
and the love we had for you
destroyed you with its cruelty.
What is the meaning of this song without you?
What is love, now that it fails its own believers?
Only forgive our blindness, and your pain,
forgive your knowledge of our pain.

Dead to us, you cannot die.
And when we, lost ones,
wander in your city's emptiness,
you are everywhere and nowhere, as a god should be.
But we grow sick with memories, can not forget the shadow at our
        sides
that is the only remnant of the air you took away.
Be comforted, remembering the forsaken faces of the dead
who once knew love that touched to life
the stilled darkness at the centre of the smallest stone.
For though you were a god, we know that you, too, are much alone.

James Kirk

I was very near despair. My future seemed to narrow to a long, dark
tunnel with no light whatever at the end of it. I had discarded the
Christian label at that time; it seemed more honest to call myself an
unbeliever.

274

In this state of mind I went, one freezing night, to a display of Rumanian Folk Art. In glass cases at the Royal Hotel, Woburn Place, could be seen embroidered shirts, corn dollies and the like. Looking at them, I remembered something from a book by Violet Alford: in Rumania, she said, the word 'music' could be applied to the decoration on a shirt, a belt, a buckle. This thought cheered me faintly, like a ray of winter sunshine.

What I had come for was a lecture on Rumanian Folk Music. A. L. Lloyd was giving it, with illustrations on the gramophone. At one point he was telling how, in Rumania, a peasant mother would sometimes teach a song to her daughter as if it were a weapon, magic or a kind of medicine. "Learn this song," she would say. "You may not understand it now, but you will need it later." I could do (I was thinking) with a song like that right now; and even as I thought it, or before, something started happening. I was being lifted on a wave: not by any one song in particular, but by all the folk songs, ballads, blues that I had ever listened to. All the people who sang them or were sung about—happy lovers, murderers, decrepit miners, mothers rocking cradles, cheerful drunks and lechers, flogged deserters—were lifted by the wave as well. We were in it, we were on it; it was part of what we were or could be. It was as if a veil had been drawn back to let me see, for a moment, what was happening.

This wave had a more than human personality. Male or female? Both, neither, all together: it did not speak to me but let me see that I was not alone. Nobody was alone: we were alone together, travelling. We were safe, beyond our danger; whole, beyond our being broken.

What had I become aware of? I rejected the glib label 'God.' I did not want to compromise the truth of this experience. The name of Jesus did not seem appropriate though he was surely riding in the wave as well. Critically, I began to ask myself: 'Do I have this experience, or do I just imagine it? Is it nothing but possibility, like a song that is asking to be written?'

If that is all it is, that is good enough for me. That, after all, is one kind of reality, perhaps the only kind of religious reality. Song, God, a saving possibility: you must trust it, travel with it—or it is not there.

Sydney Carter

PITCH DARKNESS

It is a human soul still, and wretched. . . . From the pit of hell it cries out. So long as there is that which can sin, it is a man. And the

275

prayer of misery carries its own justification, when the sober petitions of the self-righteous and the unkind are rejected. He who forgives not is not forgiven, and the prayer of the Pharisee is as the weary beating of the surf of hell, while the cry of a soul out of its fire sets the heartstrings of love trembling.

Troubled soul. . . . God . . . has an especial tenderness of love towards thee for that thou are in the dark and hast no light, and His heart is glad when thou dost arise and say, "I will go to my Father." . . . Fold the arms of thy faith, and wait in the quietness until light goes up in thy darkness. Fold the arms of thy faith I say, but not of thy action: bethink thee of something that thou oughtest to do, and go to do it, if it be but the sweeping of a room, or the preparing of a meal, or a visit to a friend. Heed not thy feelings: do thy work.

That man is perfect in faith who can come to God in the utter dearth of his feelings and desires, without a glow or an aspiration, with the weight of low thoughts, failures, neglects, and wandering forgetfulness, and say to Him, "Thou art my refuge."

George Macdonald

GOD HIMSELF IN DARKNESS

He could not see, could not feel Him near; and yet it is "My God" that he cries. Thus the will of Jesus, in the very moment when His faith seems about to yield, is finally triumphant. It has no *feeling* now to support it. It stands naked in His soul and tortured, as He stood naked and scourged before Pilate. Pure and simple and surrounded by fire, it declares for God. . . . Without this last trial of all, the temptations of our Master had not been so full as the human cup could hold: there would have been one region through which we had to pass wherein we might call aloud upon our Captain-Brother, and there would have been no voice or hearing: He had avoided the fatal spot.

George Macdonald

3.

Men in Prison

Extracts from 'War and Peace'

(i)

(Pierre, taken prisoner by the French, is
comforted by a fellow prisoner, the
peasant Platon Karataev. For him, a life
of love and service to his fellow men
has always been the natural way to
live. Unlike Prince Andrey, he needs no
process of thought to reach the conclusion that such a life "lasts forever," and
is for all eternity a living whole.)

Close by him a little man was sitting bent up, of whose presence
Pierre was first aware from the strong smell of sweat that rose at every
movement he made. This man was doing something with his feet in
the darkness, and although Pierre did not see his face, he was aware
that he was continually glancing at him. Peering intently at him in the
dark, Pierre made out that the man was undoing his foot-gear. And the
way he was doing it began to interest Pierre.

Undoing the strings in which one foot was tied up, he wound them
neatly off, and at once set to work on the other leg, glancing at Pierre.
While one hand hung up the first leg-binder, the other was already beginning to untie the other leg. In this way, deftly, with rounded, effec-
tive movements following one another without delay, the man un-
rolled his leg-wrappers, and hung them up on pegs driven in over-head,
took out a knife, cut off something, shut the knife up, put it under his
bolster, and settling himself more at his ease, clasped his arms round

277

his knees, and stared straight at Pierre. Pierre was conscious of something pleasant, soothing, and rounded off in those deft movements, in his comfortable establishment of his belongings in the corner, and even in the very smell of the man, and he did not take his eyes off him.

'And have you seen a lot of trouble, sir? Eh?' said the little man suddenly. And there was a tone of such friendliness and simplicity in the sing-song voice that Pierre wanted to answer, but his jaw quivered, and he felt the tears rising. At the same second, leaving no time for Pierre's embarrassment to appear, the little man said, in the same pleasant voice:

'Ay, darling, don't grieve,' he said, in that tender, caressing sing-song which old Russian peasant women talk. 'Don't grieve, dearie; trouble lasts an hour, but life lasts for ever! Ay, ay, my dear. And we get on here finely, thank God; nothing to vex us. They're men, too, and bad and good among them,' he said; and, while still speaking, got with a supple movement on his knees to his feet, and clearing his throat walked away.

'Hey, the hussy, here she is!' Pierre heard at the end of the shed the same caressing voice. 'Here she is, the hussy; she remembers me. There, there, lie down!' And the soldier, pushing down a dog that was jumping up on him, came back to his place and sat down. In his hand he had something wrapped up in a cloth.

'Here, you taste this, sir,' he said, returning to the respectful tone he had used at first, and untying and handing to Pierre several baked potatoes. 'At dinner we had soup. But the potatoes are first-rate!'

Pierre had eaten nothing the whole day, and the smell of the potatoes struck him as extraordinarily pleasant. He thanked the soldier and began eating.

'But why so, eh?' said the soldier smiling, and he took one of the potatoes. 'You try them like this.' He took out his clasp-knife again, cut the potato in his hand into two even halves, and sprinkled them with salt from the cloth, and offered them to Pierre.

'The potatoes are first-rate,' he repeated. 'You taste them like that.'

It seemed to Pierre that he had never eaten anything so good. . . .

(ii)

Karataev lived on affectionate terms with every creature with whom he was thrown in life, and especially so with man—not with any particular man, but with the men who happened to be before his eyes. He loved his dog, loved his comrades, loved the French, loved Pierre, who was his neighbour.

To all the other soldiers Platon Karataev was the most ordinary soldier; they called him 'little hawk' or Platosha; made good-humoured

278

ibes at his expense, sent him to fetch things. But to Pierre, such as he appeared on that first night—an unfathomable, rounded-off, and everlasting personification of the spirit of simplicity and truth—so he remained to him for ever.

Every word and every action of his was the expression of a force uncomprehended by him, which was his life. But his life, as he looked at it, had no meaning as a separate life. It had meaning only as a part of a whole, of which he was at all times conscious. His words and actions flowed from him as smoothly, as inevitably, and as spontaneously, as the perfume rises from the flower. He could not understand any value or significance in an act or a word taken separately.

(iii)
(Retreating from Moscow, the French
take their prisoners with them.
By the camp fire at night Platon
tells his fellow prisoners a story.
In the morning, too ill to continue
the march, he is shot.)

Getting chilled by the dying fire on the previous night's halt, Pierre got up and moved to the next fire, which was burning better. There Platon was sitting, with a coat put over his head, like a priest's chasuble. In his flexible, pleasant voice, feeble now from illness, he was telling the soldiers a story Pierre had heard already. It was past midnight, the time when Karataev's fever usually abated, and he was particularly lively. As he drew near the fire and heard Platon's weak, sickly voice, and saw his piteous mien in the bright firelight, Pierre felt a pang at heart. He was frightened at his own pity for this man, and would have gone away, but there was no other fire to go to, and trying not to look at Platon, he sat down by it.

'Well, how is your fever?' he asked.

'How is my fever? Weep over sickness, and God won't give you death,' said Karataev, and he went back at once to the story he had begun.

'And so, brother,' he went on with a smile on his thin, white face, and peculiar, joyful light in his eyes, 'And so, brother. . . .'

Pierre had heard the story long before. Karataev had told it to him about six times already, and always with special joyful emotion. But well as Pierre knew the story, he listened to it now as though it were something new, and the subdued ecstasy, which Karataev evidently felt in telling it, infected Pierre too.

It was the story of an old merchant, who had lived in good works and in the fear of God with his family, and had made a journey one day with a companion, a rich merchant, to Makary.

Both the merchants had put up at an inn and gone to sleep; and next day the rich merchant had been found robbed, and with his throat cut. A knife, stained with blood, was found under the old merchant's pillow. The merchant was tried, sentenced to be flogged, and to have his nostrils slit—'all according to the law in due course,' as Karataev said—and sent to hard labour.

'And so, brother' (it was at this point in the story that Pierre found Karataev) 'ten years or more passed by after that. The old man lives on in prison. He submits, as is fitting; he does nothing wrong. Only he prays to God for death. Very well. And so at night-time they are gathered together, the convicts, just as we are here, and the old man with them. And so they fell to talking of what each is suffering for, and how he has sinned against God. One tells how he took a man's life, another two, another had set fire to something, and another was a runaway just for no reason. So they began asking the old man, "What," they say, "are you suffering for, grandfather?" "I am suffering, dear brethren," says he, "for my own sins, and for other men's sin. I have not taken a life nor taken other men's goods, save what I have bestowed on poorer brethren. I was a merchant, dear brethren, and I had great wealth." And he tells them this and that, and how the whole thing happened. "For myself," says he, "I do not grieve. God has chastened me. The only thing," says he, "I am sorry for my old wife and my children." And so the old man fell a-weeping. And it so happened that in that company there was the very man, you know, who had killed the merchant. "Where did it happen, grandfather?" says he. "When and in what month?" and so he asked him all about it. His heart began to ache. He goes up to the old man like this—and falls down at his feet. "You are suffering for me, old man," says he. "It's the holy truth; this man is tormented innocently, for nothing, lads," says he. "I did that deed," said he, "and put the knife under his head when he was asleep. Forgive me, grandfather, for Christ's sake!" says he.'

Karataev paused, smiling blissfully, and gazing at the fire, as he rearranged the logs.

'The old man, says he, "God forgive you," says he, "but we are all sinners before God," says he. "I am suffering for my own sins." And he wept with bitter tears. What do you think, darling?' said Karataev, his ecstatic smile growing more and more radiant, as though the great charm and whole point of his story lay in what he was going to tell now, 'what do you think, darling, that murderer confessed of himself to the police. "I have killed six men," says he (for he was a great criminal), "but what I am most sorry for is this old man. Let him not weep

hrough my fault." He confessed. It was written down, and a paper sent
off to the right place. The place was far away. Then came a trial. Then
all the reports were written in due course, by the authorities, I mean. It
was brought to the Tsar. Then a decree comes from the Tsar to let the
merchant go free; to give him the recompense they had awarded him.
The paper comes; they fall to looking for the old man. Where was that
old man who had suffered innocently? The paper had come from the
Tsar, and they fell to looking for him.' Karataev's lower jaw quivered.
But God had pardoned him already—he was dead! So it happened,—
darling!' Karataev concluded, and he gazed a long while straight before
him, smiling silently.

Not the story itself, but its mysterious import, the ecstatic gladness
that beamed in Karataev's face as he told it, the mysterious significance of that gladness vaguely filled and rejoiced Pierre's soul now.

Leo Tolstoy

Extracts from the Writings
of Dietrich Bonhoeffer in Prison

(i)

THE SUFFERING GOD

God would have us know that we must live as men who manage our
ves without him. The God who is with us is the God who forsakes us
(Mark 15:34). The God who lets us live in the world without the working hypothesis of God is the God before whom we stand continually.
Before God and with God we live without God. God lets himself be
pushed out of the world on to the cross. He is weak and powerless in
the world, and that is precisely the way, the only way, in which he is
with us and helps us. Matthew (8:17) makes it quite clear that Christ
helps us, not by virtue of his omnipotence, but by virtue of his weakness and suffering.

Here is the decisive difference between Christianity and all reli-
gions. Man's religiosity makes him look in his distress to the power of
God in the world: God is the *deus ex machina*. The Bible directs man
to God's powerlessness and suffering; only the suffering God can help.
'Christians stand by God in his hour of grieving'; that is what distin-
guishes Christians from pagans. Jesus asked in Gethsemane, 'Could
you not watch with me one hour?' That is a reversal of what the reli-

gious man expects from God. Man is summoned to share in God's suf
ferings at the hands of a godless world.

Christ kept himself from suffering till his hour had come, but when
it did come he met it as a free man, seized it, and mastered it. Christ, so
the scriptures tell us, bore the sufferings of all humanity in his own
body as if they were his own—a thought beyond our comprehension—
accepting them of his own free will.

CHRISTIANS AND PAGANS

Men go to God when they are sore bestead,
Pray to him for succour, for his peace, for bread,
For mercy for them sick, sinning or dead;
All men do so, Christians and unbelieving.

Men go to God when he is sore bestead,
Find him poor and scorned, without shelter or bread,
Whelmed under weight of the wicked, the weak, the dead;
Christians stand by God in his hour of grieving.

God goes to every man when sore bestead,
Feeds body and spirit with his bread;
For Christians, heathens alike he hangs dead,
And both alike forgiving.

(ii)
GOD CAN USE OUR MISTAKES

I believe that God can and will bring good out of evil, even out of the
greatest evil. For that purpose he needs men who make the best use of
everything. I believe that God will give us all the strength we need to
help us resist in all time of distress. But he never gives it in advance,
lest we should rely on ourselves and not on him alone. A faith such as
this should allay all our fears for the future. I believe that even our mistakes and shortcomings are turned to good account, and that it is no
harder for God to deal with them than with our supposedly good deeds.
I believe that God is no timeless fate, but that he waits for and answers
sincere prayers and responsible actions.

(iii)
FAITH AND PROVIDENCE

We must confront fate—to me the neuter gender of the word "fate"
(Schicksal) is significant—as resolutely as we submit to it at the right

ime. One can speak of "guidance" only on the other side of that two-
old process, with God meeting us no longer as "Thou," but also "dis-
uised" in the "It"; so in the last resort my question is how we are to
ind the "Thou" in this "It" (i.e., fate), or, in other words, how does
'fate" really become "guidance"? It's therefore impossible to define
he boundary between resistance and submission on abstract princi-
les; but both of them must exist, and both must be practised. Faith de-
nands this elasticity of behaviour. Only so can we stand our ground in
ach situation as it arises, and turn it to gain.

(iv)

WHO AM I?

I often wonder who I really am—the man who goes on squirming
under these ghastly experiences in wretchedness that cries to heaven,
or the man who scourges himself and pretends to others (and even to
himself) that he is placid, cheerful, composed, and in control of
himself, and allows people to admire him for it (i.e., for playing the
part—or is it not playing a part?).

Who am I? They often tell me
I would step from my cell's confinement
calmly, cheerfully, firmly,
like a squire from his country house.

Who am I? They often tell me
I would talk to my warders
freely and friendly and clearly,
as though it were mine to command.

Who am I? They also tell me
I would bear the days of misfortune
equably, smilingly, proudly, like one accustomed to win.

Am I then really all that which other men tell of?
Or am I only what I know of myself,
restless and longing and sick, like a bird in a cage,
struggling for breath, as though hands were
compressing my throat,
yearning for colours, for flowers, for the voices of birds,
thirsting for words of kindness, for neighbourliness,
trembling with anger at despotisms and petty humiliation,
tossing in expectation of great events,
powerlessly trembling for friends at an infinite distance,

283

weary and empty at praying, at thinking, at making,
faint, and ready to say farewell to it all?

Who am I? This or the other?
Am I one person today, and tomorrow another?
Am I both at once? A hypocrite before others,
and before myself a contemptibly woebegone weakling?
Or is something within me still like a beaten army,
fleeing in disorder from victory already achieved?

Who am I? They mock me, those lonely questions of mine.
Whoever I am, thou knowest, O God, I am thine.

Dietrich Bonhoeff

Our moments of happiness are those when we see a burning ligh
through the bars of our personal prison, when for some amazing reaso
we *look out* through the cracks; or perhaps by suffering with someor
in charity, we leap out of the prison itself, guided by the Spirit, whic
has never lost its New Testament talent for walking through bri
walls. The grace of God is in my mind shaped like a key, that com
from time to time and unlocks the heavy doors.

Donald Swar

I said to the prisoners, 'Go free,'
and to those in darkness, 'Come out and be seen.'
They shall find pasture in the desert sands
and grazing on all the dunes.
    They shall neither hunger nor thirst,
no scorching heat or sun shall distress them;
    for one who loves them shall lead them
    and take them to water at bubbling springs.
    I will make every hill a path
        and build embankments for my highways.
See, they come; some from far away,   .
these from the north and these from the west
        and those from the land of Syene.
Shout for joy, you heavens, rejoice, O earth,

284

you mountains, break into songs of triumph,
for the LORD has comforted his people
  and has had pity on his own in their distress.

The Book of Isaiah
The New English Bible

4.

Acceptance and Courage in Storm and Darkness

ACCEPTANCE

When the spent sun throws up its rays on cloud
And goes down burning into the gulf below,
No voice in nature is heard to cry aloud
At what has happened. Birds, at least, must know
It is the change to darkness in the sky.
Murmuring something quiet in her breast,
One bird begins to close a faded eye;
Or overtaken too far from his nest,
Hurrying low above the grove, some waif
Swoops just in time to his remembered tree.
At most he thinks or twitters softly, "Safe!
Now let the night be dark for all of me.
Let the night be too dark for me to see
Into the future. Let what will be, be."

Robert Fro

Thich Nhat Hanh, the Vietnamese poet, in the introduction to h
book *Vietnam: Lotus in a Sea of Fire* quotes a Zen monk of the ele
enth century: "The Lotus, blooming in the furnace, does not lose i
freshness." I am going to say no more than is said in that monk's line
verse. In the sea of fire we must bloom, like that lotus; in death w
must be brave, in decay we must be fresh.

Let me accept the poverty of millions, the homelessness of millio
and the sickness of millions and acknowledge for a minute of aw
peace that all this suffering is already on the shoulders of Christ. Befo

286

UNESCO, UNRWA, UNICEF, he is there, with the statistics, he is
head of the report of the advance party on the scene. When the prison
door closes on the political prisoner, he is there in the gloom of the cell
as you put your foot in, even before Amnesty. As you look on your skin
to see the sores, he is there before you meet the doctor who diagnoses
leprosy, and before you become eligible for help from Lepra. If the doctor never comes, and if Lepra never finds you, he is still there.

My first conclusion about the world is that God is ahead. He also
knows certain things to console him, which are not generally spot-
lighted, and which don't get into our minds because they have not the
searing power of the disastrous news that reaches us more commonly
and more quickly.

Donald Swann

THE RESURRECTED MAN

Tollund, Denmark, 1950

Inhabitant of my ancestral land,
he lay two thousand years in peat,
tanned by the earth's dark sun
and by the soil's cold heat.

The peasant cutters found him
buried in the sodden bog they mine
for fire, a braided rope around his neck:
a sacrifice to earth, a monument to time.

He wore the victim's foolish cap,
the cloak of nakedness. In earth's womb
he crouched like a full-grown foetus,
a ghost laid out in death's unfurnished tomb.

He stayed there as he fell in death:
his feet crossed, as if in sleep,
to bring him warmth and comfort;
his eyes closed, his breathing deep.

Then he was roused, uplifted by
the living man, unhoused by his own

Descendants, who dissected his repose,
Registered his fingerprints, and bared each bone.

Still he remained himself, preserved the archaic
Dignity far older than his nails and eyes
And the heartsease and sorrel of his bed: an unimpregnable
Acceptance—the faith that is the earth's, where nothing dies.

James Kirku

THE NEED

Nobody knows
Whither our delirium of invention goes.
Who turn toward time to come
Alone with heart-beats, marching to that muffled drum.
Nobody hears
Bells from beyond the silence of the years
That wait for those unborn.
O God within me, speak from your mysterious morn.

Speak, through the few,
Your light of life to nourish us anew.
Speak, for our world possessed
By demon influences of evil and unrest.
Act, as of old,
That we some dawnlit destiny may behold
From this doom-darkened place.
O move in mercy among us. Grant accepted grace.

Siegfried Sasso

A FULL CONSENT

Throw away thy rod,
Throw away thy wrath:
O my God,
Take the gentle path.

For my heart's desire
Unto thine is bent:
    I aspire
To a full consent.

Not a word or look
I affect to own,
    But by book,
And thy book alone.

Though I fail, I weep:
Though I halt in pace,
    Yet I creep
To the throne of grace.

Then let wrath remove;
Love will do the deed:
    For with love
Stonie hearts will bleed.

Love is swift of foot:
Love's a man of warre,
    And can shoot,
And can hit from farre.

Who can scape his bow?
That which wrought on thee,
    Brought thee low,
Needs must work on me.

Throw away thy rod;
Though man frailties hath,
    Thou art God:
Throw away thy wrath.

George Herbert

COURAGE

It is an ancient trouble, the brain
Capped with a cloud of melancholy;

The summer of hope dissolved in rain,
A lifework sold for a moment's folly.

Once a Christian wizard sought
A cure for the sick imagination,
And the tower of mental strength he wrought
He called 'Of philosophic consolation.'

Four centuries flew before his words,
By our first English King translated,
Found England, as the fork-winged birds
In spring, from Africa migrated.

Find her, in gloom and dampness wrapped,
And to her dripping eaves come twittering
Their promises of summer capped
With a wealth of harvest fields glittering.

Boethius was done to death
By the Ostrogoth, Theodoric.
Alfred was worn down beneath
His hopes, by a body treacherous and sick.

Their failure is a fountain still
To which my mind for courage looks,
By instinct drawn to drink my fill,
As the hart desires the water-brooks.

Richard Church

WILLOW

To understand
A little of how a shaken love
May be sustained

Consider
The giant stillness
Of a willow

After a storm.
This morning it is more than peaceful

But last night that great form

Was tossed and hit
By what seemed to me
A kind of cosmic hate,

An infernal desire
To harass and confuse,
Mangle and bewilder

Each leaf and limb
With every vicious
Stratagem

So that now I cannot grasp
The death of nightmare,
How it has passed away

Or changed to this
Stillness,
This clean peace

That seems unshakeable.
A branch beyond my reach says
"It is well

For me to feel
The transfiguring breath
Of evil

Because yesterday
The roots by which I live
Lodged in apathetic clay.

But for that fury
How should I be rid of the slow death?
How should I know

That what a storm can do
Is to terrify my roots
And make me new?"

Brendan Kennelly

WILD NIGHT

Our mountains are indifferent to it.
They go right through the earth
and are riveted on the other side.
Such weather merely bounces off them,
blunting itself on their hunched backs.

It's another story at this level.
Streams out of control career downhill.
Fields drum and buckle, tearing loose
from their fence posts. My house is adrift
in the garden, battering against the wall.

I, too, tilt with the landscape.
My mind is not on gimbals.
I'd pray if there were anyone to pray to.
I'm sure that God has stuffed his ears
with bits of cloud to drown the noise.

My salvation must be here if anywhere.
I have fired my last flare,
all I can do is hold on.
Great seas come rolling in from space.
The world rocks at its anchor.

Alasdair MacLean

Have no fear; for I have paid your ransom;
I have called you by name and you are my own.
When you pass through deep waters, I am with you,
    when you pass through rivers,
    they will not sweep you away;
walk through fire and you will not be scorched,
through flames and they will not burn you,
For I am the LORD your God,
    the Holy One of Israel, your deliverer.

The Book of Isaiah
The New English Bible

Lament no more, my heart, lament no more,
Though all these clouds have covered up the light,
And thou, so far from shore,
Art baffled in mid flight;
Still proudly as in joy through sorrow soar!
As the wild swan,
Voyaging over dark and rising seas,
Into the stormy air adventures on
With wide unfaltering wings, the way he bore
When blue the water laughed beneath the breeze
And morning round the radiant beaches shone,
So thou through all this pain
Endure, my heart, whither thy course was bound;
Though never may the longed-for goal be found,
Thy steadfast will maintain.
Thou must not fail, for nothing yet hath failed
Which was to thee most dear and most adored;
Still glorious is love, thy only lord.
Truth still is true, and sweetness still is sweet;
The high stars have not changed, nor the sun paled.
Still warmly, O my heart, and bravely beat,
Remember not how lovely was delight,
How piteous is pain,
Keep, keep thy passionate flight,
Nor find thy voyage vain.
Yea, till thou break, my heart, all meaner quest disdain.

Laurence Binyon

THE OMENS OF DISASTER

There have been all the usual signs:
The crack in the ceiling, rust
On the suspension-bridge, the crossed lines
Of communication, a bee in the dust
Of March. We have learned to ignore
The untimely flower, the rain
Pelting on one field, not on another,
The headline message in the train.

293

For these, and all signs no longer matter.
We know too well what they portend.
Though a dead bird lies in the gutter
We do not believe the gods intend
This for us, who have seen it all
So many times, and felt the scare
Telling us love is about to fail
And breath to be taken from the air.

We found that all was never lost,
Though we were sick, afraid and friendless.
We tried to heed the warnings of the past,
But still we loved, as if love were endless.
—We have listened to the cry of wolf
Too often, till we cannot fear the worst.
The crack will grow into another gulf,
But still we live, as if each day were not our last.

James Kirkup

IN THE LONG NIGHT

I would build my house of crystal,
With a solitary friend,
Where the cold cracks like a pistol
And the needle stands on end.

We would pour oil on the ingle
And for want of books recite.
We would crawl out filing single
To observe the Northern Light.

If Etookashoo and Couldlooktoo
The Esquimaux should call,
There would be fish raw and cooked too
And enough drink oil for all.

As one rankly warm insider
To another I would say,
We can rest assured on eider
There will come another day.

Robert Fros

5.

Merciful Night

Passages from The Holy Innocents

GOD SPEAKS OF HIS SON, AND OF HIS DAUGHTER NIGHT

O day, O eve, O night of the entombment.
Fall of that night I shall nevermore see.
O night, so sweet to the heart because you fulfil,
And you soothe like a balm.
Night on that mountain and in that valley.
O night, I had said so often I should never see you more.
O night, I shall see you throughout my eternity.
That my will be done. O it was then that my will was done.
Night I see you still. Three tall gibbets were raised up. And my
    Son in the middle.
A hill, a valley. They had started from that town which I had
    given to my people. They were raised up.
My Son between those two thieves. A wound in his side. Two
    wounds in his hands. Two wounds in his feet. Wounds on
    his forehead.
Some women who stood upright weeping. And that bowed head
    which dropped on his breast. . . .
And that heart no longer throbbed, which had so often throbbed
    with love.
Three or four women stood upright weeping. As for men I don't
    remember, I think there were none left.
They had found perhaps that it was too much. All was finished.
    All was consummated. It was finished.
And the soldiers went home, and on their square shoulders they
    bore the might of Rome:

It was then, O night, that you came. O night, ever the same.
Even so you come every evening and have come so many times
   since the earliest darkness.
Even so you came down on the smoking altar of Abel, on the
   corpse of Abel, on that torn corpse, on the first murder in
   the world.
O night, even so you came down on the lacerated corpse, on
   the primal, on the greatest murder in the world. It was then,
   O night, that you came.
The same that had come down on so many crimes since the beginning
   of the world;
And on so many stains and on so much bitterness;
And on that sea of ingratitude, even so you came down on my
   mourning;
And on that hill and on that valley of my desolation; it was then,
   O night, you came down.
O night, must it be, then must it be that my Paradise
Will be nothing but a great clear night which will fall on the
   sins of the world.
Shall it be thus, O night, that you will come.
It was then, O night, that you came; and you alone could finish,
   you alone could bring to an end that day of days.
As you brought that day to an end, O night, will you bring the
   world to an end?
And will my Paradise be a great shining night? . . .

O night you had no need to go and ask permission from Pilate.
   That is why I love you and I salute you.
And among all others I glorify you and among all others you
   glorify me
And you are my honour and my glory,
For you obtain sometimes the most difficult thing in the world,
The surrender of man.
The resignation of man into my hands.
I know man well. It is I who made him. He is a strange creature.
For in him operates that liberty which is the mystery of
   mysteries.
Still one can ask a great deal from him. He is not too bad. You
   must not say he is bad.
If you know how to take him you can still ask a great deal from him.
Make him give a great deal. And God knows if my grace knows
   how to take him, if with my grace

I know how to take him. If my grace is insidious, clever as a
 thief
And like a man hunting a fox.
I know how to take him. It's my business. And this liberty itself
 is my creation.
One can ask of him plenty of heart, plenty of charity, plenty
 of sacrifices.
He has plenty of faith and plenty of charity.
But what one can't ask from him, damn it, is a little hope.
A little confidence, what, a little relaxation.
A little delay, a little abandonment.
A little pause. He is always resisting.
Now you, my daughter night, you succeed, sometimes. You
 sometimes obtain just that
From rebellious man.
This gentleman's consent to yield a little to me.
Just to relax, his poor tired limbs on a restful bed.
Just to relax, his aching heart on a restful bed.
For his head, above all, to be still. It goes on far too long, that
 head of his. And he calls it work when his head goes on like
 that.
And his thoughts, no, or what he calls his thoughts.
For his ideas to be still and no longer shake about in his head
 like seeds in a pumpkin.
Like a rattle made from an empty pumpkin.
When one sees what they are, the things he calls his ideas.
Poor creature. I do not like, God says, the man who doesn't
 sleep. . . .

Now you, my daughter night, my daughter of the great cloak,
 my daughter of the silver cloak
You are the only one who can sometimes conquer that rebel
 and bend his stubborn neck.
It is then, O night, that you come.
And what you did once upon a time,
You do every time.
What you did one day,
You do every day.
As you came down one evening,
So you come down every evening.
What you did for my Son made man,
O great Charity, you do for all men, his brothers.

297

You shroud them in silence and shadow
And in healthy forgetfulness
Of the mortal anxiety
Of the day. . . .

Charles Péguy

6.
Songs of Deliverance

SONG OF THE RETURNED EXILES:
A PILGRIMAGE SONG

When the Lord delivered Sion from bondage,
It seemed like a dream.
Then was our mouth filled with laughter.
On our lips there were songs.

The heathens themselves said: "What marvels
the Lord worked for them!"
What marvels the Lord worked for us!
Indeed we were glad.

Deliver us, O Lord, from our bondage
as streams in dry land.
Those who are sowing in tears
will sing when they reap.

They go out, they go out, full of tears,
carrying seed for the sowing:
they come back, they come back, full of song,
carrying their sheaves.

Psalm 125

THANKSGIVING FOR RECOVERY FROM SICKNESS

will praise you, Lord, you have rescued me
and have not let my enemies rejoice over me.

299

O Lord, I cried to you for help
and you, my God, have healed me.
O Lord, you have raised my soul from the dead,
restored me to life from those who sink into the grave.

Sing psalms to the Lord, you who love him,
give thanks to his holy name.
His anger lasts but a moment; his favour through life.
At night there are tears, but joy comes with dawn.

I said to myself in my good fortune:
"Nothing will ever disturb me."
Your favour had set me on a mountain fastness,
then you hid your face and I was put to confusion.

To you, Lord, I cried,
to my God I made appeal:
"What profit would my death be, my going to the grave?
Can dust give you praise or proclaim your truth?"

The Lord listened and had pity.
The Lord came to my help.
For me you have changed my mourning into dancing,
you removed my sackcloth and girded me with joy.
So my soul sings psalms to you unceasingly.
O Lord my God, I will thank you for ever.

Psalm 2

GOD THE PROTECTOR: A PILGRIMAGE SONG

I lift up my eyes to the mountains:
from whence shall come my help?
My help shall come from the Lord
who made heaven and earth.

May he never allow you to stumble!
Let him sleep not, your guard.
No, he sleeps not nor slumbers,
Israel's guard.

The Lord is your guard and your shade;
at your right hand he stands.
By day the sun shall not smite you
nor the moon in the night.

The Lord will guard you from evil,
he will guard your soul.
The Lord will guard your going and coming
both now and for ever.

Psalm 120

SONG OF SERENITY: A PILGRIMAGE SONG

O Lord, my heart is not proud
nor haughty my eyes.
I have not gone after things too great
nor marvels beyond me.

Truly I have set my soul
in silence and peace.
A weaned child on its mother's breast,
even so is my soul.

O Israel, hope in the Lord
both now and for ever.

Psalm 130

Part 10

Faith Maintained as Old Age Carries Us Forward Through Death to Resurrection and to Hope of Heaven

1. Old Age
2. Death and Immortality
3. Dreams and Echoes of Heaven

"Old age comes from God, old age leads on to God, old age will not touch me only so far as he wills."

Pierre Teilhard de Chardin

1.
Old Age

AS ONE OLDSTER TO ANOTHER

Well, yes the old bones ache. There were easier
Beds thirty years back. Sleep, then importunate,
    Now with reserve doles out her favours;
        Food disagrees; there are draughts in houses.

Headlong, the down night train rushes on with us,
Screams through the stations . . . how many more? Is it
    Time soon to think of taking down one's
        Case from the rack? Are we nearly there now?

Yet neither loss of friends, nor an emptying
Future, nor England tamed and the ruin of
    Long-builded hopes thus far have taught my
        Obstinate heart a sedate deportment.

Still beauty calls as once in the mazes of
Boyhood. The bird-like soul quivers. Into her
    Flash darts of unfulfill'd desire and
        Pierce with a bright, unabated anguish.

Armed thus with anguish, joy met us even in
Youth—who forgets? This side of the terminus,
    Then, now, and always, thus, and only
        Thus, were the doors of delight set open.

C. S. Lewis

WHATEVER HAPPENS TO YOU—PRAISE GOD

On the way home I met a friend who lived alone in a ramshackle caravan on a windy site overlooking the Atlantic, a tall imposing woman in her late sixties with a crown of grey hair piled on top of her head and tied with a velvet ribbon, wearing a thick ulster and waving a stout stick, singing at the top of her voice: "O all ye works of the Lord, bless ye the Lord, praise him and magnify him for ever! O all ye hills and oceans of the Lord, bless ye the Lord! La illah illa Alla! On mani padme hum!" Like a clipper ship, its sails bellied by the wind, she advanced and like many a full-rigger she had been battered by dreadful storms from every point of the human compass: deserted by two husbands, ruined by swindlers, her only child drowned by the carelessness of her best friend—she kept his ashes in her van—and now the victim of arthritis. "God bless!" she boomed, waving and rocking towards me. "You look done in. Why *do* you totter over to Morwenstow? You ought to know better. Let go, let go! Let go of people, passions, possessions, ideals, hopes, desires, treasures—everything! To live without sorrow or bitterness you must be able to do without, to give them all up. There's always more suffering than joy." And she shouted: "O all ye beasts and birds and fishes of the Lord, praise ye the Lord! And blessed be the great God Pan!" Rolling from side to side she whirled her stick and pushed past me, bawling: "Rejoice to-day with one accord, sing out with exultation. Rejoice and praise the mighty Lord whose arm has wrought salvation!" A gallant old lady, generous, brave, and rather goddess-like herself—a dethroned Juno, cast out of Olympus for some outrageous peccadillo that offended the other divinities, and hurled down to end her troubled and troubling existence on the wave-pounded Cornish coast. The last I saw of her—the last forever: she died soon afterwards—was her stick waving while her strong voice floated over hedgerows: "O all ye winds and waves and rainbows of the Lord, praise ye the Lord! . . ."

Adelaide Ross, in her book "A Wild Flower Wreath"
describes her last meeting with one of her old friends

ONE DOES GET OLD AT LAST

Long light is over at last, evening is here,
Companion of the day:

We go slowly under branches getting bare
	Just as the books say.

Fancy, it's true, then—stiff about the knees,
	Mind and eyes a bit dim:
While we can still see, under thinning trees,
	It's time we turned to Him.

For there is something in us willing to go,
	Something that knows its time;
We do not need to feel a feather of snow
	Or see the first white rime

To know that our long day, so short, is nearly
	Spent, and it is the season
To use the little wisdom we bought so dearly
	And stored, while we could reason.

Easier far now than it was at first, love,
	No more to be possessed,
Or to possess ourselves, or things; the worst, love,
	Is over, not the best.

Ruth Pitter

LOVE'S REMORSE

I feel remorse for all that time has done
To you, my love, as if myself, not time,
Had set on you the never-resting sun
And the little deadly days, to work this crime.

For not to guard what by such grace was given,
But leave it for the idle hours to take,
Let autumn bury away our summer heaven;
To such a charge what answer can I make

But the old saw still by the heart retold,
'Love is exempt from time.' And that is true.
But we, the loved and the lover, we grow old;
Only the truth, the truth is always new:

'Eternity alone our wrong can right,
That makes all young again in time's despite.'

Edwin Mui

What are you, my soul, you lean and bloodless thing
Like a withered fig that has survived the winter?
In youth it was so different: then the blood
Sang along the veins and it was easy both to love and welcome love.
But when you are old grace conquers only by hard victories;
You are stiffened, crusted by the salt spray
After the long sea voyage.

The lanes of memory may be as green
As in the year's paradise of spring.
It is the immediate present that slips unremembered,
Yet in love's presence there is only this one moment—
A question not of time but of understanding,
As when beauty seeps through the crevices of the soul
Burning the dead wood and illuming the self's verities.—
This, only after a long journey.

So limping, my soul, we will together go
Into the city of the shining ones,
Of those whose crutches have been cast into the sea,
Whose love is garlanded across the festal stars;
And we with them will bow before the sceptred wisdom of a child.
The trembling broken years shall be restored
And these shall be our offering; for by them we shall know
Love has travailed with us all the way.

M.L., A nun of Burnham Abbe

EUPHRASY

The large untidy February skies—
Some cheerful starlings screeling on a tree—

West wind and low-shot sunlight in my eyes—
　　Is this decline for me?

The feel of winter finishing once more—
Sense of the present as a tale half told—
The land of life to look at and explore—
　　Is this, then, to grow old?

Siegfried Sassoon

A PRAYER IN OLD AGE

Bring no expectance of a heaven unearned
No hunger for beatitude to be
Until the lesson of my life is learned
Through what Thou didst for me.

Bring no assurance of redeeméd rest
No intimation of awarded grace
Only contrition, cleavingly confessed
To Thy forgiving face.

I ask one world of everlasting loss
In all I am, that other world to win.
My nothingness must kneel below Thy Cross.
There let new life begin.

Siegfried Sassoon

Thou hast made me, and shall thy works decay?
Repaire me now, for now mine end doth haste,
I runne to death, and death meets me as fast,
And all my pleasures are like yesterday;
I dare not move my dimme eyes any way,
Despaire behind, and death before doth cast
Such terrour, and my feeble flesh doth waste
By sinne in it, which it t'wards hell doth weigh;
Only thou art above, and when towards thee
By thy leave I can looke, I rise againe;

But our old subtle foe so tempteth me,
That not one houre my selfe I can sustaine;
Thy Grace may wing me to prevent his art,
And thou like Adamant draw mine iron heart.

John Donne

In the hour of death, after this life's whim,
When the heart beats low, and the eyes grow dim,
And pain has exhausted every limb—
   The lover of the Lord shall trust in Him.

When the will has forgotten the lifelong aim,
And the mind can only disgrace its fame,
And a man is uncertain of his own name—
   The power of the Lord shall fill this frame.

When the last sigh is heaved, and the last tear shed,
And the coffin is waiting beside the bed,
And the widow and child forsake the dead—
   The angel of the Lord shall lift this head.

For even the purest delight may pall,
And power must fail, and the pride must fall,
And the love of the dearest friends grow small—
   But the glory of the Lord is all in all.

Anonymou

Thou bid'st me come away,
And I'll no longer stay,
Than for to shed some tears
For faults of former years:
And to repent some crimes,
Done in the present times:
And next to take a bit
Of Bread, and Wine with it:
To don my robes of love,
Fit for the place above;

310

To gird my loins about
With charity throughout;
And so to travel hence
With feet of innocence;
These done, I'll only cry
God Mercy: and so die.

Robert Herrick

AUTUMN

The leaves are falling, falling as from far,
as though above were withering farthest gardens;
they fall with a denying attitude.

And night by night, down into solitude,
the heavy earth falls far from every star.

We are all falling. This hand's falling too—
all have this falling-sickness none withstands.

And yet there's One whose gently-holding hands
this universal falling can't fall through.

Rainer Maria Rilke

2.

Death and Immortality

THE DAY OF OUR DEATH

O Eternal and most glorious God,
Who sometimes in thy justice
Dost give the dead bodies of the saints
To be meat unto the fowls of the heaven,
And the flesh of thy saints
Unto the beasts of the earth,
So that their blood is shed like water,
And there is none to bury them;
Who sometimes sell'st thy people for naught,
And dost not increase thy wealth by their price,
And yet never leav'st us without the knowledge
That precious in thy sight
Is the death of thy saints,
Enable us,
In life and death,
Seriously to consider the value,
The price of a soul.
It is precious, O Lord,
Because thine image is stamped and
Imprinted upon it;
Precious because the blood of thy Son
Was paid for it;
Precious because thy blessed Spirit,
The Holy Ghost,
Works upon it and tries it by His diverse fires;
And precious because it is entered into thy revenue

And made a part of thy treasure.
Suffer us not, therefore, O Lord,
So to undervalue ourselves—
Nay, so to impoverish thee—
As to give away those souls,
Thy souls,
Thy dear and precious souls—
For nothing,
And all the world is nothing if the soul
Must be given for it.

We know, O Lord,
That our rent, due to thee, is our soul;
And the day of our death is the day,
And our death-bed the place,
Where that rent is to be paid.
And we know too that he that hath sold his soul before
For unjust gain,
Or given away his soul before
In the society of fellowship and sin,
Or lent his soul for a time
By lukewarmness and temporizing,
To the dishonour of thy name,
To the weakening of they cause,
To the discouraging of thy servants,
He comes to that day, and to that place,
His death and death-bed,
Without any rent in his hand,
Without any soul to that purpose,
To surrender it unto thee.
Let therefore, O Lord, the same hand
Which is to receive them then,
Preserve those souls till then;
Let that mouth that breathed them into us, at first,
Breathe always upon them,
Whilst they are in us,
And suck them into itself,
When they depart from us.
Preserve our souls, O Lord,
Because they belong to thee;
And preserve our bodies,
Because they belong to those souls.

Thou alone dost steer our boat
Through all our voyage,
But hast a more especial care of it,
A more watchful eye upon it,
When it comes to a narrow current,
Or to a dangerous fall of waters.
Thou hast a care of the preservation of those bodies
In all the ways of our life;
But in the Straits of Death,
Open thine eyes wider,
And enlarge thy providence towards us so far,
That no fever in the body may shake the soul,
No apoplexy in the body damp or benumb the soul,
Nor any pain or agony of the body
Presage future torments to the soul.
But so make thou our bed in all our sickness,
That being used to thy hand,
We may be content with any bed of thy making;
Whether thou be pleased
To change our feathers into flocks*
By withdrawing the conveniences of this life,
Or change our flocks into dust,
Even the dust of the grave,
By withdrawing us out of this life.
And though thou divide man and wife,
Mother and child,
Friend and friend,
By the hand of death,
Yet stay them that stay,
And send them away that go,
With this consolation:
That though we part at divers days
And by divers ways, here,
Yet we shall all meet at one place,
And at one day—
A day that no night shall determine:
The day of the Glorious Resurrection.

John Donn

*wool or hair

Fear death?—to feel the fog in my throat,
    The mist in my face,

314

When the snows begin, and the blasts denote
    I am nearing the place,
The power of the night, the press of the storm,
    The post of the foe;
Where he stands, the Arch Fear in a visible form,
    Yet the strong man must go:
For the journey is done and the summit attained,
    And the barriers fall,
Though a battle's to fight ere the guerdon be gained,
    The reward of it all.
I was ever a fighter, so—one fight more,
    The best and the last!
I would hate that death bandaged my eyes and forbore,
    And bade me creep past.
No! let me taste the whole of it, fare like my peers,
    The heroes of old,
Bear the brunt, in a minute pay glad life's arrears
    Of pain, darkness and cold.
For sudden the worst turns the best to the brave,
    The black minute's at end,
And the elements' rage, the fiend-voices that rave,
    Shall dwindle, shall blend,
Shall change, shall become first a peace out of pain,
    Then a light, then thy breast,
O thou soul of my soul! I shall clasp thee again,
    And with God be the rest!

Robert Browning

INVOCATION

Come down from heaven to meet me when my breath
Chokes, and through drumming shafts of stifling death
I stumble toward escape, to find the door
Opening on morn where I may breathe once more
Clear cock-crow airs across some valley dim
With whispering trees. While dawn along the rim
Of night's horizon flows in lakes of fire,
Come down from heaven's bright hill, my song's desire.

Belov'd and faithful, teach my soul to wake
In glades deep-ranked with flowers that gleam and shake

315

And flock your paths with wonder. In your gaze
Show me the vanquished vigil of my days.
Mute in that golden silence hung with green
Come down from heaven and bring me in your eyes
Remembrance of all beauty that has been,
And stillness from the pools of Paradise.

Siegfried Sasso

LORD, IT BELONGS NOT TO MY CARE

LORD, it belongs not to my care,
   Whether I die or live;
To love and serve Thee is my share,
   And this Thy grace must give.

If life be long I will be glad,
   That I may long obey;
If short—yet why should I be sad
   To soar to endless day?

CHRIST leads me through no darker rooms
   Than He went through before;
He that unto GOD's kingdom comes,
   Must enter by this door.

Come, LORD, when grace has made me meet
   Thy blessed face to see;
For if Thy work on earth be sweet,
   What will Thy glory be!

Then I shall end my sad complaints,
   And weary, sinful days,
And join with the triumphant saints,
   To sing JEHOVAH's praise.

My knowledge of that life is small,
   The eye of faith is dim,
But 'tis enough that CHRIST knows all,
   And I shall be with Him.

Richard Bax

The door of death is made of gold
That mortal eyes cannot behold:
But when the mortal eyes are closed,
And cold and pale the limbs reposed,
The soul awakes, and wondering sees
In her mild hand the golden keys.

William Blake

WHY I BELIEVE IN GOD

We believe in what we believe in. I believe in God.
Since the beginning of man we have tried to describe
   this spiritual figure.
Poets have tried, the Bible has tried, but all in vain.
For if we did, we would be like Him.
In these times of war and worry we need Him most of all.
No man can say he has never been scared to die at one time
   or another, or be sad and sorry when he sees others
   die.
When I face my darkest hour, or my death seems inevitably
   sure, all I wish is to believe in Him and die for Him,
   rather than live without Him and His watchful eye.
And may He guide me and keep me in life and in death.
May His ways be merciful when I do wrong and may He have as
   much faith in me as I in Him.
Maybe one, not very far away day, we shall find a new King
   of Peace which we do not have to find in death,
But truly, most of all, may He keep me in death as He has
   in life.

Malcolm Kaufman

There is a necessity in us, however blind and ineffectual, to discover
hat we are. Religion once supplied that knowledge, but our life is no
nger ruled by religion. Yet we can know what we are only if we ac-
pt some of the hypotheses of religion. Human beings are understand-
le only as immortal spirits; they become natural then, as natural as
ung horses; they are absolutely unnatural if we try to think of them
 a mere part of the natural world.
I do not have the power to prove that man is immortal and that the

317

soul exists; but I know that there must be such a proof, and that compared with it every other demonstration is idle. It is true that human life without immortality would be inconceivable to me, though that is not the ground for my belief.

My belief in immortality, so far as I can divine its origin, and that is not far, seems to be connected with the same impulse which urges me to know myself. I can never know myself, but the closer I come to knowledge of myself the more certain I must feel that I am immortal and, conversely, the more certain I am of my immortality the more intimately I must come to know myself. For I shall attend and listen to a class of experiences which the disbeliever in immortality ignores or dismisses as irrelevant to temporal life. The experiences I mean are of little practical use and have no particular economic or political interest. They come when I am least aware of myself as a personality moulded by my will and time: in moments of contemplation when I am unconscious of my body, or indeed that I have a body with separate members; in moments of grief or prostration; in happy hours with friends; and, because self-forgetfulness is most complete then, in dreams and day-dreams and in that floating, half-discarnate state which precedes and follows sleep. In these hours there seems to me to be knowledge of my real self and simultaneously knowledge of immortality. Sleep tells us things both about ourselves and the world which we could not discover otherwise. Our dreams are part of experience; earlier ages acknowledged this. If I describe a great number of dreams in this book I do so intentionally, for I should like to save from the miscellaneous dross of experiences a few glints of immortality.

Edwin Muir

For the only air of the soul, in which it can breathe and live, is the presence of God and the spirits of the just: that is our heaven, our home, our all-right place. . . . We shall be God's children on the little hills and in the fields of that heaven, not one desiring to be before another any more than to cast that other out; for ambition and hatred will then be seen to be one and the same spirit.

To believe in the wide-awake real, through all the stupefying, enervating, distorting dreams: the will to wake, when the very being seems athirst for Godless repose:—these are the broken steps up to the high fields where repose is but a form of strength, strength but a form of joy, joy but a form of love.

To some minds the argument for immortality drawn from the appa

318

ntly universal shrinking from annihilation must be ineffectual, seeing
ney themselves do not shrink from it. . . . If there is no God, an-
ihilation is the one thing to be longed for, with all that might of long-
ng which is the mainspring of human action. In a word, it is not im-
nortality the human heart cries out after, but that immortal, eternal
nought whose life is its life, whose wisdom is its wisdom. . . . Dis-
ociate immortality from the living Immortality, and it is not a thing
o be desired.

George Macdonald

Extracts from 'War and Peace'

(i)

(Napoleon has invaded Russia. Prince
Andrey Bolkonsky, who had fought at
Austerlitz, has a meeting with his
friend, Pierre Bezukhov)

Pierre interrupted him. 'Do you believe in a future life?' he asked.
'In a future life?' repeated Prince Andrey.
But Pierre did not give him time to answer, and took this repetition
 a negative reply, the more readily as he knew Prince Andrey's athe-
tic views in the past. 'You say that you can't see the dominion of
od and truth on the earth. I have not seen it either, and it cannot be
en if one looks upon our life as the end of everything. On earth, this
rth here' (Pierre pointed to the open country), 'there is no truth—all
 deception and wickedness. But in the world, the whole world, there
 a dominion of truth, and we are now the children of earth, but eter-
lly the children of the whole universe. Don't I feel in my soul that I
 a part of that vast, harmonious whole? Don't I feel that in that vast,
numerable multitude of beings, in which is made manifest the God-
ad, the higher power—what you choose to call it—I constitute one
in, one step upward from lower beings to higher ones? If I see, see
early that ladder that rises up from the vegetable to man, why should
uppose that ladder breaks off with me and does not go on further and
ther? I feel that I cannot disappear as nothing does disappear in the
iverse, that indeed I always shall be and always have been. I feel that
side me, above me, there are spirits, and that in their world there is
ith.'
Yes, that's Herder's theory,' said Prince Andrey. 'But it's not that,
 dear boy, convinces me; life and death are what have convinced

319

me. What convinces me is seeing a creature dear to me, and bound u
with me, to whom one has done wrong, and hoped to make it right
(Prince Andrey's voice shook and he turned away), 'and all at once tha
creature suffers, is in agony, and ceases to be. . . . What for? It cannc
be that there is no answer! And I believe that there is. . . . That's wha
convinces, that's what has convinced me,' said Prince Andrey.

'Just so, just so,' said Pierre; 'isn't that the very thing I'm saying?'

'No. I only say that one is convinced of the necessity of a future lif
not by argument, but when one goes hand-in-hand with some one, an
all at once that some one slips away *yonder into nowhere,* and you a
left facing that abyss and looking down into it. And I have looked int
it. . . .'

'Well, that's it then! You know there is a *yonder* and there is *som
one. Yonder* is the future life; *Some one* is God.'

Prince Andrey did not answer. The coach and horses had long bee
taken across to the other bank, and had been put back into the shaft
and the sun had half sunk below the horizon, and the frost of evenir
was starring the pools at the fording-place; but Pierre and Andrey, t
the astonishment of the footmen, coachmen, and ferrymen, still stoc
in the ferry and were still talking.

'If there is God and there is a future life, then there is truth and the
is goodness; and the highest happiness of man consists in striving f
their attainment. We must live, we must love, we must believe,' sa
Pierre, 'that we are not only living today on this clod of earth, but ha
lived and will live for ever there in everything' (he pointed to the sk
Prince Andrey stood with his elbow on the rail of the ferry, and as I
listened to Pierre he kept his eyes fixed on the red reflection of the su
on the bluish stretch of water. Pierre ceased speaking. There was pe
fect stillness. The ferry had long since come to a standstill, and on
the eddies of the current flapped with a faint sound on the bottom
the ferry boat. It seemed to Prince Andrey that the lapping of the wat
kept up a refrain to Pierre's words: 'It's the truth, believe it.'

Prince Andrey sighed, and with a radiant, child-like, tender look
his eyes glanced at the face of Pierre—flushed and triumphant, thou
still timidly conscious of his friend's superiority.

'Yes, if only it were so!' he said. 'Let us go and get in, though,' add
Prince Andrey, and as he got out of the ferry he looked up at the sky,
which Pierre had pointed him, and for the first time since Austerlitz
saw the lofty, eternal sky, as he had seen it lying on the field of Aust
litz, and something that had long been slumbering, something bett
that had been in him, suddenly awoke with a joyful, youthful feeling
his soul. That feeling vanished as soon as Prince Andrey returned aga
to the habitual conditions of life, but he knew that that feeling

320

hough he knew not how to develop it—was still within him.

Pierre's visit was for Prince Andrey an epoch, from which there be-
an, though outwardly unchanged, a new life in his inner world.

(ii)

(Prince Andrey, mortally wounded at
the battle of Borodino, knows that
there is no eternity apart from love.)

'Yes, love (he thought again with perfect distinctness), but not that
ove that loves for something, to gain something, or because of some-
hing, but that love that I felt for the first time, when dying, I saw my
nemy and yet loved him. I knew that feeling of love which is the very
ssence of the soul, for which no object is needed. And I know that
lissful feeling now too. To love one's neighbours; to love one's ene-
nies. To love everything—to love God in all His manifestations. Some
ne dear to one can be loved with human love; but an enemy can only
e loved with divine love. And that was why I felt such joy when I felt
hat I loved that man. What happened to him? Is he alive? . . . Loving
ith human love, one may pass from love to hatred; but divine love
annot change. Nothing, not even death, nothing can shatter it. It is
he very nature of the soul. . . .

'Love is life. All, all that I understand, I understand only because I
ove. All is, all exists only because I love. All is bound up in love alone.
ove is God, and dying means for me a particle of love, to go back to
he universal and eternal source of love.'

Leo Tolstoy

Extract from 'Uncle Vanya'

onia   My misfortune is perhaps even greater than yours, but I am
ot plunged in despair. I endure my sorrow, and shall endure it until
ny life comes to a natural end. You must endure yours, too. . . . You
nust endure your sorrow, Uncle Vanya; you must endure it. . . .
ncle Vanya   Oh, my child, I am so miserable; if only you knew how
niserable I am!
onia   What can we do? We must live our lives. Yes, we shall live,
ncle Vanya. We shall live through the long procession of days before
s, and through the long evenings; we shall patiently bear the trials
nat fate imposes upon us; we shall work for others without rest, both
ow and when we are old; and when our last hour comes we shall meet

321

it humbly, and there, beyond the grave, we shall say that we have suf
fered and wept, that our life was bitter, and God will have pity on us
Ah, then dear, dear Uncle, we shall see that bright and beautiful life
we shall rejoice and look back upon our sorrow here; a tender smile—
and—we shall rest. I have faith, Uncle, fervent, passionate faith. W
shall rest. We shall rest. We shall hear the angels. We shall see heaven
shining like a jewel. We shall see all evil and all our pain sink away in
the great compassion that shall enfold the world. Our life will be a
peaceful and tender and sweet as a caress. I have faith; I have faith. M
poor, poor Uncle Vanya, you are crying! You have never known wha
happiness was, but wait, Uncle Vanya, wait! We shall rest. We shal
rest.

Anton Chekho

STUDY TO DESERVE DEATH

Study to deserve Death, they only may
Who fought well upon their earthly day,
Who never sheathed their swords or ran away.

See, such a man as this now proudly stands,
Pale in the clasp of Death, and to his hands
Yields up the sword, but keeps the laurel bands.

Honour and emulate his warrior soul,
For whom the sonorous death-bells toll;
He after journeying has reached his goal.

Prate not to me of suicide,
Faint heart in battle, not for pride
I say Endure, but that such end denied
Makes welcomer yet the death that's to be died.

Stevie Smi

FOR A PLATONIST ON HER BIRTHDAY

The further on in time we move,
Here, as through a tangled grove,

In shifting moonlight (each a shade
By shadows fitfully betrayed)
The closer to eternity—that bright
Undifferentiated light.
Yet, stripped of their corporeal dress,
Those alone, who learned to bless,
In time, beneath time-measuring stars,
All the minute particulars,
Can bear that shrivelling radiance:
And then we may begin to dance.
Accept my words—they cannot reach
What Plato and Platinus teach—
Yet also I, perhaps, have known
How unsubstantial is the stone
(Mountains that crumble in an hour),
How real and timeless is the flower.

John Heath Stubbs

TRANSFIGURATION

I saw the grave dug in the ground,
And into it a body laid
As wood and kindling in a hearth,
And there was nothing death had made.

The hearth was cold, yet lighted
With the level flames of earth.
The soil and stones that filled it
Filled me with love and mirth.

I saw love's fire kindled,
The smoke rose through the ground
As through a chimney, into
The air that death had found.

The grave was blazing white with love,
The body lived with flame.
The smoke leapt up, the soul was borne
Back to that light from which we came.

James Kirkup

From THE DUINO ELEGIES

Part of the First Elegy

A LAMENT FOR A YOUNG MAN WHO DIED YOUNG

Who, if I cried, would hear me among the angelic
orders? And even if one of them suddenly
pressed me against his heart, I should fade in the strength of his
stronger existence. For Beauty's nothing
but beginning of Terror we're still just able to bear,
and why we adore it so is because it serenely
disdains to destroy us. Each single angel is terrible.
And so I keep down my heart, and swallow the call-note
of depth-dark sobbing. Alas, who is there
we can make use of? Not angels, not men;
and already the knowing brutes are aware
that we don't feel very securely at home
within our interpreted world. There remains, perhaps,
some tree on a slope, to be looked at day after day,
there remains for us yesterday's walk and the cupboard-love loyalty
of a habit that liked us and stayed and never gave notice.
Oh, and there's Night, there's Night, when wind full of cosmic space
feeds on our faces: for whom would she not remain,
longed for, mild disenchantress, painfully there
for the lonely heart to achieve? Is she lighter for lovers?
Alas, with each other they only conceal their lot!
Don't you know *yet*?—Fling the emptiness out of your arms
into the spaces we breathe—maybe that the birds
will feel the extended air in more intimate flight.

Yes, the Springs had need of you. Many a star
was waiting for you to espy it. Many a wave
would rise on the past towards you; or, else, perhaps,
as you went by an open window, a violin
would be giving itself to someone. . . .

True, it is strange to inhabit the earth no longer,
to use no longer customs scarcely acquired,
not to interpret roses, and other things
that promise so much, in terms of a human future;
to be no longer all that one used to be
in endlessly anxious hands, and to lay aside

324

even one's proper name like a broken toy.
Strange, not to go on wishing one's wishes. Strange,
to see all that was once relation to loosely fluttering
hither and thither in space. And it's hard, being dead,
and full of retrieving before one begins to espy
a trace of eternity.—Yes, but all of the living
make the mistake of drawing too sharp distinctions.
Angels, (they say) are often unable to tell
whether they move among living or dead. The eternal
torrent whirls all the ages through either realm
for ever, and sounds above their voices in both.

They've finally no more need of us, the early-departed,
one's gently weaned from terrestrial things as one mildly
outgrows the breasts of a mother. But we, that have need of
such mighty secrets, we, for whom sorrow's so often
source of blessedest progress, could we exist without them?
Is the story in vain, how once, in the mourning for Linos,
venturing earliest music pierced barren numbness, and how,
in the horrified space an almost deified youth
suddenly quitted for ever, emptiness first
felt the vibration that now charms us and comforts and helps?

Rainer Maria Rilke

O sure and swiftly guided plough! If pain
is where you plunge into another layer,
is not pain good? And that so long delayer
that breaks upon us in the midst of pain?

How much there is to suffer! Who could guess
there'd once been time for laughter and repose?
And yet I know, better than most of those
awaiting resurrection, happiness.

Rainer Maria Rilke

3.
Dreams and Echoes of Heaven

"There is a secret too great to be told."

HE WHO ASKED

He who asked: 'Who knows
The meaning of the snow?'
Is answered now.
'Who understands the rose?'
Is shown its mystery.

'What is that long night,
The dark day of the dead?'
To him who said
Let me see Love,' the secret sight
Is simply told, once whispered in agony.

James Kirku

LAZARUS

While Mary wept within her darkened room;
While Martha served the guests and broke her heart,
Where were you, Lazarus, those four days?

Not in the garden-tomb, cool from the sun,
But in a world of light, glory beyond
The toys of sense, the friend of Time.

'The undiscover'd country from whose bourn
No traveller returns'—
But you, bewildered Lazarus, came back,
Answering His mighty word of power:
'Lazarus, come forth!'
You stood, bound in your grave-clothes, in the sun,
While awe fell on the shaking crowd,
Your amazed soul caged dumbly in your eye.

How could you, Lazarus, speak to them of that?
Words would fall baffled back
Beating against the doors of sense,
The myth of Time.

How make the deaf to hear?
The blind to see?
So your soul kept a secret: unguessed Heaven.
Dazed, you walked softly all your length of hours,
A silent man, a quiet man, remote,
A man who guards a dream.

Joseph Braddock

THE BEAUTY OF THE WORLD IS THE GATE OF HEAVEN

Your enjoyment of the world is never right till every morning you awake in Heaven; see yourself in your Father's palace, and look upon the skies, the earth and the air as celestial joys; having such a reverend esteem of all, as if you were among the Angels. The bride of a monarch, in her husband's chamber, hath no such causes of delight as you.

You never enjoy the world aright till the sea itself floweth in your veins, till you are clothed with the heavens and crowned with the stars; and perceive yourself to be the sole heir of the whole world, and more than so, because men are in it who are every one sole heirs as well as you. Till you can sing and rejoice and delight in God, as misers do in gold, and kings in sceptres, you can never enjoy the world.

Till your spirit filleth the whole world, and the stars are your jewels; till you are as familiar with the ways of God in all ages as with your walk and table; till you are intimately acquainted with that shady nothing out of which the world was made; till you love men so as to desire their happiness with a thirst equal to the zeal of your own; till you delight in God for being good to all; you never enjoy the world. Till you more feel it than your private estate, and are more present in the hemisphere, considering the glories and the beauties there, than in your own house; till you remember how lately you were made, and how wonderful it was when you came into it; and more rejoice in the palace of your glory than if it had been made today morning.

Yet further, you never enjoyed the world aright, till you so love the beauty of enjoying it, that you are covetous and earnest to persuade others to enjoy it. And so perfectly hate the abominable corruption of men in despising it that you had rather suffer the flames of hell than willingly be guilty of their error.

The world is a mirror of Infinite Beauty, yet no man sees it. It is a Temple of Majesty, yet no man regards it. It is a region of Light and Peace, did not men disquiet it. It is the Paradise of God. It is more to man since he is fallen than it was before. It is the place of Angels and the Gate of Heaven. When Jacob waked out of his dream, he said, God is here, and I wist it not. How dreadful is this place! This is none other than the House of God and the Gate of Heaven.

Thomas Traherne

SUDDEN HEAVEN

All was as it had ever been—
The worn familiar book,
The oak beyond the hawthorn seen,
The misty woodland's look:

The starling perched upon the tree
With his long tress of straw—
When suddenly heaven blazed on me,
And suddenly I saw:

Saw all as it would ever be,
In bliss too great to tell;
For ever safe, for ever free,
All bright with miracle:

Saw as in heaven the thorn arrayed,
The tree beside the door;
And I must die—but O my shade
Shall dwell there evermore.

Ruth Pitter

ALL THE WORLD TODAY RINGS MAD WITH EXULTATION

Where wind sings green on lamb-nibbled paths
where air is brushed by the seep of sharp wings
and the sun-heaped flowers stare
a child-stare
till I could scoop them up
to lull in my arms,
that note—
is it light, water or bird?
This breath I feel on my brow
is it fragrance of pear-blossom?

I am drunk and drink for evermore
this adoration.
No song before
was ever poured in this pure modulation.
I do not know
if I am looking on
sun
earth or flower
for all the world today
rings mad
with exultation.

Sister Mary Agnes, Order of Poor Clares

LOST IN HEAVEN

The clouds, the source of rain, one stormy night
Offered an opening to the source of dew;
Which I accepted with impatient sight,
Looking for my old sky-marks in the blue.

But stars were scarce in that part of the sky,
And no two were of the same constellation—
No one was bright enough to identify;
So 'twas with not ungrateful consternation,

Seeing myself well lost once more, I sighed,
"Where, where in Heaven am I? But don't tell me!
O opening clouds, by opening on me wide.
Let's let my heavenly lostness overwhelm me."

Robert Frost

THE VISION OF PARADISE

Dark was that impenetrable door
At which we stood like shades
Waiting for admission. Then we saw
Our real shadows melt into the rock
Like sun, or wind, or rain piercing the spring's white glades.
And naturally, with no loss, no sense of shock
Or shame, we found ourselves, at last,
Re-entering the dwelling that our faith had lost.

There all was bright with sunlight and profusions.
Our shrunken hearts delighted to be rich again
With all the tender savagery of continents and oceans.
We could feel the wild blood burning in each living hand,
The breath of gods and heroes flowing in each vein.
We had entered life as if a new-found land
Had suddenly appeared familiar, and good.
And there was speech, like love, which all men understood.

James Kirkup

THERE IS A NEW MORNING

There is a new morning, and a new way,
When the heart wakes in the green
Meadow of its choice, and the feet stray

Securely on their new-found paths, unseen,
Unhindered in the certain light of day.

There is a new time, and a new word
That is the timeless dream of uncreated speech.
When the heart beats for the first time, like a bird
Battering the bright boughs of its tree; when each
To the other turns, all prayers are heard.

There is a new world, and a new man
Who walks amazed that he so long
Was blind, and dumb; he who now towards the sun
Lifts up a trustful face in skilful song,
And fears no more the darkness where his day began.

James Kirkup

Tell me, O Swan, your ancient tale.
From what land do you come, O
   Swan? To what shore will you
   fly?
Where would you take your rest, O
   Swan, and what do you seek?

Even this morning, O Swan, awake,
   arise, follow me!
There is a land where no doubt nor
   sorrow have rule: where the terror
   of Death is no more.
There the woods of spring are a-bloom,
   and the fragrant scent 'He is I'
   is borne on the wind:
There the bee of the heart is deeply
   immersed, and desires no other
   joy.

Rabindranath Tagore

THE HEAVENLY CITY

I sigh for the heavenly country,
   Where the heavenly people pass,

And the sea is as quiet as a mirror
Of beautiful beautiful glass.

I walk in the heavenly field,
With lilies and poppies bright,
I am dressed in a heavenly coat
Of polished white.

When I walk in the heavenly parkland
My feet on the pasture are bare,
Tall waves the grass, but no harmful
Creature is there.

At night I fly over the housetops,
And stand on the bright moony beams;
Gold are all heaven's rivers
And silver her streams.

Stevie Smith

Let the wilderness and the thirsty land be glad,
   let the desert rejoice and burst into flower.
   Let it flower with fields of asphodel,
   let it rejoice and shout for joy.
   The glory of Lebanon is given to it,
      the splendour too of Carmel and Sharon;
these shall see the glory of the LORD, the splendour of our God.
   Strengthen the feeble arms,
   steady the tottering knees;
say to the anxious, Be strong and fear not.
   See, your God comes with vengeance,
with dread retribution he comes to save you.
   Then shall blind men's eyes be opened,
      and the ears of the deaf unstopped.
   Then shall the lame man leap like a deer,
      and the tongue of the dumb shout aloud;
   for water springs up in the wilderness,
   and torrents flow in dry land.
   The mirage becomes a pool,
      the thirsty land bubbling springs;
      instead of reeds and rushes, grass shall grow

in the rough land where wolves now lurk.
And there shall be a causeway there
which shall be called the Way of Holiness,
   and the unclean shall not pass along it;
it shall become a pilgrim's way,
   no fool shall trespass on it.
No lion shall come there,
no savage beast climb on to it;
   not one shall be found there.
By it those he has ransomed shall return
   and the LORD's redeemed come home;
they shall enter Zion with shouts of triumph,
crowned with everlasting gladness.
Gladness and joy shall be their escort,
and suffering and weariness shall flee away.

The Book of Isaiah
The New English Bible

INDEX OF AUTHORS

When the Lord delivered Sion from bondage, 299
When the spent sun throws up its rays on cloud, 286
When the truth shines out in the soul, 147
When these in all their bravery took the knock, 147
When thou feelest that thou mayest in no wise put them (distraction;
    down, 246
When to the sessions of sweet silent thought, 266
When we entered the wood that bright spring morning, 200
When we talk of our development I fancy we mean little more tha;
    that we have changed, 195
When you say your prayers, you must go to your private room, 254
Where, in what ever-blissfully watered gardens, upon what trees, 209
Wherever faith is, the abyss of possible doubt is opened up, 216
Wherever now you are, and whoever you may be, 108
Where wind sings green on lamb-nibbed paths, 329
While Mary wept within the darkened room, 326
White is my neck, head yellow, 91
'Who be it calls me from my long whoam, 105
Who, if I cried, would hear me among the angelic, 324
Who is this that comes in grandeur, coming from the blazing East, 127
Whose woods these are I think I know, 202
With a pure colour there is little one can do, 61
Within this earthen vessel are bowers and groves, 34
With roof and shadow for a while careers, 176
Written on a gold leaf in Greek, 259

Yes, I have experienced it now, 230
Yesterday the gentle, 114
Yet in this journey back, 195
Your enjoyment of the world is never right till every morning yo*
    awake in Heaven, 327
Your love, Lord, reaches to heaven, 42
Your turbulent intensity, 151
You, through whose face all lovely faces look, 114
You who went so innocently before us, 164

ACKNOWLEDGMENTS

Acknowledgment is gratefully made for permission to include the following works or extracts from them:

Barker, Eric: "A Ring of Willows," "A Pool for Unicorns," "To a Blind Friend" (from *A Ring of Willows*, by permission of André Deutsch Ltd.).

Binyon, Laurence: "Sursum Cor" (from *Collected Poems, Volume I*, by permission of Mrs. Nicolette Gray and the Society of Authors, on behalf of the Laurence Binyon Estate).

Bond, M.: "Old Woman to Cat" (first published in *Country Life*).

Bonhoeffer, Dietrich: "The Suffering God," "God Can Use Our Mistakes," "Christians and Pagans," "Faith and Providence," "Who Am I?" (from *Letters and Papers from Prison*, Revised, Enlarged Edition, by Dietrich Bonhoeffer. Reprinted with permission of SCM Press Ltd.).

Boros, Ladislaus: "Wherever Faith Is," "A Human Being Loves," "The Final Thing," "Self-giving," "Mercy," "Humility," "Mercy of Jesus," "Silence," "The Silence of Jesus" (from *God Is with Us*, copyright Search Press Ltd., 1967, by permission of Search Press Ltd.).

Braddock, Joseph: "The Rare Moment," "The Butterfly," "Rock Daffodils," "Van Gogh," "Lazarus," "These Images," last verses from "Modes of Feeling" (from *No Stronger Than a Flower, Poems 1935–1960*, by permission of Robert Hale & Company, publishers).

Brown, Christy: "Rainbow in Exeter," "Sunday Visit," "Poem for Sean Collis," "Lines for Lioba" (from *Background Music*, copyright © 1973 by Christy Brown. Reprinted with permission of Martin Secker & Warburg Ltd., publishers).

Burnshaw, Stanley: "Blood" (from *In the Terrified Radiance* by Stanley Burnshaw. Copyright © 1972 by Stanley Burnshaw. Reprinted with the permission of George Braziller, Inc., publisher).

Carter, Sydney: "Lord of the Dance," "One More Step" (from *Green Print for Song*, by permission of Stainer and Bell Ltd., publisher); "Mother Theresa" (by permission of the National Book League); "Child," "My Believing Bones," "The New Song" (from *The Two Way Clock*, published by Stainer and Bell Ltd., by permission of the publisher); Extracts from *Green Print for Song* (published by Stainer and Bell Ltd., by permission of the publisher); "Nowhere and Never" (from *Songs of Sydney Carter in the Present Tense, Book 3*, Galliard, by permission of Stainer and Bell Ltd.).

Causley, Charles: "Ballad of the Bread Man" (from *Collected Poems, 1951–1975*, by Charles Causley. Copyright © 1975 by Charles Causley. Published by Macmillan Publishers Ltd.).

Chekhov, Anton: Extracts from *Uncle Vanya* (translated from the Russian by Marian Fell, published by Duckworth).

Christie, Agatha: "Dartmoor," "Remembrance" (reprinted by permission of Hughes Massie Ltd. from *Poems* by Agatha Christie).

Church, Richard: "The Fourteenth Day," "Friendship," "Courage" (from *Twentieth Century Psalter*, published by William Heinemann Ltd.).

Church, T.: "Something to Love" (from *Modern Psalms for Boys*, published by the University of London Press).

Cicero: Extract from *The Cloud of Unknowing* (translated by Clifton Wolters, Penguin Books Ltd., 1961, copyright © Clifton Wolters, 1961, by permission of Penguin Books Ltd., publishers).

Clark, Pitt: "A Ghosting, In Memoriam: Richard Mundy, Miller" (first published in *Southern Arts*, by permission of *Southern Arts*).

De la Mare, Walter: "Winter Company," "The Tomtit," "The Burning Glass," "The Secret" (from *The Complete Poems of Walter de la Mare*, 1969, by permission of The Literary Trustees of Walter de la Mare, and The Society of Authors as their representative).

Dickinson, Patric: "St. Stephen's Day" (from *A Bearing Beast* published by Chatto and Windus Ltd.).

French, R. M.: Extract from *The Way of a Pilgrim and the Pilgrim Continues His Way* (translated from the Russian by R. M. French, used by permission of the Seabury Press, Inc.).

Frost, Robert: "Not All There," "Rose Pogonias," "A Hillside Thaw," "The Runaway," "A Time to Talk," "Come In," "Stopping by Woods on a Snowy Evening," "Neither out Far nor in Deep," "Sitting by a Bush in Broad Sunlight," "Acceptance," "In the Long Night," "Lost in Heaven" (from *The Poetry of Robert Frost* by permission of the publisher, Jonathan Cape Ltd., and the Estate of Robert Frost).

Gasztold, Carmen de: "The Prayer of the Ant," "The Prayer of the Cock" (from *Prayers from the Ark* by Carmen Bernos de Gasztold. By permission of Macmillan, London and Basingstoke).

Grigson, Geoffrey: "The Badger," "Wild Doves," "Louis MacNeice," "Masters of Certain Arts," "Lovers Who Meet in Churches," "Encouragement on a Leaf" (from *A Skull in Salop: Collected Poems* by Geoffrey Grigson, by permission of Macmillan, London and Basingstoke).

Hamburger, Michael: "Spring Song in Winter," "Birds and Flowers Come Back to War-Scarred London," "A Child Accepts" (from *The Dual Site*, published by the Carcanet Press Ltd.); "Teesdale," "Cat," "Shakespeare Road, S.E. 24," "For a Family Album" (from *Travelling*, published by the Fulcrum Press).

Huxley, Aldous: Extract from *The Perennial Philosophy* (by permission of Chatto & Windus Ltd., publisher, and Mrs. Laura Huxley).

Kendon, Frank: "Inadequate of Words" (from *Arguments and Emblems*, published by the Bodley Head, by permission of Mrs. Celia Kendon).

Kennelly, Brendan: "To Go to Rome," "Jesus at School," "Christ's Bounty," "The Holy Man," "The Good," "Light Dying," "The Thatcher," "How Glad Are the Small Birds," "Hospitality in Ancient Ireland," "Saint, Bird, Angel" (from *A Drinking Cup, Poems from the Irish*, published by Allen Figgis and Co. Ltd.); "Birth," "Willow," "A Giving" (from *Salvation the Stranger* published by the Gallery Press).

Kenward, Jean: "The Lark's Nest," "At Christmas" (published in *Country Life*, by permission of the author).

Kiely, Jerome: "Lizard," "Miracles" (from *The Griffon Sings*, published by Geoffrey Chapman Publishers).

Kirkup, James: Extract from "Toki," "Annunciation," "In Memoriam: Bertrand Russell," "Visiting the Graves in Zoshigaya Cemetery" (from *The Body Servant* by James Kirkup, by permission of J. M. Dent & Sons Ltd.); "The Nativity at Night," "The Eve of Christmas," "The Omens of Disaster" (from *A Spring Journey*, published by Oxford University Press); "Meeting with a Stranger," "The Blind Boy," "Elegy for a Dead God," "He Who Asked" (from *The Submerged Village*, published by Oxford University Press); "Lammas," "The Resurrected Man" (from *Descent into the Cave*, published by Oxford University Press); "Transfiguration" (from *Refusal to Conform*, published by Oxford University Press); "Giving and Taking" (from *The Prodigal Son*, published by Oxford University Press); "The Vision of Paradise," "There Is a New Morning" (from *A Correct Compassion*, published by Oxford University Press); "A Poem for Christmas" (from *The Drowned Sailor*, published 1947 by Grey Walls Press, London); "Elegy for Dead Cosmonauts," "Broad Daylight," "For the Birth of a God," "Christ Cosmonaut" (by permission of the author).

Lewis, C. S.: "As One Oldster to Another," "Pilgrim's Problem," "What the Bird Said Early in the Year," "Scazons" (from *Poems* by C. S. Lewis. By permission of Collins, Publishers).

Lewis-Smith, Anne: "Epitaph," "God-daughter," "October Love" (from *Flesh and Flowers* by Anne Lewis-Smith, published by Mitre Press, by permission of the author).

MacLean, Alasdair: "Hedgehogs and Geese," "Wild Night" (from *From the Wilderness* by Alasdair MacLean. Reprinted by permission of Victor Gollancz Ltd.).

Muggeridge, Malcolm: "Mother Teresa's Home for the Dying . . ." (Abridged from pp. 39, 44, 49, 52–53, 127, 130 in *Something Beautiful for God: Mother Teresa of Calcutta* by Malcolm Muggeridge. By permission of Collins, Publishers).

Muir, Edwin: "The Days," "The Covenant," "The Bird," "The Combat," "The Heroes," "Love's Remorse," "Yet in This Journey Back" (from *Collected Poems* by Edwin Muir. By permission of Faber & Faber Ltd.); Extracts from *An Autobiography* (published by the Hogarth Press Ltd., by permission of Mr Gavin Muir and the publisher).

Newbold, Francis: "The Wood" (by permission of the author).

Nicholson, Norman: "Cowper," "The Tame Hare," "To a Child Before Birth," "New Year's Eve" (from *Rock Face: Selected Poems* published by Faber & Faber, by permission of the publisher); "The Dumb Spirit" (from *A Local Habitation*, published by Faber & Faber); "Comprehending It Not" (by permission of the author).

Odell, John: "God of Twist, Rock and Trad" (from *Modern Psalms for Boys*, published by the University of London Press).

Pascal, Blaise: Extract from *The Provincial Letters* (translated by A. J. Krailsheimer, Harmondsworth, Penguin Books Ltd., 1967, copyright © A. J. Krailsheimer, 1967, by permission of Penguin Books Ltd., publisher).

Peguy, Charles: "They Are My Son's Brothers," "God Speaks of the Children," "The Three Virtues," "The God of the Virtues Speaks of Eternity Itself," "God Speaks of His Son and of His Daughter Night" (from *Holy Innocents and Other Poems* by Charles Peguy. By permission of Harvill Press Ltd., publisher).

Phoenice, J.: "Northumbrian May" (published in *Country Life*. By permission of Mrs. Fox Hutchinson).

Pitter, Ruth: "Morning Glory," "Better Than Love," "Hen Under Bay Tree," "The Sparrow's Skull," "The Great and Terrible Dream," "Three Feminine Things," "Sudden Heaven" (from *Collected Poems 1926–1960*. By permission of Barrie & Jenkins Ltd., publishers); "The Plain Facts," "So Good of Their Kind," "Spectrum," "One Does Get Old at Last" (from *End of Drought*, by permission of Barrie & Jenkins, publishers); "A Blind Child's Christmas Carol" (by permission of *Country Life*).

Prabhavananda, Swami: Extracts from *How to Know God: The Yoga Aphorisms of Patanjali* by Swami Prabhavananda and Christopher Isherwood (by permission of Vedanta Press, publishers).

Psalms: "Part of Psalm 26," "Psalm 29," "Part of Psalm 35," "Psalm 64," "Psalm 92," "Psalm 120," "Psalm 125," "Psalm 130" (from *The Psalms: A New Translation*, by permission of The Grail, England).

Rilke, Rainer Maria: "The Stranger," "The Unicorn," "Autumn," "Beloved, Lost to Begin With," "The Merry-go-round, Jardin de Luxembourg," "Where in What Ever-blissfully Watered Garden," "O Sure and Swiftly Guided Plough . . ." (from Rainer Marie Rilke, *Selected Works*: Volume II, *Poems*, translated by J. B. Leishman. By permission of The Hogarth Press Ltd., publishers, and St. John's College, Oxford); "The Saints," "For Lotte Bielitz" (from Rainer Maria Rilke, *Poems 1906–1926*, translated by J. B. Leishman. By permission of The Hogarth Press Ltd., publisher, and St. John's College, Oxford); "The Site of the Fire" (from Rainer Marie Rilke, *New Poems*, translated by J. B. Leishman. By permission of The Hogarth Press Ltd., publisher, and St. John's College, Oxford); extracts from "The First Elegy" and "The Ninth Elegy" (from *Duino Elegies* by Rainer Maria Rilke. Translated by J. B. Leishman. By permission of The Hogarth Press Ltd., publisher, and St. John's College, Oxford).

Sassoon, Siegfried: "It Is Rumoured of God Almighty," "The Need," "Euphrasy," "A Prayer in Old Age," "Invocation," "Everyone Sang" (from *Poet's Pilgrimage*, published by Victor Gollancz Ltd. By permission of Bolt & Watson Ltd.).

Smith, S. L. Henderson: "Brambles," "Christmas Eve," "Fear" (from *Snow Children and Other Poems*, by permission of the author).

Smith, Stevie: "The Old Sweet Dove of Wiveton," "The Airy Christ," "Fafnir and the Knights," "Dirge," "Study to Deserve Death," "The Heavenly City," "Advice to Young Children" (from *Selected Poems*, published by Longman, by permission of James MacGibbon).

Squire, Aelred: "It Is a Summer Day in Burgundy," "Prayer and Silence" (from *Asking the Fathers*, by permission of the Society for Promoting Christian Knowledge).

Stubbs, John Heath: "For a Platonist on Her Birthday" (from *The Tablet* of April 19th, 1969, by permission of The Tablet Publishing Co. Ltd.).

Swann, Donald: Extracts from *The Space Between the Bars* (by permission of Hodder and Stoughton Limited, publishers).

Tagore, Rabindranath: "I Laugh When I Hear That the Fish," "Within This Earthen Vessel," "How Could the Love," "On This Tree Is a Bird," "This Day Is Dear to Me," "Tell Me, O Swan" (from *Songs of Kabir* translated by Rabindranath Tagore, by permission of the Trustees of the Tagore Estate, and Macmillan, London and Basingstoke).

Teilhard de Chardin, Pierre: "Old Age" (from *The Divine Milieu* by Pierre Teilhard de Chardin. By permission of Collins, Publishers).

Thomas, R. S.: "The Moor" (from *Selected Poems 1946–1965*, published by Hart-Davis, MacGibbon).

Thorogood, Bernard: "Crisis Face" (published in *Reform*).

Tolstoy, Leo: Extracts from *War and Peace* (translated by Constance Garnett, by permission of William Heinemann Ltd., publishers).

Waddell, Helen: "Epitaph for One Dead at Roncevalles," "The Archbishop of Sens Suggests a Visit to His Old Friend Alcuin: Alcuin Replies," "Alcuin Writes to His Friend, Arno of Salzburg, Many Leagues Away," "A Ninth Century Requiem for the Abbess of Gandesheim Who Died Young" (from *Poetry in the Dark Ages*, published by Constable Publishers, by permission of the publisher).

Whitelock, E.: "Without His Hand" (from *Modern Psalms for Boys*, published by the University of London Press).

Young, Andrew: "The Last Leaf," "Ploughing in Mist," "The Bee-orchis," "Idleness," "The Missel Thrush," "Nicodemus" (from *Complete Poems*, edited by Leonard Clark, by permission of Martin Secker & Warburg Limited, publishers).